977.3025 $5.95   W9-CJD-454
Ca
pb   Camp, Paul
                Paul Camp's
            Chicago Tribune
            restaurant guide

DATE DUE

NOV 1 3 95			

EAU CLAIRE DISTRICT LIBRARY

DEMCO

Paul Camp's
Chicago Tribune
Restaurant Guide

WITHDRAWN

Acknowledgements

All of us engaged in the business of reviewing restaurants owe a debt to those who showed us the way: *The Guide Michelin*, Gault/Millau Guides, Craig Claiborne and Mimi Sheraton. Together they raised restaurant criticism from a shady business of freeloads and puffery to a respected profession. Thanks to them and to the editors of *The Chicago Tribune*, who unfailingly provide the resources and support necessary to ensure the accuracy and fairness of my reviews.

My gratitude goes to Tasia Kavvadias. Not only does she schedule my review visits and confirm the information in my reviews for *The Tribune*, she also contributed greatly to the breadth and accuracy of this book by phoning every restaurant to reconfirm their policies. How she managed to remain good natured during her hours on the telephone with restaurateurs, who often changed their policies as the conversations went on, shall always remain a mystery. Thanks, also to John Lux, my editor at *The Tribune*, who makes me appear to be better than I am; and to Soon Har-Tan, who typed and corrected the final manuscript.

Most of all, loving thanks to Mary Connors. She suffered through countless lousy meals as my dining companion, heated arguments about content and style as my primary editor, and the frustrations as my life's companion of what seemed a never-ending project. Without her encouragement this book would never have been published.

Paul Camp
Chicago
April, 1986

PAUL CAMP'S
Chicago Tribune
RESTAURANT
★ GUIDE ★

ACADEMY

CHICAGO

EAU CLAIRE DISTRICT LIBRARY

75302

Copyright © 1986
Paul Camp

Published in 1986 by
Academy Chicago Publishers
425 North Michigan Avenue
Chicago, Illinois 60611

Printed and bound in the USA

No part of this book may by
reproduced in any form without
the express written permission
of the publisher.

ISBN 0-89733-201-6

INTRODUCTION

The *Chicago Tribune* pays me to spend its money on my indulgences in the best restaurants (and admittedly some of the worst) Chicago has to offer. Since starting as restaurant critic in 1982, I have eaten just under 2,000 meals in the line of duty. Not a bad way to make a living.

How does one become a professional eater? Luck, mostly.

I do know something about food. I studied cooking formally and can cook well myself... or used to. Being a restaurant critic leaves little time for cooking at home. I also worked for a restaurateur some time ago and got to know a bit about the business from the inside. Still, the main reason I am the *Tribune's* restaurant critic is that they needed someone to do the job, and I was in the right place at the right time.

Restaurant critics must enjoy eating out—a lot. Believe it or not, eating out in a different place for every meal, every day, every week, every year and thinking about, remembering and chronicling what you've eaten eventually becomes... well, a job. Luckily, just when it starts to get boring a new place opens, or I discover an old one that few people know about that excites and delights. All of a sudden, it's fun again.

You also have to enjoy helping consumers get the most for their restaurant dollars. While I like restaurants and the people who run them, I consider myself an advocate for the customer, who deserves good food and good treatment for his or her money.

A Guide for Consumers

Many of the nearly 2,000 meals I've consumed were wonderful. A few were painfully bad. Most fell somewhere in between—neither great nor awful, just

7

okay. Given the escalating cost of eating out, "okay" no longer seems good enough, which brings me to the purpose of this book.

With an estimated 16,000 restaurants in the Chicago metropolitan area, accordng to the Illinois Restaurant Association, the chances of venturing out for dinner and coming home both disappointed and broke are incredibly high. This book is dedicated to helping you minimize bad dining experiences and maximize good ones.

While I cannot change the quality of a restaurant's food or service, I can warn you about what you may expect. I cannot tell you what you will like, but I can tell you what I like and what a restaurant looks and feels like, and how much you can expect to pay if you dine there.

Obviously, this book falls far short of a complete guide to all 16,000 Chicago restaurants. At the rate I'm going, it would take another 26 years just to visit them all. Yet, this book is the most complete, up-to-date and accurate guide we know of, thanks to the editors and management of the *Chicago Tribune*.

The *Tribune* encourages me to be sure of what I write, financing as many visits as necessary to "get it right." Every restaurant is visited anonymously at least twice before a review appears in the paper. If two visits lead to different conclusions, a third visit or more is required. I have visited some restaurants as many as six or seven times before writing about them. The cost can be astronomical.

Accentuating the Positive

Some people complain—none of the restaurateurs, mind you—that I never write anything negative about restaurants. This is not true. First, these critics fail to notice that I rarely write anything entirely positive about any restaurant I review. Second, many of the restaurants I visit never make it into the newspaper. I see no reason to bludgeon a little ethnic restaurant or neighborhood eatery that has lousy food and service. They will put themselves out of business—or, more accurately, their lack of customers will—quite nicely without my help.

Others, usually restaurateurs, complain that I never tell the restaurateur's side of the story. There is some truth to this accusation. But why should consumers be bothered with the restaurateur's problems? Unless restaurant operators are willing to discount prices when the food or service isn't up to snuff, then the customer who pays full price has every right to expect full value for his or her dollar no matter what problems the restaurateur may have that day.

The reviews in this book reflect my personal opinion about what makes a restaurant good or bad. I assume that the vast majority of readers simply want to go out and have a good time. They want to come home feeling they received good value for their money, whether the total price comes to $10 or more than $100. A few readers, I call them restaurant groupies, want to know about the latest in restaurant styles and culinary innovations. The reviews note these whenever possible.

My three and a half years of eating out convince me that despite the occasional loser, Chicago has a vast number of high-quality restaurants. Claims on behalf of other cities notwithstanding, the number of ethnically diverse restaurants in Chicago exceeds that of any American city, including New York, San Francisco and New Orleans, the cities most often cited as dining meccas.

Indeed, Chicago may be the country's most underrated city for its culinary achievements. All of which makes my job the best in Chicago journalism.

A Couple of Caveats

At press time, all addresses, telephone numbers, hours, credit cards and reservation policies have been checked and double-checked. However, restaurants seem to get some kind of perverse enjoyment from changing their hours and policies. Please use the information here as a guide. If you want to be absolutely sure of current policies, phone ahead.

Don't forget that restaurants come and go here as fast as the wind changes. Fifty percent of all new restaurants, even the good ones, close within three years, according to the Illinois Restaurant Association. Luckily, there are always replacements. But, phone ahead if you aren't absolutely sure the restaurant of your choice is still with us.

PRICES

Restaurants thrive on change. Revisions of prices, usually upward, occur without notice. So instead of specific prices, I've given price ranges in each listing.

The ranges are based on the price of a dinner for one, including appetizer or soup, salad, entree, dessert, tax and tip. Note that neither wine nor liquor, both of which can add greatly to the price of a meal, is included in the price range. Note also that these are average prices, and a person ordering the most expensive dishes at a modestly priced restaurant could push the bill up to the moderately expensive category. Likewise, judicious choices can provide an inexpensive meal in a restaurant classified as moderately expensive.

The average price ranges given per person are as follows:

Inexpensive:	less than $10
Moderate:	$10–$25
Moderately expensive:	$25–$40
Expensive:	More than $40

TIPPING

Tipping is a problem. It causes consumers discomfort because they are confused about who gets what and how much. The problem is even worse in restaurants simply because there are more people to tip. Tipping should be considered a tool, a means of indicating pleasure or displeasure.

Servers, most of whom are paid minimum wages or less, depend on tips to earn a liveable income. The standard tip for a waiter or waitress is 15 to 20 percent. A tip is not mandatory. It should be adjusted up or down as the situation dictates.

In most situations, it's easy to identify who's responsible for good or bad service. Rudeness or gross errors are easy to pinpoint. Slow service or long pauses between courses may be the fault of either the server or the kitchen. Try to figure out which it is. If the kitchen is at fault, complain to the owner or manager rather than penalizing the waiter or waitress.

When the restaurant has both a captain who announces the specials, makes suggestions and takes orders and a waiter who delivers the food, the traditional 15 to 20 percent tip should be divided between the two, with roughly one-third going to the captain and two-thirds to the waiter. Again, use your own judgment on this. If the waiter does all of the work and the captain does little more than hand you the menu and take the order, he deserves little more reward than the acknowledgement of his existence.

Increasingly, restaurants make the division of the tip automatically. However, at some restaurants if you do not divide the tip between waiter and captain, the captain gets nothing. If your charge card provides separate areas for the two tips, you can compensate for restaurant policy if you like.

Bus boys generally get a share of the waiter's tips automatically, so you need not leave a tip for the bus boy. However, if the bus boy performs some useful extra service, such as bringing a pack of cigarettes, an extra tip should be given, usually 50 cents.

The old practice of slipping the maitre d' $20 to get a good table ahead of others has pretty much disappeared. That was probably never as effective a technique as the movies made it out to be. However, if you are a regular at a particular restaurant, you may wish to tip the maitre d' $5 to $10 from time to time for making sure that you get the table and service you desire. Maitre d's who actually know their customers by name and take especially good care of them are few and far between, and deserve special acknowledgement. Under most normal circumstances, however, the maitre d' expects no tip.

The sommelier or wine steward is often overlooked in the tipping scheme. When the sommelier is helpful in choosing a wine, a tip of two dollars a bottle, irrespective of the price of the bottle, is appropriate. If the steward simply fetches and uncorks a wine you have selected, no tip is necessary, although it may still be expected at expensive restaurants.

Coat checking is a service that should be offered free to patrons of a restaurant. When a fee is charged, no tip is necessary. However, when free service is offered, a tip of 50 cents to a dollar per garment is appropriate. Use your judgement, taking into consideration the price range of the restaurant you're in and the number of items you check.

I hate the institution of washroom attendants. Usually they catch you with your pants literally down and with no change for a tip. Most often the attendant is more an embarassment than a service. Nevertheless, the normal tip is 25 to 50 cents—provided the attendant actually does

Star ratings are a mixed blessing. On the positive side they offer you quite a quick reference to the overall quality of a restaurant and force me to take a firm stand. To that end, there are no half stars in this book. There's no hedging.

On the negative side, stars are a gross generalization of a restaurant's worth. Restaurants are not only the food they serve, but also their appearance, their attitude toward their customers and, in a real sense, their position in contemporary society as a whole. Star ratings encompass all of this.

A two-star restaurant might well serve a four-star meal. Likewise, it could serve a no-star meal. That's what averages are all about.

To minimize error, no *Tribune* review appears without at least two visits to the restaurant and often more. Each visit involves at least two people, sometimes more than two, so that a wide range of food can be sampled. This sampling includes not only different main courses—fish, poultry, game, red meat, and vegetables—but also different preparations and saucing.

Still, it is my opinion that counts. I taste everything on everyone's plates and make up my own mind. I may respectfully listen to the comments of others in my party, but the reviews are based on my reactions, not theirs. The ratings in this book may differ slightly from those previously published in the *Tribune*, not only because they have been updated, but because I do not always agree with other *Tribune* restaurant reviewers.

This is an important distinction to you. Reviewing restaurants is a subjective business at best. What I like, you may not like at all. What I dislike you may love. That doesn't really matter as long as I am consistent. You can read my reviews and judge my opinions by your own standards, which will tell you how likely you are to like or dislike a restaurant I review. Therefore it is critical that these reviews be based on my opinions and no one else's.

My judgement of the quality of the food represents about 70 percent of the star rating. Price, or value for the dollar spent, represents another 15 percent. The remaining 15 percent of the rating is divided among service, cleanliness, ambiance and comfort.

Some confusion inevitably arises when a little neighborhood storefront Thai restaurant gets two stars and a beautiful, sophisticated French restaurant gets only one. How can this be?

There are two answers to this question. First, on an absolute basis, the humble Thai eatery may serve better food than the glitzy French place.

Second, the following legend appears with every *Tribune* review: "This rating reflects the reviewer's opinion of the food in relation to price compared to similar restaurants in the Chicago area."

Therefore, the two-star Thai restaurant is rated in relationship to other Thai restaurants, while the French restaurant competes with other French restaurants. The two do not compete with each other for a rating.

PROBLEMS

What happens when you don't get what you pay for?

Too often people pay the bill, walk out the door never to return and spread the word among their friends that a restaurant is bad without ever letting the restaurant manager or owner know. As a paying customer you have a right to complain when things go wrong.

Most restaurateurs try to do a good job, want your return business and appreciate your immediate criticism when something goes wrong. If service is rude or careless, ask for the manager or owner and complain. If the food is not good or not what you ordered, send it back. Make the kitchen aware of its errors.

Don't be intimidated by a fancy place with exotic-sounding dishes and waiters with condescending attitudes. Even if you don't know how to pronounce the name of a dish or how it's prepared, it should taste good. If it doesn't, let your server know. Quietly accepting poor service or bad food does nothing to improve the restaurant or help you and your fellow diners.

If all else fails—you have complained, you have left no tip and you are still not satisfied that the wrongs will be corrected—write a letter to the owner documenting your experiences and send a copy to me. I will place your letter in our file on the restaurant and be mindful of the problems you mention when I make my next review visit.

ENJOY

It is my sincere hope that this book will introduce you to some restaurants you didn't know about, and remind you of some old favorites you may have forgotten. Most of all I hope the book helps increase your enjoyment of dining out in Chicago. And may your only problems result from the temptations of great food.

Now I'm going on a diet!

RESTAURANTS BY CUISINE

Alsation
Hibbeler's

Afghanistan
Helmand, The

American
Acorn On Oak
Ambria
American Grill
Amerique
Army & Lou Restaurant
  & Lounge
Arnie's Cafe
Bar Harbor
Barney's Market Club
Bencher's Club Room
Bencher's Grille
Bennigan's Tavern
Blue Mesa
Bijan
Billy Goat Tavern &
  Grill
Bob Chinn's Crab House
Boston Blackie's
Carson's—The Place For
  Ribs

Chicago Claim Co.
Cricket's
Dixie Bar & Grill
Don Roth's River Plaza
Ed Debevic's Short
  Orders/Deluxe
Foley's Grand Ohio
Grillade, La
Lem's
Hackney's
Hamburger Hamlet
Hy's Of Canada
Lawry's—The Prime Rib
Mallory's On Wells
Mary D's
Murphy's Bleachers
95th, The
Periwinkle
Philander's
Printer's Row
Pump Room, The
Randall's
R.D. Clucker's
R.J. Grunts
Rue Saint Clair
Sage's
Santa Fe Cafe

Sessions Pullman Club
Showboat Sari-S II
Sinclair's
Staley's Of Chicago
Star Of Chicago
Star Top Cafe
Sweetwater
Timbers Charhouse
Tony Roma's A Place For
  Ribs
Top Notch Beefburger
  Shop
Walnut Room
Winnetka Grill

Armenian
Casbah
Sayat Nova

British
  (English/Irish/Scottish)
Atlantic Restaurant
Cafe Royal

Cajun/Creole
Maple Tree Inn
Ragin' Cajun

Chinese
Dee's Restaurant
Dragon Palace
House Of Hunan

Imperial Cathay
Mandar-Inn
Mandarin Garden
On The Tao
Pago Pago
Panda's
Shi Hu
Szechwan Kitchen
Wok's

Continental
Ash Manor
Bakery, The
Biggs
Cottage, The
Edgewater Beach Cafe
Nierman's
Star Top Cafe
Zodiac

Cuban
Castellano's
Tania's

Eclectic
Beverly Hills Cafe
Foley's First Street
Gordon
J. P. 's Eating Place
Stats
Tamborine

Ethiopian
Mama Desta's Red Sea
  Restaurant

French
Avalon
Bastille
Boheme, La
Louis' Bon Appetit
Albert's Cafe And
  Patisserie
Cafe D'Artagnan
Cafe Du Parc
Cafe Provencal
Carlos Restaurant
Chardonnay, The
Chez Paul
Ciboulette, La
Cochonnet, Le
Dining Room At The
  Ritz Carlton, The
Fontaine, La
Four Farthings
Francais, Le
Froggy's
Grand Cafe, Un
Jackie's
Jimmy's Place
Meme Chose, La
Perroquet, Le
Plumes, Les

Tallgrass
Titi De Paris, Le
Toulouse
Tour, La
Vichyssois, Le
Yoshi's Cafe
Yvette

Fondue
Geja's Cafe

Georgian
Kavkaz

German
Berghoff
Binyon's
Golden Ox
Heidelberger Fass
Schulien's

Greek
Courtyards Of Plaka,
  The
Greek Islands
Parthenon
Roditys

Indian
Bombay Palace
Standard India

Italian
Abati
Aurelio's
Avanzare
Bacchanalia
Bruna's Ristorante
Cafe Angelo
Cafe Spiaggia
Capannina, La
Carlos & Carlos
Carlucci
Chef Eduardo's
Convito Italiano
  Restaurant
Corona
Crema Dolce Cafe
Da Nicola
Danilo's
Father & Son Pizza
Florentine Room
Fricano's
Gene & Georgetti
George's
Gondola, La
Grand Wells Tap
John's Restaurant And
  Pizzeria
Leona's
New Rosebud Cafe
Papa Milano
Riccardo
Riggio's

Caffe Pranzo
Sogni Dorati
Spiaggia
Strada Ristorante, La
Taste Of Italy
T. Colombo's And
  Oscar's
Vicinato, Il

Japanese
Benihana Of Tokyo
Happi Sushi
Ko Chi
Ron Of Japan

Korean
Gin Go Gae
Shilla Restaurant

Mexican
Abril
Costa Azul
Matador, El
Plumas, Las
Salvador's
Su Casa
Villita, La

Pizza
Father & Son Pizza
Gino's East
Pizzerias Uno & Due

Polish
Arcadia

Portuguese/Brazilian
Rio's

Seafood
Annabelle's Fish Market
Cape Cod Room
Charley'sCrab
Chestnut Street Grill
Davis Street Fishmarket
Dearborn Street Oyster
   Bar
Don's Fishmarket And
   Tavern
Fricano's
Ireland's
King Crab Tavern &
   Seafood Grill
Maple Street Pier
Nick's Fishmarket
Shaw's Crab House &
   Blue Crab Lounge
Tango
Tap Root Pub
Turbot
Waterfront Restaurant,
   The

Serbian
Miomir's Serbian Club

Spanish
Cafe Ba-Ba-Reeba!

Steaks
Eli's The Place For
   Steaks
Gene & Georgetti
Grand Wells Tap
Hy's Of Canada
Morton's
Palm, The

Thai
Ananda
Arun's
Bangkok Star
Pattaya
Siam Square
Sri Uthai
Star Of Siam
Thai Room

Vietnamese
Mekong Restaurant
Mimosa Cafe
Song Huong
Yugoslavian
Yugo Inn Restaurant &
   Bar

RESTAURANTS BY LOCATION

Downtown
Bar Harbor
Bencher's Club Room
Bencher's Grille
Benihana of Tokyo
Bennigan's Tavern
Berghoff
Beverly Hills Cafe
Binyon's
Cafe Angelo
Dearborn Street Oyster Bar
Florentine Room
Nick's Fishmarket
Pago Pago
Printer's Row
Salvador's
Staley's of Chicago
Star of Chicago
La Strada Ristorante
Walnut Room

Near North
Abati's
Acorn on Oak
Ambria
Amerique

Ananda
Arnie's Cafe
Avanzare
Bastille
Biggs
Bijan
Billy Goat Tavern & Grill
Blue Mesa
Bombay Palace
Boston Blackie's
Albert's Cafe and Patisserie
Cafe Royal
Cafe Spiaggia
Cape Cod Room
Carson's—The Place for Ribs
Charley's Crab
Chef Eduardo's
Chestnut Street Grill
Chez Paul
La Ciboulette
Convito Italiano Restaurant
Corona
Crema Dolce Cafe

Cricket's
Dining Room at the
    Ritz-Carlton, The
Dixie Bar & Grill
Don Roth's River Plaza
Ed Debevic's Short
    Orders/Deluxe
Eli's the Place for Steak
Foley's First Street
Foley's Grand Ohio
Geja's Cafe
Gene & Georgetti
George's
Gino's East
Golden Ox
Gordon
Grand Wells Tap
Hamburger Hamlet
Hibbeler's
House of Hunan
Hunan Palace
Hy's Of Canada
Imperial Cathay
Ireland's
J. P. 's Eating Place
King Crab Tavern &
    Seafood Grill
Lawry's—The Prime Rib
Lino's
Mallory's on Wells
Maple Street Pier
Morton's

95th, The
Palm, The
Papa Milano
Pattaya
Perroquet, Le
Pizzerias Uno & Due
Plumas, Las
Pump Room, The
Randall's
Riccardo
Ron of Japan
Rue Saint Clair
Sage's
Salvador's
Sante Fe Cafe
Sayat Nova
Shaw's Crab House &
    Blue Crab Lounge
Showboat Sari-S II
Sogni Dorati
Spiaggia
Standard India
Star of Siam
Stats
Su Casa
Sweetwater
Szechwan House
Tamborine
Tap Root Pub
Tony Roma's A Place for
    Ribs
Toulouse

24

Tour, La
Turbot
Waterfront
Wok's
Yvette
Zodiac

North
American Grill
Arun's
Ash Manor
Bakery, The
Bangkok Star
Boheme, La
Cafe Ba-Ba-Reeba
Cafe D'Artagnan
Cafe du Parc
Cafe Provencal
Carlos Restaurant
Carlucci
Carsons—The Place for
  Ribs
Casbah
Chardonnay, The
Chicago Claim Co.
Cochonnet, Le
Da Nicola
Davis Street Fishmarket
Dee's Restaurant
Don's Fishmarket &
  Tavern
Edgewater Beach Cafe

Fontaine, La
Four Farthings
Fricano's
Froggy's
Gin Go Gae
Grand Cafe, Un
Grillade, La
Hackney's
Happi Sushi
Heidelberger Fass
Helmand, The
Jackie's
Jimmy's Place
Kavkaz
Ko Chi Restaurant
Meme Chose, La
Leona's
Mama Desta's Red Sea
  Restaurant
Mandarin Garden
Mekong Restaurant
Miomir's Serbian Club
Murphy's Bleachers
On the Tao
Panda's
Periwinkle
Plumes, Les
Ragin' Cajun
R. D. Clucker's
Riggio's Caffe Pranzo
Rio's
R. J. Grunts
Schulien's

Shi Hu
Shilla Restaurant
Siam Square
Sinclair's
Song Huong
Star Top Cafe
Szechwan Kitchen
Tango
T. Colombo's and
  Oscar's
Thai Room
Timbers Charhouse
Villita, La
Winnetka Grill
Yoshi's
Yugo Inn

Northwest
Abril
Annabelle's Fish Market
Arcadia
Avalon
Bob Chinn's Crab House
Carlos & Carlos
Carsons—The Place for
  Ribs
Castellano's
Dragon Palace
Father & Son Pizza
Francais, Le
Hackney's
Happi Shushi
Sage's

Sayat Nova
Sri Uthai
Tania's
Titi de Paris, Le
Vichyssois, Le

South
Army & Lou Restaurant
  & Lounge
Aurelio's
Louis' Bon Appetit
Cottage, The
John's Restaurant and
  Pizzeria
Lem's
Mandar-Inn
Maple Tree Inn
Mary D's
Nierman's
Sessions Pullman Club
Taste of Italy
Top Notch Beefburger
  Shop

Southwest
Bacchanalia
Bruna's Ristorante
Courtyards of Plaka, The
Greek Islands
New Rosebud Cafe
Parthenon
Roditys

Tallgrass
Vicinato, Il

West
Atlantic Restaurant
Barney's Market Club
Benihana of Tokyo
Capannina, La
Carsons—The Place for
  Ribs
Chicago Claim Co.
Costa Azul
Danilo's
Gondola, La
J. P. 's Eating Place
Matador, El
Mimosa Cafe
Philander's
Sage's
Salvador's

RESTAURANTS BY PRICE

Inexpensive
Acorn On Oak
Arcadia
Aurelio's
Billy Goat Tavern &
  Grill
Boston Blackie's
Dearborn Street Oyster
  Bar
Ed Debevic's Short
  Orders/Deluxe
Father & Son Pizza
Mama Desta's Red Sea
  Restaurant
Mekong Restaurant
Mimosa Cafe
Murphy's Bleachers
Pizzerias Uno & Due
Salvador's
Shi Hu
Showboat Sari-S II
Siam Square
Song Huong
Sri Uthai
Thai Room
Top Notch Beefburger
  Shop

Moderate
Abril
Abati's
Albert's Cafe and
  Patisserie
Annabelle's Fish Market
Ananda
Army & Lou Restaurant
  & Lounge
Arnie's Cafe
Arun's
Atlantic Restaurant
Bacchanalia
Bakery, The
Bangkok Star
Barney's Market Club
Bastille
Bencher's Grille
Benihana of Tokyo
Bennigan's Tavern
Berghoff
Biggs
Bijan
Blue Mesa
Bob Chinn's Crab House
Bruna's Ristorante

Cafe Angelo
Cafe Du Parc
Cafe Spiaggia
Casbah
Castellano's
Chardonay, The
Chicago Claim Co.
Cochonnet, Le
Corona
Costa Azul
Courtyards Of Plaka, The
Crema Dolce Cafe
Da Nicola
Danilo's
Dragon Palace
Edgewater Beach Cafe
Foley's First Street
Fricano's
Froggy's
Geja's Cafe
Gin Go Gae
Gino's East
Gondola, La
Grand Wells Tap
Greek Islands
Hackney's
Hamburger Hamlet
Heidelberger Fass
Helmand, The
Hibbeler's
J. P. 's Eating Place

John's Restaurant and Pizzeria
Kavkaz
King Crab Tavern & Seafood Grill
Tap Root Pub
Taste Of Italy
T. Colombo's And Oscar's
Timbers Charhouse
Tony Roma's A Place for Ribs
Vicinato, Il
Villita, La
Walnut Room
Wok's
Yugo Inn Restaurant & Bar
Yvette
Zodiac

Moderately Expensive
American Grill
Amerique
Ash Manor
Avanzare
Bar Harbor
Bencher's Club Room
Beverly Hills Cafe
Binyon's
Bombay Palace
Cafe Ba-Ba-Reeba!
Louis' Bon Appetit

Cafe D'Artagnan
Cafe Royal
Capannina, La
Carlos & Carlos
Carlucci
Carson's—The Place For
 Ribs
Charley's Crab
Chef Eduardo's
Chestnut Street Grill
Convito Italiano
 Restaurant
Cottage, The
Cricket's
Davis Street Fishmarket
Dee's Restaurant
Dixie Bar & Grill
Don's Fishmarket And
 Tavern
Don Roth's River Plaza
Eli's The Place For
 Steaks
Foley's Grand Ohio
Four Farthings
Gene & Georgetti
George's
Golden Ox
Grand Cafe, Un
Grillade, La
Happi Sushi
House Of Hunan
Hy's Of Canada

Imperial Cathay
Ireland's
Lawry's—The Prime Rib
Lino's
Mallory's On Wells
Mandar-Inn
Maple Street Pier
Maple Tree Inn
Mary D's
Nierman's
Philander's
Plumes, Les
Rue Saint Clair
Sage's
Shulien's
Sessions Pullman Club
Shaw's Crab House &
 Blue Crab Lounge
Star Of Chicago
Stats
Su Casa
Sweetwater
Turbot
Vichyssois, Le
Waterfront Restaurant,
 The
Winnetka Grill

Expensive

Ambria
Avalon
Boheme, La
Cafe Provencal
Cape Cod Room
Carlos Restaurant
Chez Paul
Ciboulette, La
Dining Room At The
    Ritz Carlton, The
Florentine Room
Fontaine, La
Francais, Le
Gordon
Jackie's
Jimmy's Place
Morton's
Nick's Fishmarket
95th, The
Palm, The
Perroquet, Le
Printers Row
Pump Room, The
Randall's
Ron of Japan
Sinclair's
Sogni Dorati
Spiaggia
Strada Ristorante, La
Tallgrass

Tango
Titi De Paris, Le
Toulouse
Tour, La
Yoshi's Cafe

RESTAURANTS BY STAR RATING

Poor
Hy's Of Canada
Rue Saint Clair
Tony Roma's A Place For
   Ribs

Fair
Abati's
Annabelle's Fish Market
Ash Manor
Bangkok Star
Bencher's Club Room
Benihana Of Tokyo,
   downtown
Bennigan's Tavern
Beverly Hills Cafe
Cafe Royal
Chez Paul
Davis Street Fishmarket
Grand Wells Tap
Hamburger Hamlet
Hibbeler's
Meme Chose, La
Pago Pago
Plumas, Las
Pump Room, The
Rio's

Rodity's
Shi Hu
Showboat Sari-S II
Sweetwater
Szechwan Kitchen
Tap Root Pub
Wok's

One Star—★
Abril
Acorn On Oak
Albert's Cafe And
   Patisserie
American Grill
Amerique
Ananda
Arnie's Cafe
Atlantic Restaurant
Aurelio's
Bakery, The
Bar Harbor
Barney's Market Club
Bastille
Benihana Of Tokyo,
   Lombard
Berghoff
Biggs

Billy Goat Tavern & Grill
Binyon's
Blue Mesa
Boheme, La
Boston Blackie's
Bruna's Ristorante
Cafe Angelo
Cafe Du Parc
Cape Cod Room
Carlucci
Carson's—The Place For Ribs
Castellano's
Charley's Crab
Chef Eduardo's
Chicago Claim Co.
Corona
Cottage, The
Crema Dolce Cafe
Cricket's
Dearborn Street Oyster Bar
Dee's Restaurant
Dixie Bar & Grill
Don's Fishmarket And Tavern
Dragon Palace
Edgewater Beach Cafe
Father & Son Pizza
Fontaine, La
Four Farthings

Fricano's
Geja's Cafe
Gene & Georgetti
Gin Go Gae
Gondola, La
Hackney's
Heidelberger Fass
Imperial Cathay
Ireland's
J. P. 's Eating Place
Star Of Siam
Stats
Su Casa
Tamborine
Tango
Tania's
Taste Of Italy
T. Colombo's And Oscar's
Top Notch Beefburger Shop
Vicinato, Il
Villita, La
Walnut Room
Waterfront Restaurant (The)
Yugo Inn Restaurant & Bar
Yvette
Zodiac

Two Stars—★★

Arcadia
Army & Lou Restaurant
  & Lounge
Arun's
Avanzare
Bacchanalia
Bijan
Bob Chinn's Crab House
Bombay Palace
Cafe Ba-Ba-Reeba!
Cafe Spiaggia
Capannina, La
Carlos & Carlos
Casbah
Convito Italiano
  Restaurant
Cochonnet, Le
Costa Azul
Courtyards of Plaka,
  The
Da Nicola
Danilo's
Don Roth's River Plaza
Ed Debevic's Short
  Orders/Deluxe
Eli's The Place For
  Steaks
Florentine Room
Foley's First Street
Foley's Grand Ohio
Froggy's
George's

Gino's East
Golden Ox
Gordon
Grand Cafe, Un
Greek Islands
Grillade, La
Happi Sushi
Helmand, The
House Of Hunan
Jimmy's Place
Kavkaz
Louis' Bon Appetit
Mama Desta's Red Sea
  Restaurant
Mandar-Inn
Maple Street Pier
Mekong Restaurant
Nick's Fishmarket
95th, The
On The Tao
Pattaya
Philander's
Pizzerias Uno & Due
Randall's
Riggio's Cafe Pranzo
Ron Of Japan
Sessions Pullman Club
Shilla Restaurant
Siam Square
Sinclair's
Sogni Dorati
Song Huong

Sri Uthai
Star Top Cafe
Strada Ristorante, La
Thai Room
Timbers Charhouse
Toulouse
Turbot

Three Stars— ★ ★ ★
Ambria
Cafe D'Artagnan
Cafe Provencal
Chardonnay, The
Chestnut Street Grill
Ciboulette, La
Dining Room At The
    Ritz Carlton, The
Jackie's
Lawry's—The Prime Rib
Lem's
Maple Tree Inn
New Rosebud Cafe
Plumes, Les
Printer's Row
Shaw's Crab House &
    Blue Crab Lounge
Spiaggia
Titi De Paris, Le
Tour, La
Vichyssois, Le
Winnetka Grill
Yoshi's Cafe

Four Stars ★ ★ ★ ★
Avalon
Carlos Restaurant
Francais, Le
Morton's
Perroquet, Le
Tallgrass

RESTAURANTS OPEN ON SUNDAY

Abril
Abati's
Acorn On Oak
Albert's Cafe and
  Patisserie
American Grill
Annabelle's Fish Market
Ananda
Arcadia
Army & Lou Restaurant
  & Lounge
Arnie's Cafe
Arun's
Ash Manor
Atlantic Restaurant
Aurelio's
Avalon
Avanzare
Bacchanalia
Bangkok Star
Barney's Market Club
Bastille
Benihana of Tokyo
Bennigan's Tavern
Biggs
Bijan
Billy Goat Tavern &

Grill
Blue Mesa
Bob Chinn's Crab House
Bombay Palace
Bruna's Ristorante
Cafe Angelo
Cafe D'Artagnan
Cafe Du Parc
Cafe Royal
Cafe Spiaggia
Capannina, La
Cafe Cod Room
Carlos Restaurant
Carlos & Carlos
Carlucci
Carsons—The Place For
  Ribs
Casbah
Castellano's
Chardonnay, The
Charley's Crab
Chestnut Street Grill
Chez Paul
Chicago Claim Co.
Ciboulette, La
Costa Azul
Courtyards Of Plaka, The

Crickets
Da Nicola
Dee's Restaurant
Dining Room At The Ritz Carlton, The
Dixie Bar & Grill
Don's Fishmarket And Tavern
Don Roth's River Plaza
Dragon Palace
Ed Debevic's Short Orders/Deluxe
Edgewater Beach Cafe
Eli's The Place For Steaks
Father & Son Pizza
Four Farthings
Le Francais
Fricano's
Geja's Cafe
Gin Go Gae
Gino's East
Golden Ox
Gordon
Grand Wells Tap
Greek Islands
Grillade, La
Hackney's
Hamburger Hamlet
Happi Sushi
Heidelberger Fass
Hibbeler's
House Of Hunan
Imperial Cathay
Ireland's
J. P. 's Eating Place
John's Restaurant and Pizzeria
Kavkaz
King Crab Tavern & Seafood Grill
Ko Chi Restaurant
Meme Chose, La
Lawry's—The Prime Rib
Lem's
Leona's
Louis' Bon Appetit,
Mama Desta's Red Sea Restaurant
Mandar-Inn
Matador, El
Mekong Restaurant
Mimosa Cafe
Murphy's Bleachers
Nierman's
On The Tao
Panda's
Papa Milano
Parthenon
Pattaya
Periwinkle
Pizzerias Uno & Due
Pump Room, The
Randall's

R.D. Clucker's
Riccardo
Riggio's Caffe Pranzo
Rio's
R.J. Grunts
Ron Of Japan
Rue Saint Clair
Sage's
Salvador's
Santa Fe Cafe
Sayat Nova
Sessions Pullman Club
Shaw's Crab House &
    Blue Crab Lounge
Shilla Restaurant
Siam Square
Sinclair's
Song Huong
Spiaggia
Sri Uthai
Staley's of Chicago
Standard India
Sweetwater
Szechwan Kitchen
Tallgrass
Tango
Tania's
Tap Root Pub
Taste Of Italy
T. Colombo's And
    Oscar's
Thai Room

Timbers Charhouse
Tony Roma's A Place For
    Ribs
Tour, La
Vichyssois, Le
Villita, La
Walnut Room
Waterfront Restaurant,
    The
Winnetka Grill
Wok's
Yoshi's Cafe
Yugo Inn Restaurant &
    Bar
Yvette

ABATI'S
Italian
Rating: Fair

60 E. Walton St.   280-7788
Hours: Sun–Thurs 11 am–midnight, Fri & Sat 11–1 am
Price range: Moderate
Credit cards: A   C   D   M   V
Reservations: Accepted

From the outset, let it be said that Abati's attracts a large following of diners with a gimmick: "Abati's Original Flamed Pizza." It should also be noted that I don't think much of theatrics for the sake of theatrics.

Here's the bit: the waiter arrives tableside with a deep-dish pizza and a jigger of a "secret" concoction. With a bit of fanfare, he pours the booze over the pizza and flicks his Bic until the pizza bursts into flames. The result: tomato sauce extinguishes the fire pretty quickly, leaving the end of each pizza slice tasting mostly of alcohol. Yuck!

In a town known for its terrific pizza, this is a really bad idea. The other fare here includes ribs, Italian specialities, average salads and the like. None of it is terrible, but none of it's very good either.

The people who serve here are incredibly nice and the decor is pleasant. Silly theatrics can be fun if that's what you're after. Just don't expect great food.

★ ABRIL
Mexican

2607 N. Milwaukee Ave.   227-7252
Hours: Daily 11 am–12 pm
Price range: Moderate
Credit cards: A   M   V
Reservations: Accepted
Handicap

By no means the best Mexican restaurant in Chicago, but far from the worst, this cheery place offers traditional fare at relatively modest prices.

Abril means April in Spanish and with bright lighting, hanging plants and festive Mexican folk designs under clear epoxy on the table tops, the restaurant has a warm, springlike ambiance. In the small bar in the back of the room there is a hanging piñata, that can be lowered so that children can take a prize from its open top.

The warmth and friendliness of the place carries over to the waiters in their white shirts and pants with red or green cumberbunds. Service is efficient and pleasant.

Appetizers include the usual offerings. Pizza ala Mexicana, described on the menu as six small flour tortillas filled with cheese, Mexican sausage, onions, tomato sauce and topped with melted cheese and cilantro, are neither pizza nor Mexican but taste good. Flautas, large tortillas filled with chicken and topped with guacamole and sour cream, have a generous amount of chicken and good flavor. Rice, refried beans and shredded iceberg lettuce come on the side.

Deep fried whole red snapper, covered with a melange of tomato, pepper, carrots, olives and celery, tastes a tad fishy, but the topping, heavily seasoned with cumin, helps improve the flavor.

In general, the food here isn't as toned-down for the "gringos" as it is in many other places, which is a nice difference. The low prices attracted a mixed crowd from Hispanic families to yuppies singles, reflecting the ethnic and economic mix of the Abril's Logan Square neighborhood.

★ ACORN ON OAK
American

116 E. Oak St.   944-6835
Hours: Mon–Sat 11:30 am–10:30 pm, Sun 4:30–9 pm

Price range: Inexpensive
Credit cards: A
Reservations: Recommended

Long a favorite of people who live near Oak Street, for its congenial bar and reasonable prices, this remains one of the few places in the area where one can dine in comfort and still walk out arms and legs intact. It also is one of the few late-night places open to 4 a.m. Mon.-Sat., with a lively piano bar.

The claim to fame here is an excellent hamburger. The Acorn burger, with green pepper and onions incorporated into the meat before cooking, is one of the best examples of this genre in Chicago. It could have a few more onions, but the meat is fresh, the outside is charred, the inside moist and cooked as ordered. This burger, or a more standard version, comes on sesame buns with onion, tomato, pickle and lettuce as well as good, large steak fries.

The restaurant has the warmth of a friendly neighborhood eatery, but, befitting its upscale surrounds, the decor here is a darned sight classier. Inside the entrance, a bar stretches toward the small dining room. At lunch the atmosphere tends to be subdued and a little blue-haired-ladyish. On busy nights the crowd livens up considerably.

★ ALBERT'S CAFE AND PATISSERIE
French

52 W. Elm St.,   751-0666
Hours: Tues–Fri 10 am–9:30 pm, Sat 9 am–9:30 pm,
*   Sun 9 am–8 pm*
Price range: Moderate
Credit cards: Not accepted
Reservations: Not accepted

Albert's Cafe sits behind its older and more formal brother, Biggs. Like Biggs', Albert's offers terrific value for a

41

downtown restaurant; a full dinner with a couple of glasses of wine will run two persons $25. The cafe is unpretentious and fun.

Located in a carriage house, the tiny room has only 10 tables. In marked contrast to the dark, stained interior of the main house, the cafe is bright and cheery. And while the young servers here could take a few lessons from the more polished waiters in the main restaurant, they make up for small gaffes with pleasant demeanor.

A pastry case at the front of the room displays pastries and tortes in a glass case, a broad selection, with more than a few winners. Thus, this is a good place for late-night espresso and desserts.

Soups are excellent, entrees less pleasing but a good value for the price. (BIGGS, page 82.)

★ ★ ★ ★ AMBRIA
Nouvelle cuisine

Belden-Stratford Hotel, 2300 N. Lincoln Park West
472-5959
Hours: Mon–Thurs 6–9:30 pm, Fri&Sat 6–10:30 pm, closed
    Sun
Price Range: Expensive
Credit cards: A   C   D   M   V
Reservations: Necessary

Restaurant critic Mimi Sheraton complains that Ambria smells of wax, but I would rather think of its giving off the fragrance of a well-oiled operation. It must take gallons of wax to maintain the miles of darkly stained wood in this splendid art nouveau room which, despite its large size, affords diners a sense of privacy.

Ambria opened to almost instant critical acclaim. That must have been pretty heady stuff for Richard Melman, who had proven his business acumen with such lighthearted Lettuce Entertain You restaurants as R.J. Grunts and Fritz That's It, but had yet to prove that he could succeed with a restaurant devoted to fine cuisine and careful service. Heady, too, for Melman's partner, chef Gabino Sotelino, whose thoughtfully creative Nouvelle cuisine won the rave reviews.

Ambria was one of the first restaurants in Chicago (Le Perroquet was the first) to seriously present excellently prepared nouvelle cuisine. With the novelty of nouvelle long since faded, Ambria must now depend on well-conceived flavor combinations, drop-dead presentation and attentive, knowledgeable service.

Jaded diners may grouse that Ambria has become downright boring. Indeed, the menu has not changed much, although the nightly specials follow the latest food trends. Surprisingly, the prices have not escalated greatly over several years of operation. One caveat: the price of the long list of enticing specials runs considerably higher that the menu offerings, even though the exciting combinations often justify the stiff tariff.

Appetizers continue to be one of the restaurant's strong points. Among the best: fresh, mousse-like foie gras, carpaccio, tender pieces of flavorful meat in a green vegetable sauce, dusted with parmesan cheese; the pate of duck, venison, chicken liver and head cheese patés big enough for two to share; a costly but wonderful mix of smoked eel, salmon and Beluga cavier served on baby lettuce leaves.

Meats are served rare. The menu boasts that the prime rib-eye is cooked 15 seconds on each side. The calves liver served with a crusty coating of mustard seeds and pan drippings is no exception. All of the fish entrees are specials here. The mixed grill (turbot, salmon and swordfish one night) is perfectly prepared with three sauces.

As in all Melman's restaurants, desserts here are sweet and seductive. Worth a visit on their own merit: fresh blueberry tart with a thick, buttery crust, white chocolate mousse sauced with smooth, bitter dark chocolate, flourless chocolate cake with freshly made whipped cream, and some of the best coffee to be found in any Chicago restaurant.

An extensive and expensive wine list supports the meals. Some half bottles are available. The wine steward is both knowledgeable and helpful, without all-too-common pretension. Bargains are few, but the steward can be an invaluable guide to them.

Jackets are required and blue jeans are not allowed.

★ AMERICAN GRILL
American

1913 Waukegan Road, Glenview   998-6070
Hours: Mon–Fri 11:30 am–2:30 pm, Sun–Thurs 5:30–9:30
*   pm, Fri & Sat 5:30–10 pm*
Price Range: Moderately expensive
Credit cards: A C D M V
Reservations: Recommended
Handicap

This strip of Waukegan Road has the feel of fast-food heaven. Indeed, this restaurant is housed in a former Sambo's restaurant shell, although you'd never know it.

Billed as a second generation, California-style restaurant, American Grill does have an open, breezy feel. A greenhouse-like glass front may have a chilling effect in the midst of Chicago's snowy winters, but light colors and plants try to call up sunny California.

An amalgamation of everything trendy, the restaurant doesn't quite succeed at making any real statement. Because wood grilling is in, there's a wood grill, even a trendy vertical spit. Since carry-out is in, there's a carry-out counter. And since noisy, open dining is in, the room is open and can be noisy.

Still, the mesquite-grilled seafood and chops are prepared

skillfully, if simply. A wood-burning oven turns out thin crust pizzas, topped with goat-cheesy sorts of things, that taste okay but could give California-style pizza a bad name. Veggies come on the side with entrees, warmed but too crisp to call cooked.

Servers mean well and try their best, but often are woefully ill-informed about the menu. California wines dominate the limited list, with some good values.

Despite its problems, American Grill certainly provides a much-needed alternative to the plastic castles of fast food.

★ AMERIQUE
American

900 N. Franklin St.   943-6341
Hours: Mon–Fri noon–3 pm, Tues–Thurs 6–9 pm, Fri & Sat
*   6–10 pm, closed Sun*
Price range: Moderately expensive
Credit cards: M   V
Reservations: Accepted
Handicap

Amerique definitely leaves an impression on people. Some love it, others hate it and more than a few don't know what to make of it. The debate centers on Amerique's interior, rather than on its food. The location, out of the mainstream, suggests a pioneering spirit, which is reinforced by the striking high-tech interior. Concrete floors, white walls studded with a mix of colored light bulbs and fluorescent tubes—originally bare and glaring, now more subdued behind a curtain—and metal frame chairs with black plastic tubes forming the backs and sets, combine to give the room a sleek, contemporary appearance.

Amerique's staff is warm and friendly, from the doorman who greets diners and later hails cabs—often running several blocks before he finds one—to the knowledgeable, attentive servers.

A low-ceilinged bar area lies down a short hall just inside the door of the L-shaped space. The small, jet-black bar sports pillars, again neon-lighted.

In her early twenties, chef-owner Jennifer Newbury possesses great energy, enthusiasm and creativity. Some inconsistencies plague the kitchen, but Newbury's cuisine shows promise, and surely will develop over time.

Wisely, the young chef keeps her menu limited to three appetizers and six entrees. A few specials augment the printed menu, highlighted by interesting combinations of fresh ingredients. Simple preparations predominate, with light sauces which let the natural flavor of the main ingredient shine through.

For starters, try the marinated goat cheese in a pool of mildly garlicky olive oil flecked with bits of pepper, or escargot in puff pastry or, best, charcoal grilled oysters and sausage with a mignonette sauce.

Leaf lettuce with just the right amount of good vinaigrette gets shredded into bite-sized pieces for the dinner salads, included in the price of the entree. Far too many restaurants do not bother with this nicety, which makes salad eating much more manageable. Duck, steak and seafood round out the entrees. The chef favors powerful sauces over delicacy. At times they work, other times they don't.

Desserts fall into that gray area between delightful and disasterous. Best bets include the cheesecakes with fruit toppings, chocolate hazelnut cake and fresh fruits.

ANNABELLE'S FISH MARKET
Seafood
Rating: Fair

2375 S. Arlington Heights Rd., Arlington Heights
439-1028
Hours: Mon–Thurs 11:30 am–10 pm, Fri 11:30 am–11 pm,
Sat 4:30–11 pm, Sun 4–10 pm

Price range: Moderate
Credit cards: A   C   D   M   V
Reservations: Accepted
Handicap

1105 Skokie Blvd., Edens Plaza, Wilmette
256-0110
Hours: Sun–Thurs 11:30 am–10 pm, Fri & Sat 11:30 am–11 pm
Credit cards: A   C   D   M   V
Reservations: Accepted for five or more
Handicap

This pleasant restaurant has brightened considerably since the days when it was called Christopher's. A hostess leads diners down a short flight of stairs to the dining room with brick and peach-colored walls, dark green carpeting and green upholstered chairs. At the center of the restaurant is an oyster bar, largely unused except on busy evenings. To the right is a large bar with a real fireplace that is used on chilly evenings. Wooden tables lack cloths, but have dark green cloth napkins.

Annabelle's claims that its proximity to O'Hare ensures that its fish is the freshest available in the area. Indeed, the fish is fresh, but too many heavy, complicated preparations mask its quality. Stick to the simple grilled, broiled and steamed fish.

Fried calamari starts out fresh, but the starchy, greasy coating on many of the tender squid morsels ruins an otherwise promising starter. Those who enjoy raw fresh clams and oysters will fare better with the raw bar. The house salad that comes with the meals might be avoided altogether. The garden salad of tomato and leaf lettuce is absolutely drowned in a passable dijon dressing. Spinach salad offers no better alternative—a few croutons scattered across fresh spinach smothered in a mediocre cucumber dressing.

With salads comes what is described as sourdough bread, although it has no hint of sourdough flavor. So much for the bad news... The good news is that entrees are large and good, if the simple preparations are chosen. Try the lobster, steamed mussels or shrimp, or have them all in a "shellfish bucket" with red potatoes.

Fish from the grill or broiler, such as bluefish, not often seen in this area, salmon, swordfish and marlin, are also good.

For dessert, try the good Italian ice creams or Boston bonbons—cubes of ice cream covered with a not-so-rich, but adequate chocolate.

Servers are friendly and helpful, but long waits can occur between courses even on slow nights. Annabelle's easily could be a fine restaurant if it stuck with what it does best and corrected what are essentially minor problems with salads, breads and sauces.

★ ANANDA
Thai

941 N. State St.   944-7440
Hours: Lunch Tues–Sat 11:30 am–2 pm, Dinner Tues–Thurs
*   5–10 pm, Fri & Sat 5–10:30 pm, closed Mon*
Price range: Moderate
Credit cards: A   M   V
Reservations: Accepted

When Ananda (which means "infinity" in Thai) opened in 1983 it was a decidedly different—and long overdue—addition to the Thai dining scene. Unlike almost all other storefront Thai restaurants, which provided good examples of this sophisticated complex cuisine, it had a civilized, white-clothed interior with exposed brick walls, hardwood floors, a menu in perfect English and good tableware. In short, a serious restaurant that opened the way for other classier Thai restaurants although none has Ananda's class. Its proximity to a school dictates that, by law, it can have no liquor license.

The kitchen can be a bit uneven. There are more than 60 items on the regular menu, as well as a small number of daily specials. While the menu advises "it is best not to diminish the efforts of the chef by combining dishes," the temptation to sample a wide selection is irresistible.

Appetizers: deep-fried squid stuffed with pork sausage; moist grilled pork satay served with cold, pickled cucumbers and excellent peanut sauce for dipping; paw pia tod, crisp fried egg rolls filled with shrimp and vegetables; larb chiengmai, beefsteak tartare garnished with fresh vegetables (try to ignore the fact that it looks a lot like a Gainesburger).

The most interesting of four soups: gang jued kai muen, steamed pork-filled rolled omelet with tomato and onion, must be ordered 24 hours in advance. The spicy hot shrimp soup with lemon grass is super, a tangy broth with enough fire to make it interesting without setting off extra alarms.

Salads are not what Westerners might expect. Plaa goong, a cold mixture of shrimp, lemon grass, ginger, bamboo shoot, fresh coriander, celery onions and peppers, blazes on the tongue but makes a refreshing interlude before the hot courses.

To turn up the heat to the point of meltdown: gai pad naw mai, stir-fried chicken in a punishing pepper sauce with onions and bamboo shoots. For those without asbestos palates: guey teow Ananda, wide rolled rice noodles and fresh shelled shrimp in an excellent mild sauce.

Don't be put off by the hot and spicy labels on the curries. They're not all that hot, and these are some of the most complex dishes to be sampled here. Delicate and fragrant, sweet and pungent, the coconut-based broth of the tom kha gai covers a generous amount of juicy white meat complemented by mushrooms, ginger and bamboo shoots.

★★ ARCADIA
Polish

2943 N. Milwaukee Ave.   342-1464
Hours: Daily, 10 am–10 pm
Price range: Inexpensive
Credit cards: Not accepted
Reservations: Accepted
Handicap

Although hardly plush by really posh standards, this little Polish restaurant rises above the normal diner-esque decor of most other ethnic spots around town. Beige clothed tables sit surrounded by dark wooden chairs in a room with gray-beige walls and brown carpeting. There's a small bar on the right at the back, and oil paintings on the walls lighted by sconces.

The atmosphere is homey, particularly on the frequent occasions when large Polish-speaking groups sip vodka poured straight from the bottle and exchange stories. Often whole families dine here in their finery.

More ambitious than most, the menu offers a variety of Polish as well as French and continental dishes, like Chateaubriand. Nevertheless, prices for a full meal generally run under $10.

Polish cuisine is Arcadia's reason for being. Start the meal with the cold platter of preserved meats and pickles big enough for two-and-a-half people. Or try the pickled herring.

Home-made soups with above-average flavor are a must. Chicken noodle soup is almost noodle soup with a little chicken broth so chock full is it of excellent firm noodles. The full-flavored broth with carrots is topped with fresh parsley and dill. The hearty mushroom soup with noodles is also sprinkled with fresh dill. Another dish worth trying— zurek, sausage and boiled egg soup—tastes better than it sounds.

Polish sausage has gotten a bad name because of the over-preserved, uninspired commercial versions on the market. Here, the exceedingly rich, somewhat coarse, sausage has a wonderfully full, smoky flavor. Exceptionally thin pastry wraps the ground meat filling of the pirogis. Huge rolls of stuffed cabbage filled with finely textured meat and rice are excellent.

Roast pork with prunes has dried slightly from overcooking, but the combination works well in a good, rich gravy. Mashed potatoes and sauerkraut with beans come on the side with this entree.

Roast duck stuffed with apples could use more apple stuffing. It is extremely moist and tender, however, with very little fat under the somewhat disappointingly flaccid skin. A good red cabbage slaw and ordinary frozen French fries are served with the duck.

Portions are exceptionally large for the price, so desserts may be unnecessary, but they are good if equally filling. Try the almond-chocolate-raisin cake if it's available—a unique combination of tastes and textures.

There may be communication problems and waits between courses can be long when the restaurant is crowded, but everyone who works here is so deferential and friendly it really doesn't matter. To get into the spirit of things order a bottle of vodka and sip away.

For the price, Arcadia is an exceptional restaurant that everyone who enjoys ethnic eating should try.

★★ ARMY & LOU RESTAURANT & LOUNGE
American/Soul

420 & 422 E. 75 St.   483-6550
Hours: Mon, Wed & Thurs 11 am–11 pm, closed Tues, Fri &
*   Sat 11 am–midnight, Sun 9 am–10:30 pm*
Price range: Moderate

Credit cards: A C D M V
Reservations: Accepted

Hospitality is very much in vogue here. Owners Charles and Mary H. Cole are on hand every day to make sure the food is top-notch and the service is efficient and friendly.

The food is good old, down-home Southern soul. But the surroundings are a good deal classier than most soul-food restaurants. Dark wood paneling, white-clothed tables, banquettes and soft lights lend elegance to the unpretentious room.

The food runs the gamut of soul specialities. Thick, hearty soups—chicken, bean and split pea—are a must. Smoky ribs taste great, with little fat and a slightly sweet, slightly spicy sauce. Fried chicken is crisp and moist and so is the deep-fried fish. Chicken and dumplings are available on certain days.

Side dishes include greens seasoned with smoky bacon—a classic. Fried sweet potatoes and cornbread are also great.

Pies and cobblers end meals on an appropriately sweet note.

Portions are generous and prices unbelievably low. All ingredients are good quality and fresh. There's nothing nouvelle or prissy about this fare. It's honesty and intense flavor define what southern country cooking is all about.

★ ARNIE'S CAFE
American

1030 N. State St.   266-4800
Hours: Sun–Thurs 11:30 am–10:30 pm, Fri & Sat 11:30 am–
*   11:30 pm*
Price range: Moderate-moderately expensive
Credit cards: A C D M V
Reservations: Not accepted
Handicap

Hungry Rush Street revelers find this glass box cafe fronting Newberry Plaza on State Street, an excellent vantage point from which to watch the passing parade. Crowded and noisy at times, this room offers far-ranging fare, from moderately priced burgers to rather expensive grilled fish and steaks. However, keep in mind that owner Arnie Morton considers himself a saloon keeper. Essentially this place is just that: a saloon.

While more expensive entrees don't turn out badly here, for the price, it makes more sense to choose more comfortable restaurants. However, for a couple of drinks and some of the less expensive offerings, Arnie's ain't bad.

One of its unique selling points is its hamburger bar. Just as clothes make the man (or woman), for some people the go-with-its make the burger. There's a help-yourself topping bar with an awesome myriad of toppings: raw onions, french-fried onions, olives, pickles, barbeque sauce, mayonnaise, catsup, mustard, zucchini chunks, creamed spinach, cole slaw, chili, cheese sauce, bacon bits and more.

And, the burger's not shabby either: a large, high-quality ground beef burger served on a fresh bun. Other sandwiches and chili are available, as are reasonably priced fish and chicken entrees.

★★ ARUN'S
Thai

3434 W. Irving Park   539-1909
Hours: Wed–Mon 5–10 pm, closed Tues
Price range: Moderate
Credit cards: A   D   M   V
Reservations: Accepted
Handicap

One of the classiest storefront Thai restaurants, Arun's also ranks among the best in the area. Unlike those that reproduce only traditional Thai dishes. Arun's shows some creative flair that raises it a cut above most.

The tiny dining room seats fewer than 30 and has light, natural wood, and white-clothed tables and comfortable black chairs. Framed Thai prints hang on the beige-gold papered walls. The effect is bright, cheery and tasteful.

The single waiter responsible for all the tables gets to know regulars and treats all diners in a friendly, professional manner. He can provide invaluable information about the dishes, as well as guidance to the best offerings of the day, some of which do not appear on either of the two menus.

One menu lists daily specials, the other regular menu items. Among the appetizers, marinated pork or beef satay is moist and tender with a somewhat spicy peanut sauce and cucumber salad on the side. Crisp, delicately fried wontons come with a light plum sauce and an excellent, sweet-hot pepper sauce for dipping. Tightly wrapped with a thin, greaseless dough and filled with fresh ingredients, the egg rolls put most Chinese versions to shame.

The aromatic, clear-brothed, spicy shrimp soup is just this side of heaven. Two can share one portion, but four will wish for more. In general, portions here are not as large as in most Thai restaurants.

Among the entrees, don't miss the red snapper when it's available. Deep fried to a crunchy deep brown on the outside, the meat stays juicy and tender inside. Topped with fresh vegetables, sliced mushrooms and ground pork, this is one of the best versions of this dish anywhere. Likewise, Arun's garlic prawns tantalize with their rich, slightly spicy flavor. More subtle beef with oyster sauce mixes complex seasonings with tender meat, as does the fried red curry pork.

Indeed, everything served at this little Thai eatery rises above average. Some dishes far exceed expectations for a modest restaurant. Arun's size dictates making reservations in advance and its lack of a liquor license also requires a bit of planning for those who wish to drink something other than soda, Thai coffee or tea with dinner.

ASH MANOR
Continental
Rating: Fair

1600 W. Diversey Pkwy.   248-1600
*Hours: Lunch Tues–Fri 11:30 am–2:30 pm, Dinner Tues–Thurs
       5–10 pm, Fri & Sat 5–11 pm, Sun 4:30–9 pm, closed
       Mon*
Price range: Moderately expensive
Credit cards: A   C   D   M   V
Reservations: Accepted

What a nifty place for a romantic evening out... if only the food lived up to the turn-of-the-century surroundings.

No question, this place is handsome. To pass through the wrought iron gate in front is a step back in time. On the first floor of this three-story house, two dining rooms open to the right and left of a central entry hallway. Upstairs are a third dining room and an opulent bar.

Lighting from cut-glass chandeliers is low and intimate. Pastel walls hung with what appear to be old oil paintings, miles of original wood and mouldings and white-clothed tables with candles and fresh flowers complete the feeling of turn-of-the-century elegance.

The food is passable. It probably suffices for those who come here for a romantic evening, but anyone who concentrates on what she or he eats will find few delights.

Appetizers include good snails, slightly overcooked, rubbery mussels, excellent cream of vegetable soups and nightly specials that often are the best choice.

Uninspired salads come with entrees. Ingredients are fresh, but over dressed.

Grilled fresh seafood starts with quality ingredients, but suffers from overcooking that quickly dries out a dense fish like tuna. Again, quality veal is used here, but the saucing is heavy-handed. One night the veal was totally overwhelmed by its topping of prosciutto, mushrooms and cheese.

Desserts include a cloyingly sweet bread pudding and good chocolate mousse. Service is friendly and efficient. The knowledgeable servers make every effort to please. The limited wine list offers some good wines at moderate prices.

At its best, Ash Manor offers a wonderful evening out in classic surroundings. At its worst, it simply disappoints, but is rarely a disaster. There are better restaurants in the area where good food enhances the romantic setting.

★ ATLANTIC RESTAURANT
British and Irish

7115 W. Grand Ave.   622-3259
Hours: Mon, Wed, Thurs 3–11 pm, Fri 3 pm–1 am, Sat
*   noon–midnight, Sun 10 am–11 pm*
Price range: Moderate
Credit cards: M   V
Reservations: Accepted
Handicap

"Unassuming" hardly describes the exterior of this restaurant at the western edge of the city. Inside the front door, things don't look up all that much. To the right, racks hold travel brochures promoting excursions to the world's exotic destinations. Step through the next door, however, and the warmth of a British/Irish pub washes over you.

Dart enthusiasts usually gather around the board in the corner to the left, with spectators stretched along the bar to cheer on the lively matches. Just beyond the bar, Irish folk musicians entertain several nights a week from a small stage.

The large dining room lies ahead. There's nothing fancy about this place. Booths flank both walls, with tables in the middle of the room that can be pushed together for large groups that seem to gather here. Reproductions of British and Irish artifacts dot the walls. Huge wrought-iron chandeliers topped with red railroad lanterns wired for electricity provide lighting. In sum, the place looks a wee bit down-at-the heels as befits a proper down-home pub.

Massive quantities of plain food will fill the heartiest of eaters at generally reasonable prices. Although divided between British, Irish, Welsh and Scottish cuisine, the menu—heavy on prime rib, steak and meat pies or stews—has a certain sameness.

Those with big appetites might start with the Gaelic delight appetizer, a selection of grilled corned beef—good when it's not overcooked—excellent Irish bacon, mild black pudding (blood sausage), a rather undistinguished pasty pork sausage and wedges of tomatoes. Four can easily split this appetizer. Other beginnings include baked clams, somewhat greasy deep-fried marinated artichoke hearts and shrimp cocktail.

The roast beef with Yorkshire pudding is an exceptionally good buy. Several large slices of well-done roast beef are moisturized by thin gravy, both a notch above good diner food. A boiled potato and surprisingly dense, slightly eggy Yorkshire pudding come on the side. Fish and chips neither disappoint nor delight. Large in quantity and not at all fishy, if nothing else, the portion is healthy and filling. Shepherd's pie features an exceedingly light and tender crust over a full-bodied, stew-like mix of beef and vegetables in gravy. Again, this superior dish is as filling as the devil.

Add to the main courses the soup, which changes nightly (leek one evening tasted more of chicken broth than leeks, but the thick split-pea broth rivals the best anywhere) and

57

salad swamped by your choice of dressing. Most diner wad-
dle contentedly out of the place without sampling the desserts. A good thing, too, because the desserts here are
d-i-s-m-a-l.

The English trifle is a weary mix of jello, fruit and canned
whipped cream. The chocolate eclair looks and tastes as if it
came out of the freezer case.

Nevertheless, with its British beers on tap, music, genial
down-to-earth staff with lilting brogues, Atlantic can provide a satisfying evening for Anglophiles, Irishmen and just
about everyone else suffering from over-exposure-to-
nouvelle-trendy disease.

★ AURELIO'S
Italian

18162 Harwood Ave., Homewood   798-8050
Hours: Sun, Tues–Thurs 4–11:30 pm, Fri & Sat 4 pm–1 am,
       closed Mon
Price range: Inexpensive
Credit cards: Not accepted
Reservations: Accepted for large parties only
Other: Free parking
Handicap

A chain of 19 restaurants started by Joe Aurelio in
Homewood in 1959, Aurelio's serves one of the best thin-
crust pizzas around, a cross between the ultra-thin crust version you might find at Spiaggia and Ike (Pizzaria Uno)
Sewell's deep-dish invention. The kitchen staff makes up
each pie fresh, so there can be a bit of a wait.

To fill in the time, try the antipasto salad: good aged provolone with slices of excellent ham, a few slices of pepperoni, tomatoes, diced black olives, green olives and red
peppers filling a platter of iceberg lettuce chunks. It's easily
enough for two.

In fact, portions in general are huge. The menu even

warns that Aurelio's pizzas tend to be larger than most and have "more quantity than you may be used to." Amen to that. The small size looks large, the medium giant, and the large is beyond description. A small one will stuff two hungry people. Served on a stainless steel cooling rack, the golden brown, bready crust stays crisp throughout the meal despite its heavy toppings. The mushrooms come out of a can, but all other ingredients taste fresh.

Those with really big appetites may want to go for the "Super Six," a pie topped with sausage, cheese, green pepper, ham, pepperoni and mushrooms. "Filling" would not adequately describe it.

Spinach pie, highly touted on the menu, provides an interesting alternative to pizza: spinach sauteed and marinated in Mama Aurelio's "Secret Seasonings," then baked with a tomato sauce and mozzarella cheese.

The young waitresses tend to be polite and helpful. Decor varies greatly. In Homewood, where the chain got its start, a greenhouse-like, glass-enclosed dining room fronts a two-story renovated warehouse. Natural wood predominated inside this rather elaborate eatery, with old stained glass used over skylights and intermittently throughout the tri-level dining room.

★ ★ ★ AVALON
French

Hamilton Hotel, 400 Park Blvd., Itasca   773-4000, × 3164
Hours: Dinner Mon–Sat 6–9:30 pm, Sun brunch 10 am–2:30
*   pm, closed for dinner Sun*
Price range: Expensive
Credit cards: A D M V
Reservations: Recommended
Handicap

Chances are, you'll never get a truly bad meal in a

hotel restaurant. But it's even less likely you'll eat a great meal in one. The Avalon, located in Stouffer's Hamilton Hotel in Itasca, is an exception to the latter rule. The Avalon does make for an expensive night out. It is also somewhat pretentious. But this hotel dining room is consistently far above average.

There's a good deal of pomp and ceremony here. The dining room is large but built on two levels with glassed-in private rooms for large parties and enough space between the white-clothed tabled to maintain a sense of privacy. the high, multi-level ceilings, plush booths and carpeting keep noise levels down even when the room is full. Walls are white with a good deal of dark wood and brass trim that makes for a sort of old-world/modern decor.

The service is ceremonious: waiters present carts of food and simultaneously remove the domed lids from entrees, mix soup at the table and carefully spoon dressing onto salads.

The long and tempting list of specials reveals some of the best work this restaurant has to offer. One night's cold appetizer special, a small lobster with an herb vinaigrette, was exceptional, the perfectly cooked, moist lobster meat sliced vertically along the body nicely complemented by a light dressing.

Other appetizers worth trying include; an artichoke bottom filled with finely chopped fresh tomatoes and a thin slice of goose-liver paté covered with melted cheese, accompanied by a mustard sauce; Avalon cold filet, raw filet mignon sliced thin and served in olive oil, lemon and fresh herbs with a garnish of finely cut cornichons, onions, carrots and olives; cold terrines, a regular menu offering that changes nightly.

As for Avalon's lobster bisque, concocted at the table with Armagnac-flavored broth and rich cream, the fussy presentation makes for great theatre but the bisque ends up inadequately mixed, and partly cold.

Sorbet to "cleanse the palate"—pear, grapefruit and apple—faithfully reproduce the flavor of the fruit, but they are quite icy. The salads are a better bet. Special smoked goose salad, just gamey enough to be interesting, comes with a selection of greens, including chicory, and is served with a hot walnut vinaigrette spooned on with restraint at the table.

Game plays a major role on the menu. Twin roasted quail, a regular offering, may turn some people off then the two tiny birds are presented, dwarfed on the oversized white plate. But they are perfectly roasted, stuffed with a smooth, complex and flavorful mushroom duxelle and a tiny pearl onion. This dish is served with a truffle sauce. Oyster mushrooms star in the roast breast of duckling with Grand Marnier sauce; they're done to perfection with an almost meat-like flavor that dresses up what would otherwise be a rather ordinary dish. Mushrooms, this time fresh shiitakes, also are key in the sauteed medaillons of Provimi veal in Madeira sauce. Fresh salmon comes served in a sauce of red wine and ginger. All entrees come with vegetables: slender French green beans, carrots, and, recently, tiny sliced eggplant.

Choices from the dessert cart include a very good three-layered chocolate mousse cake, the specialty of the house and well worth sampling. An apple tart—really a glorified apple pie—disappoints with its heavy, tough pastry crust and mundane filling. The Bavarian-style strawberry cheesecake special, with an unbelievably light cheesecake filling between two layers of sponge cake, is excellent. Also outstanding: strawberries sabayon from the regular menu, a half dozen fresh berries topped with a kirsch/sabayon sauce, then glazed under the broiler. Browned on the top and resembling a puff pastry, this incredible dessert is a study in contrast, the cold richness of the cream in the middle against the warmth of the glazed top.

The after-dinner drink cart presented at the end of the meal is a real killer. Be forewarned that sampling one of the rare brandies or liqueurs will add greatly to the bill, their merit notwithstanding.

★★ AVANZARE
Italian

161 E. Huron   337-8056
Hours: Lunch Mon-Fri 11:30 am–2 pm, Dinner Sun–Thurs
*   5:30–9:30 pm, Fri & Sat 5:30–10:30 pm*
Price range: Moderately expensive
Credit cards: A C D M V
Reservations: Recommended
Handicap

A brass plaque on the wall next to the coat room notes that Zakaspace designer Spiros and Peter Zakas re-designed the interior of what had been Johnny's Steak House. Avanzare is open, sleek and modern in the Italian style, defined by marble columns. To the right, after a hall-way entrance, is a large bar with enough seating and stand-ing space to make Avanzare a good place to drink as well as to eat. Most evenings after work and more than a few after-noons, this bar fills with advertising, marketing and film production types who work in the area.

Facing the bar is an L-shaped banquette, a small dining area, in dark wood with dark green upholstery. Behind this banquette is the main dining area, with banquette and table seating. The ceiling is high, and huge windows with white cafe curtains bound Avanzare, which spills outside in warm weather.

A large pink and green neon clock marks time over the bar; happily, time seems to linger here. The service is atten-tive but far from rushed. While not all of the food is excep-tional, nearly all of it is very good.

The net effect is at once casual (coat and tie not required) and exciting, comfortable and stylish. Conversations mingle, people watch people; Avanzare, one of the city's first "grand cafes," is a place to see and be seen.

Not precisely a northern Italian restaurant (although that's how it's billed) or a novelle Italian sibling of Ambria (as some had predicted), Avanzare is instead Richard Melman and chef Dennis Terczak's version of northern Italian. The food is Italian in approach, light by design, yet uniquely Chicagoan in style. There are many traditional northern Italian dishes on the menu, but these are intermingled with some strictly Terczak fare.

Appetizers include some of the real jewels on the menu. The carpaccio, raw sirloin sliced so thin one can read through it, is garnished with freshly grated cheese and comes with a tomato vinaigrette. The dish looks great and tastes better. Indeed, all the presentation at Avanzare is beautiful. The medaglione di tonno crudo, raw tuna, avacado and onions with a soy marinade, is also sliced thin; it is fresh and excellent. Grilled vegetables with various sauces please, as do steamed mussels. The cozze con salsa di pomodori come in a tomato sauce with fresh herbs and cheese. There's more than enough for one. For veal lovers, there's vitello tonnato, scallopine of veal in tuna sauce (an appetizer in the evening, an entree at lunch.) Arugula, which has become something of a cult dish, is offered here as secco di manzo—sundried beef, arugula, watercress and a vegetable vinaigrette. The sun-dried beef is not special (the carpaccio is better) but for arugula addicts the dish will provide the needed fix. Soup specials are offered daily. Two sampled were tomato with basil and green pea with prosciutto. Both were excellent.

Pasta portions are large and can easily be shared. Early on, there were problems with the pasta, which today are mostly solved, Try the capelli d'angeli vellutati con broccoli—angel hair pasta, goat cheese and broccoli.

The grilled veal chop entree (costoleta di vetello) alone may be worth a visit. The liver with sausage (fegato alla griglia con salsiccia) is also excellent. Both come with light sauces, which provide an incentive to consume the fresh, crusty bread. The petto di pollo giovannelli lives up to its billing as crisp, sauteed breast of chicken with red wine sauce, but while juicy and nicely presented, it tastes a tad bland. Grilled fish generally turns out well, but at times is overcooked and dry.

The desserts are a fitting end to the meal. The granite and gelati (ices and ice creams) are made fresh daily. The chocolate hazelnut cake is nicely balanced and not too sweet.

★★ BACCHANALIA
Italian

2413 S. Oakley St.   254-6555
Hours: Mon, Wed, Thurs 11 am–11 pm, Fri 11 am–midnight,
        Sat 4–11:30 pm, Sun 3–8 pm, closed Tues
Price range: Moderate
Credit cards: Not accepted
Handicap

Expect no wine-induced orgies, despite the images the name conjures up. This little family-owned restaurant with a paneled bar up front, trellises decorated with plastic grapes and red tablecloths, serves simple home-style Italian specialties without much fanfare.

Skip right over the good, but ordinary appetizers for the better-than-average pastas. The full-flavored, red meat sauce puts most others to shame. Try it over surprisingly light gnocchi or spaghetti, cooked al dente. The filling canneloni alla romana, two large noodles stuffed with ground meat and baked in the red sauce with mozzarella and parmesan cheese, is a meal by itself.

Among the entrees, the moist, garlicky chicken Vesuvio deserves attention. It's hard to go wrong ordering one of the veal dishes built on a foundation of quality meat. Although the veal parmigiana is popular here, like most versions of this dish the sauce, mushrooms and cheeses overwhelm the veal. Simpler preparations such as the piccante or lemone are preferable.

Seafood—red snapper, baked turbot, shrimp and perch round out the entrees. For an extra $2 over the entree price you get a full dinner—one of the hearty soups, salad and ice cream in addition to the main course.

Service is friendly. But as the menu warns, good food takes time to prepare. You may experience long waits between courses, particularly when the restaurant is busy. One of the wines from the reasonably-priced list can help pass the time.

★ THE BAKERY
Continental

2218 N. Lincoln   472-6942
Hours: Tues–Sat 5–11 pm, closed Sun & Mon
Price range: Moderate
Credit cards: A C D M V
Reservations: Recommended

Taking potshots at this restaurant has become a favorite pastime of restaurant critics. Indeed, chef Louis Szathmary puts up plenty of targets. On the other hand, several things speak well of The Bakery: its consistency, efficient service and value offered for the price. I rate it "good," despite its considerable failings. The Bakery, which stretches across two or three storefronts on Lincoln Avenue, has been around since 1962. The chef is a veritable public relations marvel. As a result, his following among conventioneers and out-of-towners probably outpaces his local popularity.

The best way to have a great evening at The Bakery is to know the chef or, conversely, be somebody the chef knows. He will then take great care of you. And because he makes his rounds to each table virtually every evening, regulars at the restaurant get to be known quickly.

Initial greetings can be gruff. A member of a party arriving early may end up consigned to what appears to be an oversized coat room until the rest of the party arrives. Diners must thread their way from one room to the next past servers' and busboys' staging areas—and the servers and busboys themselves—in order to get to their seats.

The dining room itself is rather pleasant. There are country print curtains on the windows, light walls and white-clothed tables. Unfortunately, many tables are so close together that a party of two can suddenly become a party of four. To avoid this, couples should ask for a table along the wall.

In fact, it's clear that The Bakery caters to a business crowd, which is a good thing, in a sense. There are several areas of the restaurant devoted to large tables of six, eight of even 10 persons. The effect is one of a fairly loud restaurant lacking in privacy, perhaps the real reason The Bakery gets such a bad rap. Appetizer, soup, salad, most entrees and dessert are included for $23. Some appetizer and entree specials cost an additional $3–$5.

Meals begin with a basket of good, very crusty, slightly yeasty bread and a complimentary paté—recently, a mixture of goose liver, duck liver and chicken liver cooked in beef and chicken stock that was very smooth and light, but disappointingly tasteless.

Soup follows the paté. A cream of cauliflower soup, with rather large chunks of cauliflower, is quite good. A salad of intensely smoky Coho salmon with carrots and apples in homemade mayonnaise comes next, an unusual but pleasing combination.

The house green salad as the next course seems a bit redundant. The leaf lettuce topped with tomato, carrot, feta cheese and crumbled egg drowns under a cloyingly sweet vinaigrette.

Appetizers, soups, salads and entrees change with the season or at the whim of the chef. Entrees generally shine. For example, the medaillons of pork, pounded extremely thin, dredged in flour and sauteed and covered with a variety of wild mushrooms, is a terrific dish. Cornish game hen, stuffed with a bread and smoky Viennese sausage dressing, although a little dry, is a very good dish, especially with the champagne and orange-flavored sauce.

The list of desserts is quite impressive but this is misleading because the desserts on the whole are rather disappointing.

If the limited wine list on the table doesn't have something to your liking, be sure to ask the chef for help. Szathmary has some wonderful wines stowed away for those who show an interest.

BANGKOK STAR
Thai
Rating: Fair

927 Irving Park Rd.   935-3032
Hours: Thurs–Tues 4:30–10 pm, closed Wed
Price range: Moderate
Credit cards: A M V
Reservations: Accepted

One of the area's more popular storefront Thai eateries, Bangkok Star is very crowded on Friday and Saturday night. However, while some dishes rise above the norm, others fail to reach it. The inconsistency of the kitchen when the restaurant gets crowded forces a "fair" rather than "good" rating. Those who wish to try this restaurant probably should go on a week night, when the kitchen is not over-taxed.

This tiny, plain restaurant provides a waiting area furnished with two benches flanking a coffee table stocked with magazines. A gungy, old-fashioned bar across the street comes in handy for beer, since Bangkok Star serves no liquor. The servers are extremely friendly.

Start with pork satay, fresh skewered pork cooked moist and tender and served with a thin, spicy peanut sauce for dipping and a cucumber salad. Bypass the spring rolls; the filling falls short of garden-fresh. Instead, try one of the spicy salads with ground pork or chicken, green onions, hot red peppers and coriander presented on a leaf of cabbage or lettuce.

The mild yellow curry has a somewhat grainy, mild coconut broth, with moist chunks of chicken with potatoes (a bit too mushy) and vegetables; it's fragrant and flavorful. Coho salmon comes with a wonderful sweet-and-sour sauce packed with straw mushrooms and carrots, although one night the fish tasted a little fishy, dry and overcooked.

But prices are reasonable, the place comfortable and many dishes superb. Crowds are a mixed blessing, and sometimes they're the undoing of this friendly little restaurant.

★ BARNEY'S MARKET CLUB
American

741 W. Randolph St.   372-6466
Hours: Mon–Fri 11 am–11 pm, Sat 5–11 pm, Sun 5–10 pm
Price range: Moderate
Credit cards: A C D M V
Reservations: Recommended
Handicap

"Yes, sir, Senator!" greets the maitre d'. "Yes, sir, Senator," again when the waitress approaches the table.

How could anyone dislike a place where everyone is a senator and the food ain't half bad? Of course, this statement indicates that the food may not be half good either. Most of it is, though, particularly if you like this sort of thing.

Apparently, senators prefer to dine on meat. While some seafood offerings give options for non-meat eaters, the keynote of this place is steak. Although Barney's does not rank with the best steak houses in town, its beef is pretty good and its prices lower than many competitors'.

Barney's shies away from trendy cuisine and decor. The place looks much the way it must have when it opened in 1919. Big, comfortable wooden chairs surround big wooden tables in a room with lots of big wooden pillars and dark mouldings.

One of Chicago's landmark restaurants, Barney's fell on hard times in the '60s and '70s. Finally, new owners took over and breathed new life into the place. Service is friendly and generally efficient, even when the place is crowded. The food is straightforward.

Steaks come cooked as ordered, charred on the outside and juicy inside. Liver, a little overdone but fresh and smothered with onions, will please those who like it. Barbecued ribs will please only those who enjoy them sweet.

A basket of good rolls begins meals. Soups generally are winners. The salad bar has extensive, if uninspired, selections of good fresh produce and a myriad of toppings. Crisp, lightly salted shoestring potatoes are perfection, as are the onion rings. For dessert, several different cheesecakes make the best choice. Barney's offers nothing fancy, but decent food at reasonable prices and turn-of-the-century charm makes it a fun place for lunch or dinner.

★ BAR HARBOR
American

203 N. LaSalle   977-0100
Hours: Lunch Mon–Fri 11 am–2:30 pm, Dinner Mon–Fri 5–10
      pm, Sat 5–9 pm, closed Sun
Price range: Moderately expensive
Credit cards: A D M V
Reservations: Accepted

At a time when restaurants have assumed a role in
Chicago's booming theater scene, Bar Harbor has great star
potential. Befitting its transportation building location, this
second floor restaurant may be the only place in town where
diners can sample trendy fresh mesquite-grilled seafood
while they watch the cars of the Lake-Dan Ryan El slide by
at eye-level outside.

Through some marvel of modern architecture the noise of
the train barely penetrates the dining room. The motion can
be distracting, but viewed as an urban art form, the periodic
tableau vivants, formed unwittingly by the commuters on
the passing trains, provide endless entertainment. As long as
the other diners don't mind, on request the waiter will open
the blinds to the view.

Owner Bill Bronner, who also owns TooJay's restaurant,
makes his first foray into "fine dining" with Bar Harbor. An
amalgam of cliches—oyster bar, mesquite grill, fresh seafood, vertical rotisserie, kitchen open to the view of diners'
—the 185-seat restaurant manages to exceed the sum of its
parts with a well-rounded menu that offers sufficient variety
without overwhelming diners with options.

The oyster bar just beyond the maitre d's stand and a lobster filled tank might mislead diners into thinking this is a
seafood restaurant. Seafood dishes make up roughly a third
of the offerings, but as the wall mosaics depicting a steer,

hog and lamb suggest, there is more to this menu than sea-food.

Duck filled ravioli with a sage beurre blanc leads the list of appetizers. Delicate al dente pasta wraps around a slightly herby filling of ground duck, immersed in butter with fresh sage, a bargain at $2.95. Crab cakes, unlike the thick, eggy version at Shaws, have pure crab flavor, but the crisp coating turned out burned one night. The spicy sausage in the baked, stuffed oysters completely overshadows the natural goodness of the exquisitely plump mollusks. Fried calamari stuffed with shrimp, crabmeat and bread crumbs, served with two Cajun remoulade sauces, is another example of too much of a good thing. Plain old battered and fried calamari would be better.

Luckily few dishes are overwrought. The chef takes a light-handed approach to most of the preparations, grilling, roasting and sauteeing with simple sauces. For example, the mixed seafood grill features a selection of two or three fresh fish each evening—sea bass, lake whitefish, salmon, brill, blue fin, among them—with two or three different sauces, generally excellent. An oddly lumpy shrimp mousseline spoils an otherwise fine mesquite grilled rainbow trout.

One of the best entrees, a grilled breast of chicken, comes with a wonderful Balsamic vinegar sauce augmented by the orange-soy sauce chicken marinade. Roasted chicken from the rotisserie coated with crusted pesto sauce turned out moist and tender, but the pesto coating lost its punch from the grilling.

Veal, calves liver, steak and pastas round out the menu. Good quality beef goes into the grilled strip steak, cooked somewhat less than the medium rare ordered. Although the ravioli turns out perfectly cooked, linguini primavera sampled at lunch one day had a gummy texture that ruined the dish despite its good flavor.

Simple but good house salads with a chive house dressing or optional herbed buttermilk or blue cheese dressings come with entrees. A fresh hot roll, sometimes white bread, sometimes whole wheat, sometimes an excellent whole wheat-cheese, is served at the beginning of meals.

By all means save room for dessert. The chocolate bomb, half a snowball-sized mound of rich, creamy chocolate wrapped in chocolate pastry in a pool of fudge sauce—heaven for chocolate lovers. Also good are the dense carrot cake, cheesecakes, apple strudel with caramel sauce. The only miss is the hazelnut cake with layers of meringue so hard that a chisel might have been a more appropriate instrument of destruction than a fork.

Reasonable prices highlight the limited selection of wines, listed without vintages even though most are vintage wines. Among the chardonnays the David Bruce or Mark West, priced at $19.95 and $18.25 respectively, are good bets.

Bar Harbor's good value and unique view of urban transportation make it well worth sampling. If train watching isn't your cup of tea, the glassed-in kitchen that juts out into the dining room offers an alternative bit of theater.

★ BASTILLE
French

21 W. Superior St.   787-2050
Hours: Lunch Mon–Fri 11:30 am–3 pm, Dinner Mon–Thurs
*   5–10 pm, Fri & Sat 5–11 pm, Sun 5–9 pm*
Price range: Moderate
Credit cards: A M V
Reservations: Recommended
Other: Valet parking

This restaurant has become so famous for its Bastille Day and nouveau Beaujolais celebrations held outdoors in huge tents, that people often forget that it is one of the best places around town for a reasonably priced French meal. The food may not be great, but it's generally good.

On the right inside the front door of the strange-looking building that houses this restaurant, a small bar holds waiting diners and, occasionally, serious drinkers. A nitrogen-charged wine keeper allows customers to sample a variety of French and Californian wines by the ounce or the glass.

Up a flight of stairs to the left of the bar lie two dining rooms. The one in the back with booths offers more privacy. Above the wainscoting hangs an interesting, if incongruous, mix of old French posters, signs and contemporary posters for the many Bastille events.

Friendly servers wear white butcher aprons and usually are efficient and attentive. However, service can slip during busy hours.

The food has had its ups and downs over the years, depending on who's doing the cooking. At this writing, it is quite good. Each day, one dish gets the nod as a special, such as couscous on Saturday. Traditional French favorites like steak and fries or duck appear on the printed menu. Look to the list of daily specials for creativity.

Pristinely fresh fish grilled over wood comes with sauces that change with the catch and the day. Meat dishes with interesting combinations of ingredients and saucing head the special card.

Fresh oysters, country style patés and smoked salmon will get things off to a good start. A plate of carrots in a light mayonnaise comes to the table immediately with a basket of good French bread. Some of the best French fries in town come in a small basket with all entrees: thin, crisp and lightly salted.

A good flourless chocolate cake leads the dessert list. Fruit tarts look tempting, but often sit on a tough, overworked crust.

★ BENCHERS GRILLE
American

Sears Tower, 233 S. Wacker Dr.   993-0096
Hours: Mon–Fri 11 am–8 pm, closed Sat & Sun
Price range: Moderate
Credit Cards: A   D   M   V
Reservations: None

BENCHER'S CLUB ROOM
American
Rating: Fair

Sears Tower, 233 S. Wacker Dr.   993-0096
Hours: Mon–Fri 11 am–3 pm, Mon–Sat 5–9 pm, closed Sun
Price range: Expensive
Credit cards: A   D   M   V
Reservations: Recommended
Other: Occasional free transportation to local theaters

Everyone sighed in relief when the Levy Organization took over the food service in Sears Tower. Finally there would be good food in Chicago's most famous building. Unfortunately the Benchers restaurants don't live up to the promise.

Benchers is two restaurants occupying one space. Blaring rock music sets the stage for equally loud after-work revelers in a large bar to the left of the main entrance. This bar forms a sort of singles no-man's-land between the casual Benchers Grille and more formal Club Room.

Unfortunately, in addition to its role as a meeting place for single professionals, the bar acts as a holding area for diners waiting to get into Bencher's Club Room. The frenetic pitch of this bar may shock diners who expect a calming evening in the formal dining room.

Benchers Club Room has banquettes with comfortable

seating, lots of wood and sedate music. High ceilings and glass walls along one side provide a light, airy atmosphere that befits a good seafood house. However, those interested in great seafood would do better at the Levy organization's Chestnut Street Grill in Water Tower Place.

A small number of appetizers leads the menu. Crisply coated fried calamari turns out well. Plump, fresh oysters on the half shell have been cut from their shells, so most of their juices are lost before serving. Large New Orleans-style butterflied shrimp arrive in a pool of spicy oil, which is visually unappealing but tastes great. The only loser is the ravioli, in meat- and cheese-stuffed versions with a tough pasta wrapper topped with grated Parmesan cheese. A good, red meat sauce helps but doesn't save this appetizer, which should be left to Italian restaurants that know what they're doing.

Small leaf salads come with all entrees, with just enough good, creamy mustard vinaigrette. Special salads are available for an extra charge.

Shrimp, lobster and a good number of fresh fish lead the entrees. Clearly fresh, the wahoo, a Hawaiian fish, has excellent flavor, but the dense fish is cooked to the texture of dry cardboard.

There are plenty of meat and poultry dishes for those who don't care for seafood. These also are grilled over wood. Thick lamb chops ordered medium-rare arrive perfectly cooked with only the slightest hint of gaminess. Tiny boned, grilled quail pick up slightly smoky flavor from the grill that blends well with their naturally gamy taste. Grilled breast of chicken is plain, but turns out moist. All entrees come with a large portion of vegetables, such as sliced zucchini, twice baked potato or rice that may taste too much of soy sauce.

Following the philosophy that great desserts make happy diners, a tempting tray of sweets contains some of the best bets found here. While these desserts lean more heavily on sugar than flavor, they certainly will satisfy one's sweet tooth. Especially good is the turtle pie, with its dual saucing of chocolate and caramel. The smooth, pleasing filling for a pumpkin walnut pie sits on a thick shortbread crust that tends to be tough. Chocolate cake alternates with raspberry mousse for the chocolate gateau and doesn't have much flavor. Cheesecakes are rich and sweet.

Service here is friendly and conscientious, but lacking in depth of knowledge about the food. A limited wine list offers no half bottles, but a reasonable selection of white wines are reasonably priced.

However, price is generally a problem in the Club Room. Prices reflect the owners' self-image of the place as a fine-dining institution. In other words, a meal here will set you back a pretty penny. So while the food isn't bad, the preparations are incredibly simple, too simple to justify the heady prices. Diners pay a hefty premium mostly for the restaurant's location.

That's where Benchers Grille comes in. The Grille, which stretches off behind the left side of the noisy bar is more casual and far less costly. Dining here takes place at the circular food counter or the bar flanked by booths, perfect for people-watching. At the back, another dining room activates when things start jumping, but avoid that far less interesting room if possible.

Buffalo wings, the hot spicy fried chicken wings, fried mozzarella, stuffed mushrooms and the like, form the list of appetizers in this casual restaurant. Highly touted salads may not live up to their billing. Chili three ways doesn't approach the Steak-n-Shake chili that inspired it. But the half-pound burgers that range from $5-6, depending on your choice of toppings, are good. So are the other sandwiches, grilled steak, fries and the seafood items that round out the menu—after all, the kitchen is essentially the same.

You could skip all of this in favor of the winning hot fudge sundae: two scoops of high quality vanilla ice cream on a thick, rich brownie all napped with chocolate sauce. It redefines super sundae.

If eating at Sears Tower is a must, the choice is Benchers Grille over the Club Room. Even though five or six bucks still may be expensive for a burger, the Grille offers a better value and more fun for your money than the Club Room.

BENIHANA OF TOKYO, Downtown
Japanese
Rating: Fair

166 E. Superior St.   664-9643
Hours: Lunch Mon–Sat 11:30 am–2 pm, Dinner Mon–Thurs
*   5:30–10:30 pm, Fri & Sat 5:30–11:30 pm, Sun 4–10*
*   pm*
Price range: Moderately expensive
Credit cards: A   C   D   M   V
Reservations: Recommended

★ BENIHANA OF TOKYO, Lombard
Japanese

747 Butterfield Rd., Lombard   325-4440
Hours: Lunch Mon–Fri 11:30 am–2:30 pm, Dinner Sun–Thurs
*   5–11 pm, Fri & Sat 5–midnight.*
Price range: Moderately expensive
Credit cards: A   C   D   M   V
Reservations: Recommended
Handicap

Along with technology, the Japanese exported some of the best beef in the world to the Unites States, some of which can be found at Japanese steak houses. Benihana, with its showy preparations and communal-style eating, is

77

probably the best known of this genre. It is a bit brash and brassy, perfect for entertaining business people and large families.

Dinner includes appetizer, soup, salad, main course and dessert. Choices are minimal: only one soup, a good oniony broth, salad that won't win any prizes and a shrimp appetizer cooked at the table and served with two sauces.

All of the dishes sampled were cooked to perfection. However, the simplicity of the preparations—the epitome of Japanese cooking—can lead to boredom. For example, Benihana's seafood combination of lobster tail, prawns and scallops cooked on the grill gets monotonous. The relatively bland dipping sauces don't help much.

Of course, a steak house depends on its steak. Unfortunately, while the steak at Benihana is by no means terrible, it doesn't come near the famed Kobe either. It lacks flavor and is not as tender as it ought to be.

The big, noisy Lombard Benihana gets a star for its sushi bar, which its downtown sister lacks. Because the two sides of the restaurant are separate, steak house patrons cannot start meals with a sushi course that would greatly vary the meals, but at least they are offered a choice.

Both restaurants offer desserts (fresh pineapple, ice cream and sherbet), but given the large portions and rich steak sauces, dessert is really unnecessary.

BENNIGAN'S TAVERN
American
Rating: Fair

225 N. Michigan Ave.   938-9080
Hours: Mon–Thurs 11 am–midnight, Fri & Sat 11 am–1 am,
*   Sun 11 am–11 pm*
Price range: Moderate

Credit cards: A C D M V
Reservations: Not accepted
Handicap

The full name hints that as a restaurant, Bennigan's makes a great tavern. It attracts a large, loyal following of younger downtown workers more intent on drinking away the day's woes and lining up dates for the weekend than on enjoying the food.

However, even in this age of light beer, light wine and generally lighter drinking, a long night of reveling without sustenance leads to an even longer, hang-over next morning. Therefore this much-advertised place serves food.

The decor attempts to harken back to a time when life seemed simpler, and dates were often arranged. Brass fixtures, lightly stained oak and old photographs create a comfortable atmosphere.

Simple dishes—decent hamburgers, somewhat soggy nachos, quiches and salads, along with steaks and seafood dishes of average to a-little-better-than average quality—make up the menu. The real selling point is that prices are relatively low, something hard to find in a restaurant just north of the Loop.

So Bennigan's isn't a bad choice for a drink and a quick food fix. By the same token, unless singles-mingling is the object, it's not a restaurant you should go out of your way to try.

★ BERGHOFF
German

17 W. Adams St.   427-3170
Hours: Mon–Thurs 11 am–9:30 pm, Fri & Sat 11 am–10 pm,
*   closed Sun*
Price range: Moderate

Credit cards: A M V
Reservations: Accepted for parties of five or more
Other: Reduced parking rates after 5 pm

Who could fail to like a restaurant that has operated continuously since 1898; a restaurant that proudly displays liquor license Number 1, the first issued after Prohibition; a restaurant where an army of waiters in black trousers, white aprons and tuxedo jackets efficiently-and usually pleasantly-serves 2,000 meals and more daily; a restaurant that exudes the atmosphere of old Chicago?

Who else but a legion of restaurant critics?

True, the "factory" food rarely rises to great heights, but the Berghoff continues to serve reasonably good food at extremely reasonable prices by downtown standards.

From the start, founder J. Berghoff didn't want diners hanging around any longer than necessary. He wanted to sell more meals, a philosophy to which the management ascribes to this day. So service is almost too fast.

The bar at the east end of the restaurant bustles with men and women at lunch and after work. One of the last brass-rail, stand-up bars around, it deserves preservation as a national institution. Sandwiches and oyster bar are available.

The menu in the main dining room starts out with a full page of drink suggestions, headed by the Berghoff private-stock bourbons so smooth you won't know they're knocking your socks off until you stand up—or try to.

The menu remains solidly rooted in the past although some specials, like the grilled Hawaiian mahi mahi and the hot meat on cold green salads, may surprise.

But German specialities made Berghoff's reputation and continue to sell well: Gschnaetzlets, a stew made from tender chucks of veal, smoked thuringer, wiener schnitzel, breaded veal cutlets and good steaks are fresh and good, except for a tendency to be overcooked.

Dinner entrees include a choice of two items from a long

list of side dishes: an average tossed salad, baby beets, good creamed spinach, excellent sauerkraut and utterly disappointing spaetzles and potato pancakes.

It may not be the best food in the area, but the Berghoff does give customers an honest meal for an honest price, which is more than can be said for many a fancier place.

BEVERLY HILLS CAFE
Eclectic
Rating: Fair

312 W. Randolph St.   782-3355
Hours: Lunch Mon–Fri 11:30 am–2:30 pm, Dinner Mon–Fri
*   5–9 pm, Sat 5 pm–midnight*
Price range: Moderately expensive
Credit cards: A C D M V
Reservations: Accepted

This pretty dining room manages to capture the spirit of California despite its basement location. Cafe tables sit under umbrellas in the bright, sky-lighted atrium where an indoor waterfall provides a soothing backdrop of sound for lunch and dinner.

To the right, diners wait in a large bar. Toward the rear is another low-ceilinged dining room that opens onto the bright cafe. Both dining areas are pleasant, comfortable and light with lots of natural oak.

The food and service are inconsistent. Servers can be friendly, knowledgeable and efficient, or more interested in cutting a real estate deal with the diner seated two tables down. It depends on one's luck.

The same is true of the kitchen. At times, such items as grilled fish excel. At other times, a dish as simple as chicken salad fails dismally, with an uninspired curry powder dressing and dried-out raisins that should have been thrown out.

Nevertheless, salads tend to be a safe choice here. A steak salad comes with strips of decent meat cooked to order on a bed of greens with avocado and tomato. Standard spinach salad turns out well.

Seafood items are fresh and prepared with care. Pasta dishes don't fare so well. They tend to be over-cooked and gummy.

Run-of-the-mill cheescakes and fresh fruits are the best choices for desserts. The wine list features California wines; there are few bargains and only a moderate selection.

Beverly Hills Cafe could be a great little place if the inconsistencies in food and service were smoothed out. Until then, dining here is a gamble. If you hit the right combination of food and service you can win; if you don't, you lose.

★ BIGGS
Continental

1150 N. Dearborn St.   787-0900
Hours: Daily 5 pm–midnight
Price range: Moderate
Credit cards: A M V
Reservations: Accepted

Biggs built its reputation 20 years ago. Some of the food it serves today may even date back that far. While the ornate dining rooms provide comfortable dining in an atmosphere many consider romantic, the food at Biggs has long since lost its luster.

Aware of the problems, the owner now encourages the kitchen to become more adventurous. A recently updated menu continues to offer such classics as beef Wellington, which certainly has merit when properly prepared. Specials often show creativity and promise.

Biggs does offer its customers a bargain. The fixed price dinner is only $17.50 or $24.50. Your best strategy is to stick to the nightly specials. The chef seems to take extra care in the preparation of these—simple poached salmon in champagne sauce or succulent pheasant with veal mousse stuff-

ing, for instance. Other special items might include two delicious roast quail, grilled swordfish, sauted fresh salmon
with two sauces and half pan cooked chicken with fresh
herbs.

Despite its ups and downs over the years, Biggs still enjoys great popularity, especially among conventioneers. The
service is smooth and professional, the dining rooms excel
as examples of Victoriana.

Best bets among the desserts include the fruit tarts and
fresh fruits rather than the cakes, which tend to have poor
texture and be exceedingly sweet.

By the way, Bigg's has a little brother—Albert's Cafe and
Patisserie, located in the carriage house in back. Despite its
relative youth, Albert's shows promise (see page 41).

BIJAN
American
Rating: Fair

663 N. State St.   944-0445
Hours: Lunch Mon–Fri 11:30 am–3 pm, Sat & Sun noon–3
pm, Dinner Sun–Thurs 5:30–11 pm, Fri & Sat 5:30–
midnight
Price range: Moderate
Credit cards: A D M V
Reservations: Accepted

More bar than restaurant, Bijan's boasts stained
wood and glass garage-type doors that protect diners in in-
clement weather and open to create the atmosphere of an
outdoor cafe when the weather is nice. At the back of the
room, an open-to-view kitchen holds center stage. A large
bar area, which takes up about half the total space, stretches
front to back on the left side of the room. Over the dining
area on the right side of the room hangs a huge painting—a
sort of bright, abstract desert scene. Piped-in music can be

frenetic, but the restaurant itself is relaxed, a cross between neighborhood tavern and trendy cafe.

It's obvious that a tremendous amount of attention went into the design of this restaurant. Unfortunately, the same kind of attention to detail has yet to reach the small kitchen.

For drinks and conversation, Bijan holds its own with any local watering hole. Despite some decent dishes however, the food fails to live up to the promise of the decor.

The interesting melange on the menu at first appears attractive. There are only five appetizers and five entrees, augmented by nightly specials—usually an indication that the kitchen wants to do a limited number of things and do them well. Unfortunately, while that may have been the intention here, it has not become the reality.

Among the appetizers, try the mushrooms with mozzarella or the chicken fingers. Both breaded, deep-fried dishes come with sauces—a blistering mustard sauce with the chicken and a spicy salsa with the mushrooms. Neither dish is the stuff of fond memories, but they are certainly acceptable.

Grilled items—fresh fish, a lamb and beef kabob and strip steak—make the best choices among the entrees. The unlikely combination of mild halibut grilled and served with a horseradish sauce works surprisingly well. The lamb and beef of the kabob arrives cooked a perfect medium-rare, and wonderfully flavored by a marinade. Served on an overcooked, starchy bed of rice, the meat with mushrooms, pepper and tomato has an excellent tart flavor with rosemary overtones. A good but uninteresting salad comes with the entrees. Salad Bijan, a mix of romaine, spinach, fresh vegetables, cheese and egg, can be substituted for $4.75 extra. Choose the vinaigrette over the blue-cheese dressing.

Dessert offerings change nightly. The best sampled was a chocolate marble cheesecake that approached greatness. A flourless chocolate cake looked and tasted like a brownie—

not bad for a brownie, but not great for a flourless chocolate cake.

Obvious care has been taken to make Bijan a comfortable place; it's a waste that the kitchen suffers from bouts of indifference. Although prices are kept low, there is no reason why the kitchen should not be more careful and consistent.

★ BILLY GOAT
American

Lower level at 430 N. Michigan Ave., entrance on
Hubbard St.   222-1525
Hours: Mon–Fri 7–2 am, Sat 10–3 am, Sun noon–2:30 am
Price range: Inexpensive
Credit cards: No way
Reservations: Don't even try

The second corner of the "Bermuda Triangle" (see Riccardo's listing) and reportedly home of the "cheeseburger-cheeseburger-cheeseburger" skit made famous by Saturday Night Live, the Billy Goat is something of a Chicago institution, especially among newspaper folks.

Yes, Mike Royko does stop in for a beer and a shot from time to time along with most of the rest of the staff of *The Chicago Tribune* and *Chicago Sun-Times*, both only steps away. Lots of old newspaper clips, all mentioning the Goat, bylines and photos of journalistic luminaries past and present, line the walls of this somewhat grungy, down-home basement bar.

Traditionally a stop at the Goat comes in the middle of a long night of drinking when the hamburgers seem to taste better than they really are. One colleague swears that a single cheeseburger topped with bacon staves off hangovers better than any known cure.

The burgers are decent, not great, served on a fresh bun

with do-it-yourself toppings of onion and dill pickles, no fries, but bags of Jay's chips.

But you don't go to the Billy Goat for fine cuisine. You go there for food, a beer or two, lively conversation with friends and perhaps, to sober up enough to find your way home.

★ BINYON'S
German/American

327 S. Plymouth Ct.   341-1155
Hours: Mon–Sat 11:30 am–10 pm, closed Sun
Price range: Moderate for lunch, moderately expensive for dinner
Credit cards: A   D   M   V
Reservations: Accepted

This restaurant is the stuff of which family traditions are made, one of the last good examples of what Chicago restaurants are (or used to be) all about. That alone makes it worthy of support. While not exciting, the food never fails to be fresh and good.

One can eat on all three levels of this landmark restaurant. However, the first two floors have more old, woody, turn-of-the-century atmosphere. The top floor, the only one open late, is rather dull.

Many patrons are older business people and shoppers, but a younger crowd is beginning to discover the place. White-clothed tables surrounded by comfortable large chairs provide a relaxed, semi-formal feeling, which is quickly offset by the noisy diners and exceptionally speedy service.

The staff are helpful, efficient and, unlike the Berghoff's, tend not to rush diners even when the place is bustling. The food is classic—fresh ingredients and large portions, well prepared and reasonably priced.

Breads provided in a basket are excellent; steaks and chops cooked to order are of good quality. Scallops are a value, and other broiled or sautéd seafood, while plain, is pristinely fresh.

The famous turtle soup makes a good beginning, although it's not as thick and rich as turtle soup served in Philadelphia, where it became a legend. Other appetizers include fresh oysters, chopped chicken liver and baked shrimp. Portions are large for the price, making this one of the better spots in the Loop.

★ BLUE MESA
American/Southwestern

1729 N. Halsted   944-5990
Hours: Lunch Mon–Fri 11:30 am–2:30 pm; Dinner Mon–
*   Thurs 5–11 pm, Fri & Sat 5 pm–midnight, Sun 5–10*
*   pm*
Price range: Moderate
Credit cards: A   M   V
Reservations: Accepted for large parties weeknights only
Handicap

In cold weather, a well-tended fireplace burns in the front room of this eclectic restaurant. In warmer months, an outdoor patio opens for dining.

Walls are plastered to simulate white adobe, with round, wooden pillars and exposed beams supporting the ceiling. Wide-planked wood flooring, comfortable green upholstered chairs and reasonably large clothed tables afford comfort in the open room to the left of the bar, the middle of the restaurant. In the dining room to the right, a large number of booths afford more privacy.

Although our "windy waitress," may not be typical of the servers here, she behaved very strangely from the start. Not once was there any eye contact, and she said bluntly that one appetizer would be enough—the customers ordered two anyway—but she brought only the one she had suggested!

Despite this, for about $30 a couple, Blue Mesa offers some of the most interesting food to be found anywhere at that price, in a pleasant, homey atmosphere that has won a large and loyal following. The no-reservation policy can create long waits on busy nights.

A mix of French, American and Mexican billed as Southwestern, the food in general is good and sometimes excellent. Smoked trout served as an appetizer comes on a bed of lettuce with two lemon wedges, olives and a sour-cream dip tinted pink from the hot peppers in it. The trout is smoky, moist and good.

Veal with pine nuts and tomato sauce with wild mushrooms sounds chancey in a place like this, and it is. The veal has a strange, almost slimy exterior from an unfortunate coating of flour, and the inside has a greasy texture which is the consistency of runny rubber. The combination should be flavorful, but the dish is tasteless. The excellent, slightly spicy Spanish rice and wedges of yellow squash on the side can't quite make up for the failed main course.

The blue-corn chicken enchiladas are good enough, however, to make up for the failed entrees. The blue-green enchiladas topped with sour cream and a parsley garnish are wrapped around a filling of shredded chicken and earthy spices. A serving of Spanish rice, hominy, iceberg lettuce and tomato came on the side.

Nanima, an incredibly light custard that seems to melt on the tongue, is topped with a sugar cookie and a sprinkling of fresh cinnamon. The coffee is good.

If the prices were higher, the inconsistency of the food and service would undo this restaurant. But reasonable prices and some outstanding food justify its "good" rating.

★★ BOB CHINN'S CRAB HOUSE
American

393 S. Milwaukee Ave., Wheeling   520-3633
Hours: Mon–Fri 11:30 am–2:30 pm, Dinner Mon–Thurs 4:30–
*   10:30 pm, Fri & Sat 4:30–11:30 pm, Sun 3–10 pm*
Price range: Moderate
Credit cards: A D M V
Reservations: Accepted for large parties only
Handicap

There might be a bit of a wait to get into Bob Chinn's
Crab House, but the seafood's super quality at moderate
prices is worth it. The young servers are pleasant and enthu-
siastic and rush you a little, adding to the casual, almost festive atmosphere. The pleasant and unusual interior is
marred only by tacky tableware.

The attraction here is the food, and nearly everything is
super-fresh. Appetizers are uneven; the all-you-can-eat salad
and raw seafood bar is excellent and from 4:30 to 6:30 costs
only $2.95 with entree. But the New England clam chowder
and seafood gumbo (both $1.75) are disappointing—one
too watery, the other too spicy. The salt-encrusted garlic rolls
are for the bravest garlic addict only.

When at the Crab House, don't miss the fresh Dungeness
crabs flown in from Alaska. These delicacies, rarely found
fresh this far from the Pacific, are steamed and served plain
or in a garlic sauce. Either way, they are perfectly cooked.
The menu has a large variety of char-grilled fish, ranging
from $8.50 to $11.95, as well as daily specials. All are fresh
and excellent. In the foyer, fresh lobsters share the saltwater
tank with the crabs. Live from Maine, they cost $15.95 and
are cooked to mouthwatering perfection. The snow crab,
however, was a tad dry and stringy, either from freezing

or overcooking. The only other disappointment among the entrees is the hot spicy shrimp, which also did not seem fresh. For non-fish-eaters, there's steak, barbequed ribs and chicken. The rib-eye steak is large, cooked as ordered but somewhat tough and fatty. All entrees come with coleslaw (average) and steak fries (mushy) or parsley potatoes (good).

The dessert selection is small. A cheesecake is reasonably good and the black raspberry ice is excellent. The wine list is also limited, but well-chosen and well-priced.

All in all, this is one of the better places for fun suburban dining in a pleasant atmosphere and at a good price.

★ LA BOHEME
French

The Laundry Mall, 566 Chestnut, Winnetka   446-4600
Hours: Lunch Tues–Sat 11:30 am–2:30 pm, Dinner Tues–Sat
        6–10 pm closed Sun & Mon
Price range: Expensive
Credit cards: A C D M V
Reservations: Accepted

A great many people rave about this restaurant, but my experiences here have never lived up the the advance notices. While not bad, the food does not equal food served at the better French restaurants around town, and the prices are steep.

Decorating a shopping center space for a French restaurant can't be easy, and while the high-backed chairs, dark-stained wood, hanging tapestries and low lighting make a valiant attempt to create country-French atmosphere the total effect is somewhat short of French colonial.

Service is unpolished at best. One night, a server kept stopping by to see if the group was ready to order, "because I want to go home." On another evening, a bottle of white was brought to the table, but the half-bottle of red ordered at the same time came only after the entrées and had no time to breathe before being poured.

The food could salvage this place, but it falls flat far too often. Duck with an ordinary orange sauce turns out dry and tough, with grossly overdone green beans, carrots and zucchini on the side. Rabbit fares no better—dry and stringy, but with a good sauce of onions and mushrooms in wine. Veal Normande, with a good calvados cream sauce, works better.

Although the menu changes frequently, appetizers might include scallops with pernod sauce and acidic tomatoes that ruin an otherwise interesting dish; good, grilled mushrooms with a touch of olive oil; or fresh asparagus with a lemony Hollandaise sauce.

A high point of meals here is the salad, a mix of lettuce, mushrooms, tomato and cucumber, lightly dressed.

Desserts may include fresh berries with zabaglione sauce or a rich crème caramel. A good wine list for the size of the restaurant offers a few bargains. Dinner for two can easily run more than $70. So while the food here is okay, there's better French food to be enjoyed elsewhere for the price.

★ ★ BOMBAY PALACE
Indian

50 E. Walton   664-9323
Hours: Lunch Mon–Fri 11:30 am–2:30 pm, Sat & Sun 11:30–
*   3:00 pm, Dinner Sun–Thurs 5:30–10:45 pm, Fri & Sat*
*   5:30–11:15 pm*
Price range: Moderately expensive
Credit cards: A   C   D   M   V
Reservations: Accepted
Handicap

Without question the prettiest and most sophisticated setting for Indian food in town, Bombay Palace now also serves the best of this complex cuisine. Top honors used to be held by Gandhara at 720 N. Rush, which was destroyed by fire and is under reconstruction at this writing.

Pale blue walls, pink tablecloths and dark pink carpeting give this converted Magic Pan restaurant a contemporary look that would suit any sophisticated cuisine. Back-list cutouts in the walls display small Indian figurines, which give about the only hint that you are in an ethnic restaurant. Although Bombay Palace is part of a chain of restaurants—four in this country, three in Canada, and one in London—it doesn't seem chain-like.

Dining is on two levels, since booths are partitioned by sweeping sheets of gray-tinted glass, a sense of intimacy prevails, despite the restaurant's rather large size.

Start with the exceptionally delicate shammi kabab, finely minced lamb with egg, lentils, onion and garlic—wonderful—or the sampler of Indian appetizers. Don't overlook the fine salads listed under "tid bits" on the back of the menu.

Be sure to try a few Indian breads, the basic roti or nan, or the more complex versions stuffed with potatoes, chicken or onion. These light tandoori oven-baked breads go well with almost any selections.

Everything among the entrees turns out well, none of it so spicy as to scare off the weak-of-stomach. Keema masala, small bits of chicken seasoned with ginger, garlic, onion, tomato, yogurt and green peas, doesn't look like much, but it makes a pleasing combination. Tandoori chicken turns out moist, although not as flavorful as it could be. Barra kabab, tender pieces of lamb, and seeka kabab, spicy, minced lamb formed into a sausage-like roll and cooked on skewers, are both done in the tandoori oven. They have no hint of gaminess and will win over even those who think they loathe lamb. Lamb pasanda in a smooth yogurt-cream sauce with thin slices of almond is also good.

Most of these dishes can be ordered as one of the special combination meals, which include vegetables, lentils, rice and nan. Vegetarians will appreciate the large selection of meatless dishes.

Desserts include kulfi, Indian ice cream flavored with rosewater and ground almonds, mango ice cream and creamy Indian rice pudding.

Professional servers make sure that dining here goes smoothly. However, when they are asked for help in ordering, they suggest only the combination platter.

★ ★ LOUIS' BON APPETIT
French

302 S. Main St., Crown Point, Ind.   219-663-6363.
Hours: Tues–Sat 5:30 until it's over, Sun 11 am–2 pm, closed
    Mon
Price range: Moderately expensive
Credit cards: A C D M V
Reservations: Accepted
Handicap

Bon Appetit is not only a restaurant in the country (for Chicagoans, at any rate) it's also a French country-style restaurant with a relaxed, friendly atmosphere difficult to find in the city. The informality is part of the charm, and a welcome relief from the uptight, self-conscious dining found elsewhere. But be forewarned: an evening at Louis' is just that—an entire evening. The pace here is s-l-o-w, slow and comfortable.

The restaurant itself is in a converted old house that looks like a funeral home from the outside. But inside, the atmosphere is down-to-earth, with a few antiques, curtained windows and plenty of room between tables. Eating here is more like eating at a friend's house than in a restaurant.

The food, is not the nouvelle cuisine so popular in recent years. This is hearty French-country fare, with an emphasis on regional dishes and a heavy emphasis on game. The food is rich and the portions plentiful, so come prepared to be filled to capacity.

Four special appetizers (included in the price of the entrees) are offered each evening. Fall examples include pumpkin/leek soup, French onion soup, vegetable crepe and homemade sausage. Probably the best of these is the sausage—bologna, to be exact, but not the plastic-tasting stuff that masquerades as bologna in supermarkets. This is the real thing, topped with small chunks of potatoes, richly sauced and sprinkled with fresh parsley.

Twenty steamed mussels in a white wine sauce are served plump, fresh and free of grit, but the mussels are slightly rubbery from spending a bit too much time over the steam. The broth—white wine, cream and fresh herbs—is rich and made for spooning from the bowl or dunking with the white bread. Fresh foiê gras is served in an individual ramekin and flecked with bits of truffle. At the center is a large chunk of truffle, a pleasant surprise. The paté is full-bodied and smooth, but too cold. If it's not easily spreadable, it's best to let it warm to room temperature so the flavor can develop.

Salad (included in the entree price) can be ordered before or after the entree. After is the right choice, because the mix of greens with a few slices of tomato and mustard vinaigrette is unspectacular and can easily be passed up to leave room for dessert.

Some of the best dishes at Louis' are among the entrees, which include fresh-fish specials and several steaks, as well as venison, goose, duck and rabbit.

Wild duck breast is served in four large medaillons (the breast of two ducks, the waiter says) done rare—really rare. The meat is moist, tender, full-flavored and good. It's served with an extremely peppery sauce that works well to cut the gaminess of the duck.

The goose confit (goose preserved in its own fat), a special one night, is nicely sauced. The large slices of goose breast appear to by dry, but inside the meat is moist and delicious. Cassoulet, a house specialty, is said to feature duck and goose. In fact, it comes with a lot more: lamb, ham, chicken and sausage. A quart-sized French cast-iron pan is brought to the table, from which diners help themselves. It's large enough to serve two.

Loin of lamb is a super choice when it's offered as a special. The medaillons of meat, done medium-rare, are juicy, mild-flavored, tender and beautifully sauced. Entrees come with vegetables on the side; one night there were sauteed cucumbers, pea pods and carrots.

Among the desserts, the most interesting is the chocolate cheese cake, a good cheesecake that could stand alone but instead has been completely coated with high-quality chocolate. The crisp chocolate outer layer contrasts nicely with the creamy textured cheesecake inside. For those who crave both chocolate and butter, the Bon Appetit cake is a dessert made in heaven.

The fairly extensive wine list emphasizes French wine, with prices ranging from $10 for a good 1978 Beaujolis to some fine expensive vintages. For lighter meals at a very low tariff, there is a fixed price menu ($9.95) with less extensive offerings.

On balance, Louis' Bon Appetit is a wonderful place for a relaxed dinner of good, filling, French-country food.

★ BOSTON BLACKIE'S
American

164 E. Grand Ave.   938-8700
Hours: Mon–Sat 11 am–midnight
Price range: Inexpensive

Credit cards: A C D M V
Reservations: Not accepted

A prime filet mignon for $8.95? Believe it. At Blackie's, prices are low, but quality is high. Beef dominates the menu. Half-pound burgers are cooked over charcoal precisely as ordered and served on a sesame bun or kaiser roll. Tomato, dill pickle and a scoop of cole slaw from Carson's come on the side—all for less than $5. Good steak fries, a big fried onion loaf that should be shared by two or more, potato skins and salad cost extra.

In addition to the steaks and burgers there are chops and sandwiches—corned beef, hot dog, chicken and pork. All of the food is simple and far better than average.

Two TVs, one at each end of the room, pulsate with rock videos. Lightly stained wood, lots of brass, ceiling fans and mirrors give the room an art-deco/modern look. Servers are extremely pleasant and efficient.

★ BRUNA'S RISTORANTE
Italian

2424 S. Oakley   254-5550
Hours: Mon–Fri 11 am–10 pm, Sat 11:30–11 pm, Sun 2:30–10
*   pm*
Price range: Moderate
Credit cards: A M V
Reservations: Accepted

At first glance, this restaurant in Little Italy seems to be just a bar. But the next room is a homey affair usually packed with neighborhood regulars. The feel is a good deal like eating in someone's kitchen—a good old-fashioned Italian kitchen, at that.

Chalkboard specials augment extensive menu offerings. By all means, start with mussels in a heady marinara sauce when it's available. Mopping up the sauce with the good Italian bread is not only permissible, but good form.

Other starters include a good marinated mixed seafood salad, typical anitpasto and shrimp. House salads are large, but mundane.

Sample some of the above-average pastas, but make sure to go for the homemade pastas rather than the prepacked varieties. Avoid dishes such as stuffed shells and lasagna in favor of noodles with excellent pesto, tomato-cream or ragu sauces.

Interesting special such as braised rabbit raise this restaurant a cut above many of the others in the area. However, the kitchen has a tendency to overcook both pastas and entrees.

Like the salad, desserts are typical and not particularly fetching. The wine list offers a good selection at moderate prices.

Friendly servers fit the homey atmosphere. The reasonable prices and large portions make this a good bet for a casual evening out.

★ **CAFE ANGELO**
  Italian

225 N. Wabash Ave.   332-3370
Hours: Mon–Fri 11:30 am–11 pm, Sun noon–11 pm
Price range: Moderate
Credit cards: A   C   D   M   V
Reservations: Accepted
Other: Free parking for dinner

It's hard enough for a restaurant to be situated in a hotel, but this cafe is in a Quality Inn motel downtown—not exactly one of the city's most famous hotels. Signs announce its presence to foot and auto traffic, but by modern marketing standards these signs are pretty tame.

Modern marketing, however, is apparently of less interest to Cafe Angelo owner Angelo Nicelli than good food (for example, he built a greenhouse addition to his suburban home to grow fresh basil for the pesto served in his restaurant). Nicelli describes himself as owner/chef, but someone else seems to do the cooking, because Nicelli usually greets customers and supervises the smooth-running front of the house.

Your best bet is to eat at Cafe Angelo during the lunch hour. The service then (as at all times) is excellent, so lunch can be obtained quickly or eaten leisurely. Moreover, twice as many lunches as dinners are served, so the best kitchen and front-of-the-house help are in the restaurant.

Another strategy is to order pasta dishes as entrees. About a dozen different pasta dishes are offered at the bargain price of roughly $5 or less for portions large enough to be shared by two as an appetizer. All are good. In every case, the pasta is cooked to perfection, something that should be commonplace, but is not.

Pasta with pesto made from Angelo's basil is a good choice. The pesto alla genovese is served with a choice of fettuccine, linguine or ravioli verdi. The latter, green pasta pillows filled with cheese and herbs, is also excellent simply tossed with sage butter, another menu offering. The linguine primavera comes with sauteed fresh mushrooms, onions, tomatoes, peas and prosciutto in wine. Linguine alla Norma, a variation on the primavera theme with sauteed eggplant, tomatoes, basil and peas mixed with pecorino cheese, also is excellent.

Each of the pasta dishes has the region from which the dish originated—Sicily, Lazio, Tuscany, etc.-listed with the price. Somehow it's predictable that pasta Angelo comes from Chicago, according to the menu.

A long list (21) of appetizers opens the dinner menu. Most are pretty standard fare. House salad is included with entree orders, as is the home-baked cracked wheat Italian bread. The bread is a touch of heaven, and the whole wheat makes it a welcome alternative to the white stuff most restaurants serve.

It's a mystery why a restaurant that can cook pasta so well puts so much salt on chicken and veal and overcooks the meats. In general, entrees don't fare quite so well as the pastas here, but careful choices will produce good meals.

The homemade cannoli is one of the best in the city, with a crisp outer crust and a filling flecked with chocolate chips that is at once light and rich. Strangely, one of the house specialties is Creole bread pudding—smooth, almost custard-like in texture, with a whiskey sauce.

Given the moderate prices at this restaurant (which carry over to the limited but well-thought-out wine list), some of the best pastas in the city remain a good buy at Cafe Angelo

★★ CAFE BA-BA-REEBA!
Spanish/tapas

2024 N. Halsted St.   935-5000
Hours: Mon–Thurs 5:30–11 pm, Fri & Sat 5:30 pm–midnight,
       closed Sun
Price range: Moderately expensive
Credit cards: A C D M V
Reservations: Not accepted

Call it the ultimate grazing restaurant. Call it the ultimate theater restaurant. Call it the ultimate trendy restaurant. Call it what you will... Cafe Ba-Ba-Reeba! is a reaffirmation, not that we needed one, of the talent and imagination of Richard Melman. Opened in late 1985, it was an instant smash success. No reservations are accepted so you can expect waits that stretch to two hours on weekends. Come early or late and avoid the crowds. Otherwise the temptation to soften the impact of the long wait by sampling a representative number of the 42 Spanish sherries offered dulls the senses long before you get the chance to sample the food.

With a hodge-podge of rooms, bars and dining areas that shouldn't really go together, it's possible to have a different sort of dining experience on every visit to Ba-Ba-Reeba. One might dine at one of the bars or sit at a normal table in one of the dining rooms or at a high table flanked by unmatched bar stools in another area or in a leather booth. Each mode of seating has its fans.

No restaurant offers more theater. Diners enter from Halsted through a long hallway, lined with windows so that patrons waiting in the bar to the right of the entrance can see who's coming in. Inside there is more visual stimulation that one can possibly take in during a single visit. Many of the various tapas are on display under glass; cooks bustle in kitchens open to the view of diners; murals by local artists parody the style of various masters; meats, spices and cheese hang from the ceiling; a wood-burning oven from Spain cooks away along one wall; and a whole lot more.

It's all a bit much. So much, in fact, that it's hard to remember what it is you've seen once you've seen it.

The same is true of the food. Tapas, a Spanish tradition, are small appetizer-sized portions of great variety—hot and cold, seafood, meats and vegetables, spicy and mild, as simple as a slice of sausage or as complicated as stuffed squid. Each tapas has its own distinct flavor, texture and character. The idea is to sample many different types of dishes and share with your companions.

Most of the tapas run about $3-$4. These addictive little noshes sound inexpensive, but beware. The servers recommend each person have two tapas and an entree. Before you know it with a couple of sherries, beers or glasses of wine you can build quite a bill. It's worth it.

The best way to start out is to sample as many tapas as you like, but save room for paella. This seafood casserole on a bed of saffron-infused rice is excellent here. The portion for two is easily large enough to share among four or more depending on how much gorging has gone on before it arrives.

Among the tapas by all means try the cold baked fennel with capers and anchovy napped with olive oil and the seviche-like marinated seafood with lemon, fresh coriander and red pepper. Both are unique and wonderful.

Hot tapas include wonderful grilled sausages like blood sausage, chorizo and nightly specials, swordfish with herbs, grilled shrimp with a garlicky sauce and fried tender.

There are more than thirty tapas as well as main courses like the paella, shell steak and roast pig. Tapas-sized and entree-sized salads are available. Even the potato salad is something special and with a heavy hit of garlic. The Cafe Ba-Ba-Reeba salad- a mix of greens, raddicchio, sun-dried tomato and shredded lamb- is in itself worth the visit.

Desserts include an excellent custard, chocolate pudding, rice pudding, ice creams, fresh fruits and tart-like creations. All equal the tapas in taste, texture and excellence.

Service is exceptionally efficient. Indeed, it may be too fast. It would be a gross mistake to rush. After all, if you've waited a couple of hours, you may as well take your time, sample a wide variety and enjoy yourself.

In addition to the lengthy list of sherries, a large selection of Spanish wines makes the perfect complement to the food.

★ ★ ★ CAFE D'ARTAGNAN
French

2242 N. Lincoln Ave.   *248-6543*

Hours: Sun–Thurs 5:30–9:30 pm, Fri & Sat 5:30–10 pm,
*   Closed Sun*
Price range: Moderately expensive
Credit cards: A   M   V
Reservations: Recommended

Owned by a former Le Francais sommelier and nurtured by its sister restaurant, the highly acclaimed Jackie's just two blocks north on Lincoln Ave., Cafe D'Artagnan by all rights should be as pretentious as the dickens. Yet, despite its near-Northside location, its sophisticated French cuisine and its lineage, D'Artagnan has a refreshingly casual approach to dining which makes it the best little restaurant to open in Chicago in 1985.

On warm days, Cafe D'Artagnan spills out onto a patio that fronts Lincoln Avenue, doubling the cold-weather size of this tiny, but pleasant restaurant. Given the quality of the food, the friendly, efficient service and upbeat atmosphere, one wishes it were located in a city where warm days abound year-round.

Cafe D'Artagnan makes its home in a converted house, which gives it more the feeling of a friend's sitting room than a formal dining room. Old-fashioned, floral wallpaper covers one wall of the tiny room, painted brick the other. Glass-topped tables surrounded by surprisingly comfortable wrought-iron chairs sit close together, reducing intimacy perhaps, but adding to the cafe atmosphere. And, as in any good cafe, mingling with habitues is half the fun.

D'Artagnan's lacks pretense but not the attention to detail that makes dining out a pleasure. Although it would be in the best interest of profitability to encourage diners to order, eat and leave, freeing the tables for others, servers pace meals according to the diners' wishes, encouraging them to linger, if they wish, over coffee, another glass of wine or an after-dinner drink.

For such a small restaurant, the hand-written wine list is extensive, if a bit difficult to read, with many wines offered by the glass. In addition, the list of half bottles is exceedingly large for a restaurant of this size.

The spartan menu contrasts markedly with the long list of wines. Only five appetizers, three entree salads and four entrees appear on the printed menu. Nightly specials augment these offerings. Special in the truest sense of the word, the offerings sometimes change even during the course of an evening, one being deleted, another added.

The roast pork stuffed with arugula, liver paté and mushrooms is moist, tender and flavorsome, the medium-rare pork a wonderful complement to the smooth stuffing. The full bodied madeira sauce begs to be swept from the plate with the light French bread provided for just such a purpose. No less appealing than the pork, calves liver with calvados sauce again shows a well-balanced approach. Rossettes of beef arrive seared on the outside, juice sealed within. The reduced veal stock sauce complements, again without overpowering, the meat. The chef decorates pristinely fresh grilled salmon with a garlic beurre rouge sauce as an artist might embellish a still life—just enough to add interest and direct attention to the object of primary importance.

All entrees come with a pretty arrangement of vegetables on the oversized Villery & Boch plates. Green beans and carrots or snow pea pods and baby carrots have appeared recently in a zingy, slightly tart, light butter sauce that adds greatly to the vegetables.

Appetizers presage the delights to come. A more-than-satisfying sauce pulls together the different flavors of sauteed snails and shiitake mushrooms, served on a bed of angel hair pasta flecked with sun-dried tomatoes for a surprisingly light beginning. Not quite so light, the wild mushroom and sun-dried tomatoe tart sits on a buttery sauce that adds civility to this earthy appetizer. Patés change daily.

103

Simple salads composed of greens with slices of carrot precede entrees. A light coating of mustard vinaigrette flavors the greens. Special salads are available.

Given the quality of the meal, desserts easily could be anticlimactic. Instead, they satisfy without dazzling. Light, delicate chocolate mousse cake, sliced apples arrayed on a light and flaky crust for the apple tart, and chocolate tart with raspberries win raves.

Cafe D'Artagnan is reminiscent of the early days of Yoshi's. Carefully prepared food with French underpinnings, including beautiful presentation in a comfortable, friendly environment, and reasonable prices make this an attractive alternative to stuffy evenings in haughtier joints.

★ **CAFE DU PARC**
French

2442 N. Clark St.   525-1800
Hours: Lunch Mon–Sat 11 am–4 pm, Dinner Mon–Thurs 5–
*   11 pm, Fri & Sat 5 pm–midnight, Sun brunch 11 am–*
*   3 pm, dinner 5–10:30 pm*
Price range: Moderate.
Credit cards: A C D M V
Reservations: Accepted

The younger sibling of La Fontaine, Cafe Du Parc, with outdoor dining in the summer, succeeds well enough with decent food at reasonable prices. In cool weather, the cafe occupies the lower level of the house with the more formal La Fontaine upstairs. At less than half the price of its sister restaurant, Cafe du Parc definitely offers the better value.

Appetizers include escargot in the shell with an excellent butter, garlic and wine sauce. Of the two patés, served with cornichons and mustard, the smooth chicken liver spiked with cognac and champagne is better. The coarse country paté, made with "any liver that's left," according to the server, left much to be desired. The warm artichoke with mousseline sauce is a whole artichoke that is overcooked. A squeeze from the lemon slice on the side saves the rather flat sauce. The full-flavored onion soup comes with excellent cheese melted on top. The salad consists of Boston lettuce with two tomato wedges and bits of crumbled egg. It's dressed a bit too heavily with a watery Dijon vinaigrette and sometimes topped with pimiento or artichoke.

One of the best entrees here is Couscous Casablanca, a balanced broth chock-full of vegetables, lamb and unboned chicken breast balanced with nicely steamed semolina. A spicy harissa sauce served on the side adds punch. Paella Valencianna—a large piece of unboned chicken with chunks of beef, fish and shrimp with rice—works well. The "abundant platter of freshly baked mussel" was abundant but far from fresh; covered with an herbed breading á la baked clams, the mussels have a dry texture and fishy taste.

The menu includes several one-dish meals. The combination of zucchini, broccoli, cheese and beef sausage wrapped in a puff pastry is intriguing, but the sticky cheese prevents the pastry from cooking fully and leaves the vegetables overcooked.

An excellent créme caramel tops the desserts here. The chocolate mousse has excellent texture but lacks richness. For the price, Cafe du Parc provides good value despite its somewhat uneven offerings.

★ ★ ★ CAFE PROVENCAL
French

1625 Hinman Ave., Evanston   475-2233
Hours: Mon–Thurs 6–9 pm, Fri & Sat 6–10 pm, closed Sun
Price range: Expensive
Credit cards: A C D M V
Reservations: Recommended

Regarded by many as one of metropolitan Chicago's most romantic restaurants, Leslee Reis' country French restaurant has a homey feel. Its knotty pine-paneled or fabric-covered walls, big fireplace, pink tablecloths, old French posters and soft lighting go well with traditional French dishes prepared with just enough creativity to make the meal interesting. The only problem comes with the pacing; long delays between courses occur, particularly when the room is crowded.

The food is worth the wait. Noteworthy appetizers include the wild mushroom sauté, a selection of fresh mushrooms perfectly cooked and naturally flavored, and the patés and terrines, especially the terrine of head cheese composed of different meats and vegetables in aspic and a creamy chicken liver paté. Not all appetizers excel. Only the great lentils served on the side save the somewhat dry, too-peppery and gristly sausage appetizer from disaster. The lentils have a wonderful smokey flavor supplemented with onions and bits of parsley. An escargot special one night disappointed with its lack of intensity. The plump, gritless snails swim shelless in a wine, onion and butter sauce that simply doesn't pack enough punch.

Nevertheless, it's punch that Reis believes in. The entrees proved it. Not one of the sampled dishes failed to tantalize the tastebuds. A fabulous squab dish presents crisp-skinned squab on a bed of hazelnuts, radicchio, leaf lettuce and other greens in a great sauce seasoned with pork fat. The rich squab meat, cooked medium rare and fork-tender, is balanced by the greens and slightly bitter radicchio. Equally good, the extremely smokey breast of duck, grilled rare, is complemented by tart cranberries. Slightly gamey and surprisingly tender, this duck may strike some as a tad too heavy with its wood-smoked overtones, but the combination is marvelous. The moist, barely cooked salmon has a suitably subtle, lemon-ginger butter accompaniment— perhaps too subtle with its nearly undetectable hint of ginger. An interesting combination of medium-rare, boneless saddle of lamb on a bed of confit of lemon and onions works exceptionally well, with the onions softening the slight gaminess of the meat. Potatoes and perfectly cooked vegetables—red and green peppers, squash, French green beans—come with most entrees.

Salads can be requested before or after entrees. Without prompting, the server brought a creamy celery root salad to the diner who ordered the squab on a bed of greens so that salad-like courses would not be repeated—a nice touch that unfortunately went awry one night, when the too-salty salad sent diners gasping for water. House salads are plain but adequate and come dress lightly with a mustard vinaigrette.

Meals end on a high note with dessert. Only the lemon tart, a popular house specialty, disappointed with its too-thick, albeit flaky, crust and pleasing but exceedingly eggy, tart lemon topping. The chocolate cake wrapped around a rich pistachio ice cream with whole pistachios and surrounded by a bittersweet chocolate sauce is a candidate for best dessert of the year. Coffee flan with fresh raspberries on the side captures the essence of coffee without sacrificing its smooth, creamy custard character.

In an era of mass-produced restaurants, Cafe Provencal takes a rare stand, and most of what it stands for seems right on the mark. One of the things the kitchen staff understands well is the need to harmonize ingredients, usually producing a symphony of understatement without a single garish note.

CAFE ROYAL
English and Scottish
Rating: Fair

1633 N. Halsted St.   266-3394
Hours: Tues–Sun 5–11 pm, closed Mon
Price range: Moderately expensive
Credit cards: A C D
Reservations: Accepted

Cafe Royal is a must-see restaurant, unquestionably one of the spectacular restaurant spaces to open in Chicago recently. A tremendous amount of thought, effort and money went into the open-beamed, loft-like, multi-room, multi-level space, with hardwood floors and a pleasant post-modern color scheme.

Diners enter through a two-story lobby with a bar in the center. To the right, a pianist plays classical music in a large, comfortable cocktail lounge. This lounge offers a view of the inner workings of the restaurant through a sweep of plate glass rising several feet from the floor. On a level below, cooks prepare the evening's fare.

At the rear of the cocktail lounge, a set of stairs beside the maitre d' stand leads down to an intimate wine bar. A second set of stairs to the left of the stand leads up to the dining rooms on yet another level. The main dining area faces Halsted and has the pleasant appearance of a formal English dining room, with clown dolls and antiques lining a ledge overhead. Small, private dining areas also are available, making this a terrific place for a romantic evening.

If only the same attention to detail that went into the decor were paid to all of the dishes. Granted, few places in Chicago serve English and Scottish specialties, so the culinary theme has the advantage of uniqueness. However, despite attempts to dress up the fare, many of the dishes fall far short of excellence.

One can choose from a prix fixe dinner menu at $26.50 per person or order a la carte. Avoid the hard, aspic-covered fish terrine. The venison pasty turns out better; flaky pastry dough wrapped around ground venison. Or go instead to the á la carte menu for the good stoved crab cakes, Stilton cheese fritters, Bintjes with salmon caviar or the average country paté.

House salads, a mix of shredded romaine and other leaf lettuces, carrots and tomato, come with entrees. Choose the punchy Stilton cheese dressing over the curry cream dressing, which is basically a creamy vinaigrette with curry powder mixed in.

Cod fish cooked in foil with a little lemon and parsley is fresh but exceedingly plain. The bland horseradish dressing on the side doesn't help much. The lightly sauteed julienne of peppers and carrots on the side has far more flavor. Avoid the good roast beef because of the disappointingly doughy, soggy Yorkshire pudding accompanying it. Choose instead the Black Angus sirloin, which the kitchen does well. Other acceptable entree choices include chicken gubins, pork tenderloin and the dry but flavorsome Cornish hen.

For dessert, apples Charlotte—soggy, sugared bread sprinkled with cinnamon over a bed of mushy apples—tastes a good deal better than it sounds. Cone-shaped bread pudding made with dark and white bread flecked with raisins and seasoned with too much salt comes with an excellent, rich creme Anglais.

Friendly, helpful servers work hard to make everyone comfortable. Unfortunately for this extremely handsome restaurant, the food does not measure up to the decor. Too many dishes either fail totally or taste too bland and lifeless to justify the price of $60-$80 per couple for a full meal. Still, everyone should visit Cafe Royal, if only to see it and enjoy a drink and a snack.

★ ★ CAFE SPIAGGIA
Italian

One Magnificent Mile, 980 N. Michigan Ave.   280-2750
Hours: Mon–Sat 11:30 am–11 pm, Sun 11:30 am–8 pm
Price range: Moderate
Credit cards: A   C   D   M   V
Reservations: Not accepted
Handicap

The look of this little cafe carries over from its sister restaurant next door but the prices don't, making this a terrific place for a light lunch or late-night snack.

A unique antipasto bar just inside the entrance holds tempting selections, from cold pasta salads and seafood melanges to gussied-up chicken salads ranging in price from $3 to $4. Or one can sample the exquisitely crisp thin-crust pizzas cooked in the special wood-burning oven and topped with such mouth-watering combinations as goat cheese, duck sausage and fresh herbs, or sun-dried tomatoes and a variety of cheeses. A meal can be made of these pizzas or two can share for an appetizer.

Calzones also are available, along with a limited selection of entrees including poultry, meat and seafood, grilled or simply prepared. Portions are not large and saucing is kept to a minimum, but the food is light, fresh and pleasing.

Fresh fruit with zabaglione browned under the broiler and a few pastries make fine desserts. There are some wines by-the-glass, as well as any bottle from Spiaggia's extensive list of Italian and sprinkling of French and California wines. Service is friendly, efficient and attentive, so meals can be as fast or leisurely as you desire.

★ ★ LA CAPANNINA
Italian

7353 W. Grand, Elmwood Park   452-0900
Hours: Mon–Sat 4–11 pm, Sun 2:30–10:30 pm
Price range: Moderately expensive
Credit cards: A   M   V
Reservations: Accepted
Handicap

It's understandable why Mike Rokyo wrote two favorable columns about this venerable neighborhood eatery. Despite its slick, expanded interior and minor concessions to American tastes, La Capannina shows off its Sicilian heritage without shame. Regulars from Elmwood Park (a solidly Italian community) pack the restaurant on weekends when the servers, normally very nice, attentive and helpful, tend to disappear for what seems eons. There also can be lengthy periods between courses, although given the quantity of the food, this may be more help than hindrance.

The food is pure Italian. Save the crusty Italian bread, perfectly suited for "shaving the cat," an Italian expression for wiping the bread back and forth across the plate, to soak up the fantastic fresh sauces. Salads, the usual iceberg lettuce with two wedges of ripe tomato and pickled vegetables found in Italian joints, comes before entrees and probably should be skipped in favor of the filling courses to come.

Only three appetizers are served: antipasto, raw or baked clams and insalata di mare. The antipasto, with four large sticks of aged provolone and purple Mediterranean olives augmenting the usual selection of sausages, prosciutto, pickled vegetables and lettuce, makes most others seem pretty shabby.

The menu lists no "pasta," just spaghetti, linguine and mostoccioli. All arrive a perfect al dente. For a light start, try the spaghetti alla insalata. Also great are the linguine tossed

111

in a skillet at the table with fresh tomatoes, onion and parsley sauteed in a generous amount of garlic and oil, and the linguine la capricciosa (red sauce with shrimp). The latter's sauce packs a bit of a spicy punch that makes the mouth water—and maybe the eyes as well. The traditional spaghetti with red meat sauce works well, and the rich thick sauce demands "shaving." all 20 variations on the spaghetti/linguine/mostoccioli theme can be shared as appetizers.

As in any good Italian restaurant, veal plays an important role on the menu. Choose any of the eight different preparations. The white, high-quality meat inevitably turns out fork-tender and extremely moist. The chef believes in intense flavorings. The piccata, with its host of capers, may be too rich for some tastes, while the veal al vino bianco (white wine and lemon sauce) may be too tart. Although the flank steak rolled around the mixture of provolone, onion and garlic to form braciole ala barase borders on tough, the sizable and flavorful dish bathed in a rich, slightly spicy, red sauce should please meat lovers.

A blackboard displays nightly seafood specials, including zuppa de pesce. Served from a skillet, this fresh seafood melange—shrimp, squid, fish, clams and lobster—swims in a thick, subtle tomato sauce. Except for a few tough clams, it was perfectly cooked. As for the baby clams served in white sauce, some of them had outgrown baby status; but their clear, garlicky sauce makes this a nice, light dish.

Even starting with a huge appetite, most people leave this restaurant with leftovers, so not too much emphasis need be placed on dessert. It isn't. Spumoni, cannoli and apple strudel are offered. The wine list provides a good selection of Italian wines, some rarely seen here. Prices range from around $10 to a bit over $30. An attentive waiter responded with averna to our groans after one night's strenuous overconsumption. Served steamed in a brandy snifter with a wedge of lemon, the liqueur's healing properties were amazing.

There's little wrong with this restaurant. In fact, dinner here is frighteningly addictive. Once you've sampled some of the menu offerings you want them all, despite the incredible portions.

★ CAPE COD ROOM
Seafood

Drake Hotel, 140 E. Walton   787-2200
Hours: Daily noon–11 pm
Price range: Expensive
Credit cards: A C D M V
Reservations: Recommended

Rating this Chicago seafood institution is chancy at best. When it is good it is very, very good, but when it is bad. . . . Mostly it's bad when a convention is in town or during the heavy tourist season, both of which seem to be the times I inevitably happen into the place. Then the crowds put pressure on the kitchen and the servers to make what might be a pleasant dining experience rushed and uncomfortable.

One thing almost always good at this restaurant is the oyster bar. The small, horseshoe-shaped, marble-topped bar is probably the only oyster bar in Chicago comparable in design to typical East Coast oyster bars. However, since a conservative management steadfastly believes there is a season for oysters, oysters aren't always available. The cherrystone clams are plump, fresh and tasty, served with an interesting sauce spiked with chopped onions. Six clams or oysters come on a bed of chipped ice.

The main dining room has the look and feel of a classy and classic New England fish house. Plenty of banquette seating gives a sense of privacy even at crowded times. And when waiters are not rushed, they not only know their stuff, but can also be quite charming.

The Cape Cod Room gets credit for introducing Chicago to high-quality, fresh seafood. Over time, many sharp competitors have come along, making some of the offerings here—lobster thermidor and the like—seem a bit tired and old-fashioned. Wisely, however, the Cape Cod Room for the most part keeps preparations simple to let the goodness of the fresh seafood shine through. Daily specials also help keep the restaurant in tune with the times.

An excellent snapper soup leads the list of good ways to start meals here, along with the fresh shellfish and smoked salmon. Soft-shell and stone crabs are available in season, with appropriately simple preparations. The bouillabaisse stands up well against any anywhere.

The good wine list allows plenty of latitude for choices in any price range. Desserts are not the calling card here. Save the calories.

Asking whether or not the restaurant will be especially busy when you make reservations may be the only way to ensure that the hordes don't descend to ruin your meal, and even that's not a foolproof technique.

★★★★ CARLOS RESTAURANT
French

429 Temple Ave., Highland Park   432-0770
Hours: Wed–Mon 5:30–11 pm, closed Tues
Price range: Expensive
Credit cards: A   C   D   M   V
Reservations: Necessary
Handicap

One of the area's top haute-cuisine restaurants, Carlos combines outstanding service and food that makes for very smooth dining. You don't have to know that owner Carlos Nieto worked for nearly 10 years as captain at Jean Banchet's Le Francais to notice that the service here is something special. The staff is quick, efficient, personal and never condescending.

The room is small and intimate, a pleasant, L-shaped interior, with white-clothed tables, fresh flowers, candles and Art Deco touches. Etched-glass partitions set off some tables; others are tucked into corners for privacy. A patchwork of simply framed, black-and-white photos of '30s and '40s movie stars nearly covers the upper walls. Even when the place is crowded, the noise level remains low.

No dish tastes less-than-good or looks less-than-fantastic. Chef Roland Liccioni prepares a nightly feuilletee surprise. The surprise is inside the letter-prefect puff-pastry rectangle. The nicely balanced Franco-Italian delight is filled with succulent sea scallops and spinach, underlaid with a butter sauce laced with basil and bits of tomato. A special, fresh grilled goose liver (the waiter acknowledges that the liver is from a Moullard duck) is smooth, tender and perfectly cooked, served with a tart citrus sauce. The exquisite appetizer comes with artichoke hearts, mushrooms, spinach, a sprig of chervil and some small shrimp. A pleasing, lighter appetizer is the smooth delicately herbed salmon sausage in a complementary clear sauce with basil and chopped leeks. Mushroom paté is three distinct layers of mushroom mousse, flavorful morels and more mousse. A tasty sauce generously flecked with truffle surrounds the load-shaped slice, one of Carlos' most popular items.

Soups change frequently. The lobster bisque was the only sample that didn't stand out. The house salad is unexciting but adequate. Better is the special salad with Roquefort dressing featuring radicchio, leaf lettuce and Belgian endive with lots of walnuts under a thin coat of walnut oil vinaigrette. Goat cheese and radicchio, mache, endive, mushrooms and green beans topped with three shrimp make an equally good salad. To cleanse the palate before entrees, try the fabulous pink grapefruit sorbet garnished with mint leaves. A passion fruit number is a bit too sweet, although it captures the essence of the fruit.

Veal medaillons sauteed with a confit of ginger—archly served with two peas—is excellent. The high-quality veal comes grilled to still-pink doneness in a tart, pungent sauce with three baby carrots. A special assiette of squab—small, medium rare—slices served with ravioli of mushrooms and a sweet garlic sauce—sparkles. So does the striped sea-bass special. The fresh fish is perfectly grilled, still juicy inside but cooked. It comes with a somewhat sweet, buttery sauce and little slices of grapefruit and blueberries on the side. Liver cooked medium-rare comes with rosemary and mushrooms. The fresh, rich liver is fork-tender and the rosemary sauce has piquant overtones that work well to cut the richness of the meat.

The desserts provide a fitting finale. The list changes nightly but a flourless chocolate cake and fruit tart that rival the area's best are regulars. The best dessert sampled was a mango served with fresh whipped cream and freshly made hot butterscotch sauce. The wine list is surprisingly narrow but good, from the ice dry Maitre Roidet house white to the David Bruce Zinfandel.

★ ★ CARLOS & CARLOS
Italian

1540 W. North Ave.   384-1300
Hours: Lunch Mon–Fri 11:30 am–3 pm, Dinner Mon–Thurs
*   5:30–11:30 pm, Fri & Sat 5:30 pm–midnight, Sun 5–*
*   10 pm*
Price range: Moderately expensive
Credit cards: A D M V
Reservations: Recommended
Other: Valet parking

If, as the maxim holds, there are just three keys to success in the restaurant business—location, location and

116

location—then Carlos & Carlos should, by rights, be out of business by now. Located in a culinary no-man's land between Halsted Street's burgeoning restaurant row and Bucktown, which real estate sorts describe as an area with, ah... potential, Carlos & Carlos misses the cutting edge of Chicago's trendy restaurant scene by a country mile.

Nonetheless, this young, Northern Italian restaurant, like Jimmy's Place and Gordon before it, deserves notice as 1985's off-the-beaten-track discovery.

The owners have done a miraculous job of transforming a seedy bar into a pleasantly comfortable restaurant with exposed brick walls, ceiling fans and white-clothed tables with comfortable seating.

It stands to reason that these owners should be able to accomplish such a transformation. Carlos Montiel learned how to manage the front of the room at Nick's Fishmarket, where he worked for seven years as captain and maitre d'. Chef and co-owner Eddy Montiel practiced his craft in San Francisco at Ciao and Prego restaurants.

Service exceeds expectations and, at times, the norm. On the starter plate selected by an eager-to-please waiter one evening: well-prepared scampi with a restrained topping of garlic and chives; calamari stuffed with a flavorful melange of chopped fresh seafood, capers and bread crumbs; oysters Rockefeller and antipasto.

Simplicity underscores the chef's entrees. Among the large, filling pasta dishes, Tortelloni biete, large pillows of pasta stuffed with ricotta cheese and Swiss chard and served with a simple butter and fresh sage sauce, approaches perfection. Fresh fish specials are either grilled or sauteed. Broiled veal chops come adorned with a sprinkling of fresh rosemary and sage; even the classic veal piccata shows that the chef knows how to use a light hand; a tangy lemon/butter sauce lets the taste of the veal shine through.

Despite the brothers' plan to introduce a new menu every three months, none of the current menu offerings is sufficiently unusual to draw food aficionados to this stretch of North Avenue. To develop a real following, Carlos & Carlos probably will have to include more innovative dishes.

★ CARLUCCI
Italian

2215 N. Halsted St.   281-1220
Hours: Mon–Sat 5:30–11 pm, Sun 5–10 pm
Price range: Moderately expensive
Credit cards: A   D   M   V
Reservations: Not accepted
Handicap
Other: Valet parking

Trendy and popular, Carlucci's joins the other restaurants along Halsted north of North Ave. contributing to the area's revival. This restaurant is one of the most impressive of the bunch, if not for its food, then at least for its decor.

The long, wide entry hall has an arched ceiling and *faux marbre* walls that look like real marble, but instead are an excellent paint job. Inside to the left, the large, horseshoe-shaped bar is hardly ever less than busy and usually jumps with action. Overhead a skylight gives a sense of limitless ceilings. To the left behind some columns and plants is the dining room, also with high ceilings and interesting modern paintings on the walls. Done in mahogany and grey with large mirrors so that everyone can see everyone else, this noisy dining room is another of the great cafes.

Great cafes are not great because of the food they serve, mind you. They're great because they are big, bustling, boisterous and bring together the seen-and-be-seen crowd.

Dinner starts off well, as it does in most decent Italian res-

118

taurants round town, with crusty D'Amato's Bakery bread. Appetizers include simple but good smoked fish, spicy clams marinara or steamed mussels.

Trendy as the dickens, the special house salad of arugala, radicchio, spinach and endive sounds better than it is. Stick with the regular Romaine lettuce house salad.

Pastas can soar to great heights or sour diners to this restaurant, depending on the night and the care taken in the kitchen. Fettuccini with pesto comes out al dente and flavorful. The ravioli has a bland, tasteless filling and is sauced in the same mode. Generally, however, pastas with interesting sauces such as lobster cream are good bets. If overcooked, send them back and have the kitchen try again.

Veal entrees start with quality veal and for some reason seem to receive more consistent care in the preparation than do the pastas. Six veal preparations, from standard marsala to creative specials, are offered each evening. Fresh fish specials, beef and poultry dishes round out the menu.

Desserts include rich and creamy *gelati* from the Italian *gelato* store you passed on the way in, owned by the same folks who own the restaurant. Try the flavor of your choice. Cheesecake, excellent cannoli and a special or two are also offered.

The list, dominated by Italian wines, offers some good values to those who know their way around Italian vintages. Those who don't should ask for help from the knowledgeable waiters.

The no-reservation policy combined with the trendy popularity of this place can lead to exhaustingly long waits and overindulgence at the bar that can ruin even the best meals Carlucci's has to offer. The wisest strategy is to go early or late to avoid the crowds. Or perhaps try a Monday or Tuesday evening, slow nights at most restaurants—even this one.

★ CARSON'S—THE PLACE FOR RIBS
American

Five locations:
612 N. Wells   280-9200
Hours: Mon–Thurs 11 am–midnight, Fri & Sat 11–1 am, Sun
*   2–10 pm*

5970 N. Ridge St.   271-4400
Hours: Mon–Thurs 11 am–11 pm, Fri & Sat 11 am–midnight,
*   Sun noon–10 pm*
Handicap

8617 Niles Center, Skokie   675-6800
Hours: Mon–Thurs 4–11 pm, Fri & Sat 4 pm–midnight, Sun
*   2–10 pm*
Handicap

400 E. Roosevelt, Lombard   627-4300
Hours: Mon–Thurs 11 am–11 pm, Fri & Sat 11 am–midnight,
*   Sun noon–10 pm*
Handicap

5050 N. Harlem, Harwood Heights   867-4200
Hours: Mon–Thurs 11 am–11 pm, Fri 11 am–midnight, Sat
*   noon–midnight, Sun noon–10 pm*
Price range: Moderately expensive
Credit cards: A C D M V
Reservations: Accepted for large parties only

You can go to Carson's for other things. There's good prime rib at most locations, better-than-average steaks and chops, some simple fish dishes and barbecued chicken. But let's face it, Carson's made its reputation on ribs and upon ribs it shall live or die.

I never really appreciated the attraction of Carson's ribs—

there are much better ones available in Chicago—until I tasted Tony Roma's poor excuse for barbecued ribs. That made Carson's seem a whole lot better, and raised its rating from fair to good.

My beef with the venerable Carson's bones? These assembly-line ribs (take-out orders literally come off a conveyor belt) don't measure up to those at some lesser-known houses. The ribs are big, meaty and well-cooked. You won't find too much fat on the bones, but you don't get much smokey flavor either. There can be a strong porky taste although it may be that the absence of smoke lets too much of the pork taste come through. However, the real problem is not with the ribs themselves but with the sauce. It lacks character, tastes a bit too sweet and is not very spicy at all. Carson's does have great carry-out packaging that delivers the ribs hot with their complement of good rolls and excellent cole slaw or an ordinary iceberg lettuce salad and potatoes—either skins, baked, French-fried or au gratin. On top of this, portions are large so the restaurant offers good value for the buck.

Another advantage: all of Carson's locations are friendly, homey places with big wooden chairs and no pretense. Some of the better rib places can't stake this claim. So despite the less-than-perfect ribs, Carson's continues to pack in customers who rave about its fare.

★ ★ CASBAH
Armenian

514 W. Diversey   935-7570
Hours: Daily 5–10:30 pm
Price range: Moderate
Credit cards: A C D M V
Reservations: Accepted

The Casbah is a long, narrow restaurant that can be

dreary when not crowded, but brightens considerably on weekends when the mingling conversations of many diners give life to the place. Inside the entrance, a long bar stretches down the left side of the restaurant. Here the owner either tends bar when there are customers or hangs out when there are not, sampling a little of the wine. Beyond the bar area is a two-level dining room wrapped in murals depicting Middle Eastern scenes. A brown wash and cracked plaster gives these murals a false patina of age. There is a sense of humor about this place. Men chase camels across the walls. Carpets fly overhead. The mood can turn quite festive with a full dining room. But far and away the best part of the restaurant is the food.

Start with cheese beorak, a creamy cheese baked in the flakiest of filo dough, or spinach beorak, the same dough wrapped around spiced spinach. Hommos, pureed chick peas blended with sesame seed puree, or baba ghannouj, puree of eggplant, blended with tahini sauce, come with warm pita on the side and make an excellent start to the meal. Casbah serves the best version of tabbuleh salad—parsley, mint and cracked wheat with olive oil and lemon juice—to be found in the city.

Both raw kibbeh, raw lamb blended with cracked wheat and served cold, or hot kibbeh, the same mix with the addition of onions and walnuts cooked crisp on the outside, moist and crumbly on the inside, are available. Fish specials are offered nightly. A trout special turned out moist with its spicy topping.

Entrees come with a choice of soup, tossed salad and rice pilaf or vegetables. Soups here are excellent. Desserts include baklava which seems heavier than it ought to be but tends to grow on you. The muhalabie is smooth, custard-like mixture that may strike some as bland but tends to make a pleasant contrast to the strong flavor of the entrees.

Prices are moderate and portions large. Two easily can order appetizer, soup, salad, entree and dessert for less than $40.

The Casbah is a jewel in the crown of Chicago's ethnic restaurants. It deserves far more patronage than it gets on week nights. Interesting decor, a sense of humor, good food and reasonable prices make this a restaurant no one should miss who is serious about ethnic eating.

★ CASTELLANO'S
Cuban

2529 N. Milwaukee Ave.   772-6267
Hours: Sun–Thurs 11:30 am–11 pm, Fri & Sat 11:30 am–
    midnight
Price range: Moderate
Credit cards: A C D M V
Reservations: Accepted for parties of 6 or more
Handicap

Fun at a great price, that's what Castellano's delivers. Where else can you go for an evening of live entertainment, dinner and dancing and run up a total tab of less than $50 for two? The name sounds Italian, but the food, music and dancing are pure Cuban.

The menu is in both Spanish and English, but the Spanish comes first, letting diners know where this restaurant stands. Waitresses understand and speak English, some better than others.

Although not pretentious, the dining room is exceptionally clean, with tile floors, wooden beams across the ceiling, white cloths on the tables and red cloth napkins. In the left rear corner is a separate, dark bar, but generally the lighting is bright and cheery. Bottles of wine line the back wall. The band performs from a small stand at the center of the left wall with a tiny dance floor beside it.

Prices range from about $6 to $17 for a full dinner. Billed

123

as a LeLechonera, pork palys a major role on the menu. Roast pork comes out moist, but with a stronger flavor than most Americans are used to. Boneless fried pork, browned and crisp outside yet still moist and tender within, probably makes a better choice.

Seafood lovers can split a *paella valenciana*, the classic fish stew, for $25. It takes 45 minutes or more to prepare. Other seafood offerings include lobster, shrimp and fried red snapper or kingfish.

Steaks and chicken round out the menu. Most entrees come with either casava or fried plantains on the side. Rice or black beans also generally come with main courses. Iceberg lettuce, a slice of tomato and a couple of rings of fresh onion make up the plain but fresh salad.

Desserts include flan, guava, papaya, raisin or rice pudding. Good, strong Cuban coffee is a must for coffee lovers.

For the price, there's probably no better value in food and entertainment in town.

★ ★ ★ THE CHARDONNAY
French

2635 N. Halsted St.   477-5130
*Hours: Dinner Tues–Sat 5–10 pm; wine bar opens at 4:30 pm,
        brunch Sun noon–5 pm, closed Mon*
Price range: Moderate
Credit cards: A   V
Reservations: Recommended
Handicap

When The Chardonnay first opened as a small wine bar with four or five tables and excellent if simple French fare, it seemed too good to be true. Chicago just doesn't have this sort of place. Many wines by the glass and good food at reasonable prices.

Then owner Mitch Dulin, the tall, bearded owner who

spouts reams of information about wines, allowed that he was going to expand into the storefront next door. We shuddered at the thought of expansion. Surely it would ruin this intimate little place.

It has not. Chef Charles Socher, who formerly cooked at Ambria, continues to turn out some of the best French food in town at surprisingly moderate prices.

The plain dining room with its marble-topped tables and oddly out-of-place chandeliers manages to convey the feeling of intimacy one felt before the expansion, but not the warmth. The friendly waiters with no trace of pretense help make up for the coldness of the room.

Dulin and his waiters will give mini wine seminars to anyone willing to listen when the room isn't busy and sometimes when it is. The long list of wines by the glass priced from about $2.50 to $7 makes sampling several wines during the course of dinner much more tempting than selecting a bottle. Waiters gladly make educated recommendations about which wines might go best with what dishes.

The menu changes every other week. Thus many of the dishes mentioned here may no longer be available. Indeed on some evenings the kitchen runs out of a dish or two before the end of the dinner hour. Usually new dishes are substituted so that the variety is no less limited.

Although the exact make-up of the patés changes, usually a selection is available, exquisitely presented on a bed of lettuce with garnishes and carrots carved into flowers. One night the smooth chicken liver pate flecked with truffles excelled while the coarse country paté and pork paté simply tasted great.

Usually one or more appetizers are in puff pastry. The crisp, buttery, flaky shell might be filled with mushrooms and served with a black bean sauce or with spinach and feta cheese with a tangy hollandaise. Either way this appetizer has perfect pastry and flavorsome fillings and sauces.

With only five or six entrees listed on the menu, a group of four often can sample virtually everything. Chicken appears nighty, used in many different ways. Chicken brochette, skewered, grilled and served on a bed of rice turns out incredibly moist underneath the charred outer coating of herbs heavy on cumin. Grilled baby zucchini and puree of sweet potato might come on the side.

A fish of the day often offers the best eating on the menu. Seafood is grilled, baked and sauted with sauces that range from simple herbed butter to tomato and fresh herbs.

A seafood salad served on a bed of lettuce with leaves of belgium endive looked great one night and the squid, bay scallops and tuna lightly dressed in a vinaigrette couldn't have tasted better.

Despite the moderate prices, all of the portions are incredibly large. Appetizers work well as entrees. Cheesecakes and tarts round out the menu for dessert, but don't live up to the rest of the fare. Better to save the calories for an after-dinner drink at the wonderful marble oak trimmed bar next door—very pretty with imported Italian wallpaper and barware from Scandinavia. The list of after-dinner drinks lives up to the quality of the wine list with unusual offerings like port from California.

An outdoor garden with wood-burning grill is scheduled to open for the summer of 1986, which should make this an even better place for a glass of wine or two and interesting eating. Only five tables and maybe 15 seats at the bar.

★ CHARLEY'S CRAB
Seafood

1160 N. Dearborn   337-6617
Hours: Mon–Thurs 5–10 pm, Fri & Sat 5–11 pm, Sun 4–9 pm
Price range: Moderately expensive

Credit cards: A C D M V
Reservations: Accepted
Handicap

Charley's Crab, part of Chuck Muer's ever-growing chain of seafood restaurants, has made great strides toward becoming a Chicago institution since an inauspicious start here in 1983. To recap, the restaurant brought in a 105-year-old, 28-pound lobster by the name of Sandy Claws as the prize in a charity raffle. The contest won national attention as debate raged over whether the lobster should become someone's dinner or be saved. The original lobster died before the issue was decided. But the death went unreported, and a stand-in was substituted without notice.

The story of the switch got out and Charley's Crab received some negative publicity. Eventually, someone won the second lobster, Sandy Claws II, and donated it to the Shedd Aquarium.

Charley's Crab weathered the crustacean controversy to become a much improved restaurant. The fish is exquisitely fresh, the portions large, the service attentive and the atmosphere pleasant enough. On the downside, while it's not the most expensive seafood restaurant in town, the place is hardly cheap. At these prices, diners should not have to suffer through such experiments as coconut fried shrimp: shrimp coated with beer batter, then rolled in coconut and deep fried, accompanied by an orange marmalade/horseradish dipping sauce.

Among your best bets on the restaurant's à la carte menu: Charley's bucket, whole lobster, crab, clams, mussels, corn on the cob and red potatoes; Cajun fish, one of the best renditions in town of the blackened redfish New Orleans chef Paul Prudhomme made famous; and any of the pasta dishes.

The high point of the meal may well be the desserts: peanut flan, a peanut version of pecan pie, strawberry cheese-cake, chocolate torte.

While attempts have been made to soften the painted brick walls with dark wood, fabric and prints of fish, the two side-by-side dining rooms still seem a little cold. But the friendly servers tend to make up for the warmth the decor lacks.

Owner Chuck Muer has considerable experience in opening restaurants. He runs 40 some fish restaurants in Detroit, Pittsburgh, Florida, Ohio and Washington, D.C.

This downtown location seems to be doing a land-office business. Perhaps that's because the restaurant looks like something from the suburbs, which may make it attractive for suburbanites who come in to the city for an evening out and don't know where to go.

★ CHEF EDUARDO'S
Italian

1640 N. Wells St.   266-2021
Hours: Mon–Thurs 5–10 pm, Fri & Sat 6–11 pm, closed Sun
Price range: Moderately expensive
Credit cards: A   M   V
Reservations: Necessary
Handicap

If this place is so good, why don't more people come here? Goodness only knows. Chef Eduardo's consistently plays to upbeat reviews but rarely to a full house.

A suburban-looking entrance that gives you the impression you're walking into a shopping mall probably doesn't help matters. Inside, a small bar lies straight ahead; the dining room to the left, decorated with beige walls and decent paintings, is a pleasant enough place for a meal—at least when it's not completely empty.

Waiters are friendly, if not particularly knowledgeable

about the dishes. Expect leisurely meals with some significant pauses between courses.

For appetizers, roasted pimentos and anchovies, plump mussels in a garlic-flecked wine sauce, and scallops and pesto—bay scallops browned on the outside, moist inside, served on a bed of pasta with green olive oil—all serve well.

Several good, carefully prepared pastas—linguine with marinara (also available with shell fish), fettucine with cream sauce, and the like—are served in exceptionally large portions. Ordered as a mid-course, they may leave diners stuffed; better to go for them as entrees. A simple, fresh romaine salad lightly dressed in a vinaigrette comes before entrees. The chicken with apples, raisins and broiled anchovies turns out well. On one occasion, the advertised raisins and anchovies made no appearance, but the rich cream sauce with apple and the moist chicken came off well enough without them. Veal served with marinara sauce on top of ham and cheese resembles a pizza without a crust. The rather gray veal is tender, moist and, surprisingly, not the least bit overpowered by the ham and marinara. Sweetbreads, one of the best entree choices, some simply sauteed in a lemon butter sauce and garnished with capers. All come with sauteed zucchini and carrot slices.

Fresh fruit with a dollop of whipped cream is the best strategy for dessert after such a filling meal, but the chocolate mousse cake with layers of mousse and cake topped with rich, dark chocolate may tempt beyond restraint.

★★★ CHESTNUT STREET GRILL
Seafood

Water Tower Place, 845 N. Michigan Ave.   *280-2720*
Hours: Mon–Thurs 11:30 am–10:15 pm, Fri & Sat 11:30 am–
     11:15 pm, Sun 4:30–9:15 pm, brunch 11 am–2:30 pm
Price range: Moderately expensive

Credit cards: A   D   M   V
Reservations: Accepted
Handicap

One of my two favorite restaurants for seafood in Chicago (Shaw's is the other). The atmosphere of San Fancisco's Tadich Grill is captured here, from the tile floors and wood trim to the largest selection of fresh fish cooked over wood available in the city. Although this restaurant substitutes other hardwoods for mesquite, it has mastered the art of wood grill cookery.

The grill sits in the middle of the restaurant for all to see. Watching the cooks becomes part of the fun.

Sinfully good sourdough bread can lead to far too much munching, so beware. Although the food is light, portions are quite large.

Naturally, some of the best bets on the menu come from the wood grill. Bluefish, often difficult to find in Chicago, sometimes shows up here. It grills exceptionally well. Salmon, swordfish, tuna and trout are regular grill items. All turn out charred and marked from the grill outside and moist inside—not a mean feat over such hot coals.   Fresh shell fish, steamed mussels and clams, crisply coated but incredibly tender deep-fried squid and the copious seafood salad all make good starters. If the tarter sauce tastes a tad odd, it's because it's based on potatoes, rather than simple mayonnaise.

Although simply grilled seafood headlines the menu, other seafood preparations are available. For those with extremely large appetites, the huge, spicy pot of cioppino, a tomato-base seafood stew, is truly exceptional. Those who just can't stomach seafood will find steaks and chops, also grilled to perfection.

Even if you're stuffed at this point, try the cappuccino ice cream, a rich, smooth, flavorful concoction. Cakes and pastries are also available, and good.

Attentive, efficient service helps make eating here a pleasure, as does the good wine list that includes daily specials by the glass.

The idea may have come from San Francisco, but the Chestnut Street Grill has become a notable Chicago institution.

CHEZ PAUL
French
Rating: Fair

660 N. Rush St.   944-6680
Hours: Lunch Mon–Fri 11:30 am–3 pm, Dinner 5:30–10 pm,
*   Sat & Sun 5:30–11 pm*
Price range: Expensive
Credit cards: A C D M V
Reservations: Suggested

Chez Paul long has provided fodder for the quick-witted critic's mill. None times out of ten, reviewers lambast the place for pompous service and old-fashioned, lackluster cuisines. While it's true Chez Paul isn't the trendiest of Chicago's restaurants, it probably doesn't deserve all of the nay-saying critics give it.

The room definitely has masculine overtones. Walls are black, trimmed with dark wood. White-clothed tables are surrounded by large, heavy chairs. The pattern in the plaster on the white ceilings picks up the pattern of the leaded glass windows which look out onto the more modern buildings surrounding this Victorian house. In fact, at noontime the room is populated by so many men intent on doing business—or the business of drinking—that this might be a wonderful place for nooners. A couple here could cozy up and never be noticed.

A good duck-liver paté leads the list of appetizers. Choose the onion soup over the odd-tasting vichyssoise that reminds one of nothing more than thin wallpaper paste.

House salads—a mix of fresh greens with proper amount of vinaigrette—are included with entrees. Good quality Roquefort cheese can be added to make this already fine salad something special.

The Chez Paul menu—weighted heavily toward meat, with a sufficient number of seafood items and, on the last visit, no chicken whatsoever—offers few surprises. A brochette of beef, rather large chunks of tender beef with onions and pepper in the middle is straightforward and good. The veal with calvados sauce and apples, a more complicated dish, comes from the bubble-gum school of veal: chewy. However, the dish doesn't taste bad, despite the dearth of calvados in the cream sauce.

You can, if you wish, finish off with a heavy, sweet dessert such as the peach melba: a poached peach, supposedly, with vanilla ice cream and artificial-tasting raspberry sauce.

Come to think of it . . . maybe there are some reasons why critics harp about this place. Even so, Chez Paul was one of the first restaurants to introduce Chicago to French cuisine. So perhaps a visit there *should* be a bit like stepping back in time.

★ CHICAGO CLAIM CO.
American

Three locations:
2314 N. Clark St.   871-1770
Hours: Mon–Thurs 5–10:30 pm, Fri & Sat 5 pm–midnight,
*   Sun 3:30–9:30 pm*

2124 Northbrook Court   291-0770
Hours: Mon–Thurs 11 am–10 pm, Fri 11 am–11:30 pm, Sat
*   11 am–midnight, Sun noon–9 pm*

Price range: Moderate
Credit cards: A M V
Reservations: Not accepted
Handicap

232 Oakbrook Center   789-3077
Hours: Mon–Thurs 11 am–10 pm, Fri & Sat 11 am–midnight,
*   Sun 11 am–9 pm*
Price range: Moderate
Credit cards: A M V
Reservations: For large parties only
Handicap

One of the best places for burgers in the area, and also one of the most expensive. The Claim Co. is the foundation upon which Jimmy Errant built a restaurant chain that now includes classier, non-burger joints.

Menus vary somewhat at the three locations. The Clark Street restaurant is not open for lunch; Northbrook Court and Oakbrook Center are open for lunch, and have broader menus than the downtown restaurant.

Decor at the various locations also differs somewhat, but basically carries out the California Gold Rush theme. Even the menu comes printed on a metal pan of the type prospectors used to pan for gold.

The quality of the meat that goes into this burger may justify the prices. The Motherlode is charbroiled, as ordered, and comes with lots of options: American, blue, Swiss or Cheddar cheese; sauteed or fried onions or sauteed mushrooms; barbecue or teriyaki sauce; black bread, onion roll or sesame bun. Chips come on the side. The burger also is available for take-out.

The Claim Co. offers more than burgers, but why bother? The burger is this restaurant's claim to fame.

★ ★ ★ LA CIBOULETTE
French

1260 N. Dearborn St.   944-2506
Hours: Mon–Fri 6–10 pm, Sat 6–10:30 pm, Sun 11 am–2:30 pm
Price range: Expensive
Credit cards: A C D M V
Reservations: Accepted

At first, the influence of Jovan Trboyevic over Chef/owner T. Michael Beck was obvious and, frankly, the talented young chef could not match the excellence of his former employer's Le Perroquet. However, Beck has grown to show his own style since opening this pretty restaurant.

La Ciboulette has a small bar on an upper level with a comfortable dining room below. The art-deco design creates a contemporary, somewhat masculine feeling. Reservations are honored, but the restaurant holds diners responsible for confirming them. Servers are efficient and have warmed considerably after a somewhat officious beginning. Evian bottled water sits on every table.

Appetizers start the meal on the right foot. Given the frequent menu changes, the dishes mentioned here may no longer be avilable. Potage Portugais fills a pan with a mix of seafood, vegetables and meat. This great dish should be shared, given its size. Also good are the perfectly cooked, grilled sea scallops. The Hollandaise-base, tomato-and-tarragon-spiked sauce perfectly offsets the sweetness of the moist scallops. The bay scallops and salmon caviar come in a soggy, leathery pastry, while the truffled goose liver pate with aspic arrives too cold for the flavors to mingle. A marinated mackerel salad, presented on a bed of lettuce with a coating of seasoned tomato sauce tastes great. The Ciboulette salad is good, prepared with endive and sometimes watercress, Boston lettuce and mustard greens in a light Dijon vinaigrette.

Usually, two or three seafood entrees are offered. A poached Norwegian salmon trout arrives monochromatically gorgeous, covered with a reddish/pink sauce studded with pale green seedless grapes. Another time, a pretty, green avocado sauce accompanies the fish. The sauces are mild in contrast to the strong-flavored fish. Both times the dish worked well. A grilled, black sea bass with a simple Holandaise is also nice. Breast and thigh of capon recalls a Le Perroquet dish. Served with well-prepared vermicelli, the slightly gamy capon remains moist and stands up well to the rich sauce. Grilled pork loin, two large pieces of juicy, rich, tangy smoky meat also is supported well by an equally rich, if salty sauce. Veal Normande—three big pieces of very thinly cut veal topped with mushrooms—finds salvation in the superb beurre blanc sauce served with nicely cooked noodles. Although ultra-thin, the veal was tough and cooked to dryness. A side dish of vegetables comes with entrees.

At La Ciboulette, the meal's closing comes on as strong as the beginning. The bouquet of five sweet mousses—a spectrum from chocolate to apricot—is difficult to pass up. Best is apricot, followed by lemon and raspberry. Also good are the fruit tarts and the pot de creme. All meals come with complimentary meringue mushrooms and chocolate truffles.

The wine list, is first extremely limited, has steadily improved and now offers a broad range of selections. There are few bargains, but you can find some moderately priced bottles.

★★ LE COCHONNET
French

3433 N. Sheffield   525-3888

*Hours: Mon–Thurs 5:30 pm–10:30 pm, Fri & Sat 5:30 pm–
        11:30 pm, closed Sun*
Price range: Moderate
Credit cards: A C D M V
Reservations: Accepted
Handicap

Around town lately, flashy concepts with a great deal of theater and unique food concepts—from tapas to Cajun to glorified diner food—seem to be the winners, but French restaurants definitely are "out."

Therefore one can justifiably question owners Doug and Dave Korslund and Robert Parraga's sanity in opening Le Cochonnet. Not only is it French, but also off the beaten path. Moreover, its understated decor, while pleasant has virtually no sense of theater. Indeed, just about all this restaurant has going for it is good food offered at moderate prices—a crazy idea indeed in this era of restaurant madness.

The hand-written menu changes nightly. Chef Margaret Wangelin, who formerly cooked at Monique's Cafe and briefly at Bastille, mixes such classical French regional dishes as cassoulet with her own innovations like pork chop with rosemary, walnuts and sun-dried tomatoes. Although the dominance of butter sauces lends a certain sameness to the menu, almost all of these dishes work well. Some achieve greatness.

Five or six appetizers lead the a la carte menu, getting dinner off to good start. By all means try the ratatouille if it's offered. The standard mix of eggplant, peppers, tomato and onion is finished with a topping of swiss and mozzarella cheeses melted under the broiler—simple and effective. Aged goat cheese, battered, deep fried and served with pommery mustard also hits the mark when the crisp light coating gives way to the creamy, slightly pungent cheese. Rillettes of pork and duck need the bite of the mustard served on the side to give them life, but should please those who enjoy this rich, traditional French dish. Only the carrot and leek in a remoulade dressing fail to excite. The dish tastes fine, but is not special.

A soup like tomato basil or cream of smoked chicken, is offered each evening. The tomato basil soup one night arrived lukewarm. The frothy broth might have won more praise from the basil lovers at our table if it contained more basil.

Like the rest of the menu, salads change nightly. A mix of greens with slices of beet and other vegetables in an excellent raspberry vinaigrette one evening.

Most of the seafood dishes are accompanied by a variation on a butter sauce. For example, sauteed grouper, barely cooked through, comes with a citrus beurre blanc. New Zealand amberjack, a dense fish somewhat like swordfish is served in a cucumber-orange buerre blanc. Grilled salmon is sauced with mustard beurre blanc. All of these sauces complement without overwhelming the fish, and the variations add interest, but other ideas for seafood adornment would be welcome. Preparation errs on the side of under- rather than overcooking, if it errs at all.

One of the simplest of the dishes offered also ranks among the best. A succulent pork chop topped with fresh rosemary, chopped walnuts and bits of sun-dried tomatoes takes it inspiration from the north of Italy rather than France. Likewise the tournedos of beef with a simple good green peppercorn sauce arrives cooked precisely as ordered, tender and juicy.

Good, if not exceptional, desserts provide the finale to meals here. The popular bread pudding has whiskey sauce, but you need a lot of it because the large chunks of bread held together with egg whites make a lighter than average pudding, but aren't sweet enough.

Sweetness is no problem with the cakes, which tend to be somewhat dry, dense and delicious. Chocoholics will love

137

the chocolate truffle cake. The chestnut cake is even richer than its chocolate counterpart. Creme caramel is a fine, if uninspired custard. The Normandy tart with thick slices of apple, has somewhat crude but excellent flavor. Chocolate truffles are presented free at the end of the meal.

A four course meal should cost less than $20 per person, a real bargain given the quality of most of the food. The kitchen still has a few inconsistencies to iron out, but the overall quality is high.

Service generally matches the talent in the kitchen. Friendly, attentive waiters are knowledgeable about the food they're serving. A limited wine list offers sufficient variety to match the cuisines, again at moderate prices.

The decor is simple, perhaps a bit too simple. A stripe of aquamarine rises from the floor about three feet up the wall, then gives way to lightening stripes of peach. Save for the white clothed tabled and chairs, that's about it.

★★ CONVITO ITALIANO RESTAURANT
Italian

11 E. Chestnut St.   943-2984
Hours: Mon–Sat 11:30 am–2:30 pm, Mon–Thurs 6–10 pm,
*   Fri & Sat 6–11 pm*
Price range: Moderately expensive
Credit cards: A   M   V
Reservations: For parties of three or more

For the money, Convito Italiano offers one of the best values in trendy Italian dining. Other critics have panned the place, but for my money, good food, good value and good service equal a good restaurant. The original Convito Italiano deli/wine store opened in Wilmette in 1980. Owner Nancy Barocci ventured downtown in 1985 with a second deli/wine store with a full service restaurant on the floor above.

The dining room, carved from a former apartment, lies at

the top of the stairs. Exposed brick and pink walls with windows that open to air shafts give the restaurant a clean, contemporary, open feel. Nothing adorns the walls and only white butcher's paper covers the tables.

The restaurant is popular but there's something naive about this place that's meant to be a slick downtown restaurant. The service is well-meaning, but unpracticed though gradually improving. there's no coat room, just inefficient coat trees, a problem in winter.

There's nothing naive about the food, however. The value starts in the spacious and comfortable bar, where complimentary goodies are served to waiting patrons. Generally, three or four different salamis, cheeses, olives, peppers and fresh vegetables sit on a large platter at the corner of the bar.

Convito Italiano's menu features specialties from all over Italy, a welcome break from "northern Italian." While relatively limited, the mix of regional dishes offers plenty of diversity.

In general, appetizers are kept light so diners can sample a pasta course, which can be split, as well as an entree and desert without feeling bloated. One of the lightest appetizers is the vegetable terrine, a fluffy slice flecked with bits of carrot, zucchini and other vegetables, cloaked in a lettuce leaf and bound by egg whites. The terrine itself has little flavor, but the slightly tart garlic/basil sauce served under it adds just the right zing to make this dish sing.

A good bet is the marinated frutti di mare, a selection of calamari, shrimp and plump, tender mussels in a tangy, herbed vinaigrette that looks and tastes good. A fine, if unspectacular, Romaine lettuce salad with cherry tomatoes, cucumbers and red cabbage slightly tossed with another herbed vinaigrette can be substituted for an appetizer or taken after the entree.

Linguine noir tastes like a nutty fettucine Alfredo. The just slightly chewy pasta comes with walnuts and toasted pignoli nuts in a full-bodied cream sauce rich with walnut flavor—fabulous. Some of the pasta dishes go wrong. The spinach manicotti with its bland cheese and chicken filling turned out overcooked, as did most other pastas.

On the other hand, not a single sauce for the pastas disappointed. All are full of flavor and have distinctive character, something impossible in restaurants that dip every red sauce from the same stock pot. From the simple sauce of sun-dried tomatoes to the more complex spinach gorgonzola cream sauce, all do what they're supposed to: add interest to the pasta.

Good entrees include a fish special, an excellent striped bass, scaloppine alla paesana, a superb veal dish and fresh, delicately textured liver. But the sirloin steak was tasteless, fatty and tough. Pass it up for the beef stew—chunks of lean, tender and flavorsome meat complemented by perfectly cooked vegetables.

A selection of Italian cheeses can be ordered as dessert. five cheeses—from a surprisingly mild, creamy gorgonzola to a tangy goat cheese to a brie-like semi-soft cheese—are presented with good Italian bread. For chocolate lovers, il diplomatica, a sponge cake surrounding a rich chocolate mousse in a bittersweet chocolate sauce, is nothing short of heavenly. The chocloate pudding with sabyon sauce has a strange grainy texture and lacks the intensity of great chocolate. Simple but good, the two-layer cheesecake with its rich, chewy, caramelized crust will please any sweet tooth. Italian wines dominate the list here that offers as much value as the food. Most bottles run between $10 and $20.

★ CORONA
Italian

501 N. Rush St.   527-5456
Hours: Mon–Fri 11 am–11 pm, Sat 4–11 pm, closed Sun

Price range: Moderate
Credit cards: A C D M V
Reservations: Accepted

Situated between the Chicago Tribune and the Chicago Sun-Times, and surrounded by several large advertising agencies, the Corona attracts its fair share of media types with good, honest Italian fare and fairly reasonable prices— very reasonable prices if you go in the side room, rather than the dining room, where the food is the same, the decor early diner and the prices much lower.

Fresh clams and oysters, baked clams and deep-fried shrimp lead the list of openers; all are available on a combination platter with prociutto and provolone, a portion large enough for two or more.

The main dining room looks as if it's been around for a while. It has. Full-length curtains screen diners from the street outside in this long, open room. Chandeliers hang from the high ceilings over white-clothed tables.

Pasta offerings are limited but well-cooked; the cream sauces are especially good. Entrees tend to be the typical suspects for this sort of restaurant: chicken Vesuvio, veal marsala, bracciole, steaks and the like. The veal is of high quality and is carefully prepared. Chicken dishes tend to be over-cooked, an odd occurence given the care that goes into cooking the pastas. While they're not the best in the city, steaks at Corona also aren't the highest priced, and they're properly cooked to order.

Surprisingly good desserts provide the finale. Go for the zabaglione or one of the exceptionally good cakes.

Service is more than adequate, although at peak hours servers get rushed and sometimes aren't as attentive as one might wish. Wine selections are limited and moderately priced.

★ ★ COSTA AZUL
Mexican

821 N. Ashland Ave.   *243-9244*
Hours: Mon–Thurs 8 am–midnight, Fri & Sat 8-4 am,
      Sun 8-2 am
Price range: Moderate
Credit cards: M   V
Reservations: Necessary on weekends
Handicap

Fancy, this restaurant definitely is not. One of many Mexican restaurants strung along Ashland Avenue south of Division Street, Costa Azul stands out for its fresh-tasting seafood.

Dark wooden tables surrounded by heavy wooden chairs line both walls of this long, rather narrow restaurant. About two thirds of the way back, a few steps lead up to a small bar and additional seating for diners. On the right wall, where a three-dimensional mural portrays the denizens of the deep, sharks, teeth bared, leer out into the dining room. On the other wall, plants weave through trellised arches that lead nowhere. In the front window, two simply clad ceramic maidens heft torches toward the sky.

This odd mix of decorations has its charm. But diners don't come here for the designer decor, they come for some of the finest mexican seafood around.

Appetizers include fresh oysters, seviche made from crab or fish, abalone and pico de gallo jarocho, a mix of squid, abalone and octopus topped with finely chopped tomato, onion and cilantro with wedges of avocado and half-a lime—heaven on earth (or sea).

A similar mix tops a large, whole, deep fried red snapper, crisp on the outside, moist and flaky inside.

Although camerones (shrimp) rancheros are seasoned with hot peppers, according to the menu, the sauce has little spiciness. Instead, the mix of onions, tomato and cilantro tastes closer to a semi-sweet barbecue sauce—not wholly unpleasing, but not one of the best dishes here.

Rice and salad come on the side with all entrees. Hot corn and flour tortillas, a permanent fixture on most Mexican tables that Chicago restauratuers often forget, also come with all dinners.

Those so inclined can stop by for breakfast, as do a fair number of Hispanics getting off night shifts or heading in for work.

Service is warm and friendly. A juke box offers an especially good mix of Latin music, which helps diners momentarily transport themselves from Chicago to a little coastal restaurant in Mexico—a high compliment to the owners of this restaurant that transcends the average storefront Mexican eatery.

★ THE COTTAGE
Continental

525 Torrence Ave., Calumet City   891-3900
Hours: Tues–Thurs 5-10 pm, Fri & Sat 5-11 pm, closed Sun
*   & Mon*
Price range: Moderately expensive
Credit cards: M   V
Reservations: Accepted
Handicap

The Cottage has many fans, and probably is the finest restaurant south of downtown. Energetic chef Carolyn Buster not only knows how to cook, but also cooks with creative flair. However, the restaurant is not without its problems. For one, Buster feels she can only make her customers reach so far and, thus, she edits her creativity. Two, the popularity of this restaurant can lead to service problems, with too few servers serving too many.

The interior looks like a European lodge, with dark wood and white walls. When not over-crowded it can be quite romantic. Chalkboard menus scattered through the room list the night's offerings. Entrees are priced around $20, including appetizer, soup and salad; crusty bread comes warm with butter on a citrus leaf.

Appetizers get meals off to a good start. A goose liver mousse, silky smooth with a hint of curry—is served on fresh toast triangles. Caponata, a glorified chutney made with eggplant, tomato and onions, comes with a scoop of goat cheese blended with cream cheese and herbs. The shrimp remoulade is composed of small shrimp served on a bed of lettuce with a tasty remoulade sauce and a boiled egg in the middle.

Soups are winners, especially the cream of sorrel soup when it's offered—perfectly textured with small chunks of potato and carrot, a tangy hint of lemon and served with sour cream. The cream of potato with dill is not dilly, too salty and borders on being gloppy. The salad is simple, with a well-blended vinaigrette. There is a modest wait between salad and entree but just as well, for the latter is generously portioned.

Smoked offerings such as smoked chicken are excellent. The chicken is a rich, smoky, plump and tender bird served with a rather sweet wine sauce. Steak Madagascar consists of two small beef filets covered with a richly adventurous green peppercorn cream sauce. The sauce works well but the meat is almost mushy. The fresh, baked halibut is excellently prepared, topped with julienne of green peppers, onions and almonds. Veal saltimbocca, two pieces of white, tender, quarter-inch meat sandwiching prosciutto ham and sauteed in marsala wine, is high quality but plain. A pleasing pasta complements the veal.

Desserts are inconsistent. A large piece of cheesecake can be deceptive. The three-surprise chocolate cake is a chocoholic's dream: moist chocolate cake with a chocolate mousse in the middle and a rich, chocolate sauce on the side, all topped with freshly whipped cream. Fresh peach ice cream had an off taste. Desserts cost an additional $3.25.

★ ★ THE COURTYARDS OF PLAKA
Greek

340 S. Halsted St.   263-0767
Hours: Sun–Thurs 11 am–midnight, Fri & Sat 11–1 am
Price range: Moderate
Credit cards: A   C   D   M   V
Reservations: Accepted
Handicap

Most Greek restaurants aren't known for their classy decor. However, with its salmon-colored walls, red tile floors, aquamarine bar, white-clothed tables and live music, this one offers the most sophisticated atmosphere of any Greek restaurant in town. Yet, prices at Plaka are on a par with the restaurant's more modest Halsted St. neighbors, and its food is as good if not better than theirs.
Friendly, if somewhat unpolished, servers work hard to make sure everyone has good time.

Appetizers include the ubiquitous saganaki, a rather large slice of Greek cheese flamed with brandy; *melizzanoszlata*, a puree of lightly spiced eggplant to be spread on the Greek bread presented in a basket to every table; *taramosalata*, fish ore dip; and, although it's not on the menu, mild *skordalia*, garlic flavored mashed potatoes.

Mezedes, dishes which can serve as appetizers, entrees, mid-courses or late supper, include cold octopus simmered in wine and herbs, gyros and fried meatballs. Some unusual dishes for local Greek restaurants appear among the *mezedes*, as well as elsewhere on the menu. Fried sweet-breads arrive crisply battered outside, tender and just slightly gamey inside. An assortment of four *mezedes* can be assembled for two or more for $6.75 per person.

Salads served á la carte don't live up to the creativity and excellence of the rest of the menu.

Entrees range from Greek standards such as moussaka, dolmades and pastitsio, to more unusual dishes. Beef, lamb and chicken dishes are augmented with four or five seafood offerings.

Moist broiled red snapper tastes fresh and comes with a slightly tangy light sauce of olive oil, lemon and herbs. Chicken shishkebob could have been cooked a tad less, but had excellent flavor. Both dishes come with an uninteresting rice pilafi. Two or more diners can sample 12 different specialties for $13.95 per person.

Skip the exceedingly tough baklava with watered-down honey in favor of the *sokolatina*, a pastry dough layered with chocolate custard, or the whipped yogurt with honey and walnuts.

Given the dressed-up decor, careful preparation and reasonable prices, Plaka offers the best value of all the Greektown restaurants.

★ **CREMA DOLCE CAFE**
 Italian

2 W. Elm St.,   337-2474
Hours: Mon–Thurs noon–11 pm, Fri noon–midnight, Sat 9
       am–midnight, Sun 10 am–10 pm
Price range: Moderate
Credit cards: A D M V
Reservations: Not accepted

When it first opened, this slick, bright cafe was strong on homemade Italian ice creams, ices and pastry, but weak on the rest of its cuisine. Time cures all, however, and now most everything on the menu is at least good.

Inside the door, a pastry counter lures most customers to bypass the dining room on the left. That room is tastefully decorated with brass rails, white curtains, pink walls and gray-blue carpets.

Many still come for a cup of cappuccino or expresso and one of the rich, creamy gelati. Others, mostly singles, come for a peaceful evening reading books or magazines and lingering over a single-course meal and dessert. Unlike most Gold Coast restaurants, Crema Dolce seems particularly well-suited for this sort of activity because the prices are reasonable and servers don't hurry diners to depart.

For those interested, there is a full Italian menu, and if most offerings are basic, they are no less pleasing.

For starters—all for less than $4—there are fresh oysters, fried calamari, baked clams casino, a large portion of crusty, fried brie on a sweet tomato/basil sauce an a somewhat-anemic antipasto plate of peperoni, ham, provolone and olives.

Four salads and several thin-crust pizzas are offered as well as excellent pastas cooked al dente. Penne ala crema dolce features mostoccioli with fresh, flavorful Italian sausage, green and red peppers and onions—a fine combination prettily presented. Spaghetti as a course or included on the side with entrees comes with a sweetened marinara, meat sauce or cream sauce, all pleasing.

A few specials augment the menu offerings each evening. Just slightly over-cooked chicken marsala comes smothered in fresh mushrooms with a light marsala wine and cream sauce. The veal may not be of the very highest quality, but careful, even-handed preparation makes up for any failing of meat in the picatta, served with wine, lemon and smattering of herbs.

Even a rather big meal for two costs only about $40. One person can easily get away with a satisfying meal for about $15, even with a glass of wine, although on this score, selections are grossly limited. While more expensive than the Taylor street neighborhood from which the three owners hail, this sleek eatery is a pretty good deal for the Gold Coast.

★ CRICKET'S
American

Tremont Hotel, 100 E. Chestnut St.   280-2100
Hours: Lunch Mon–Fri noon–2:30 pm, Dinner Sun–Thurs 6–
*   10:30 pm, Fri & Sat 6–11:30 pm, brunch Sat noon–*
*   2:30 pm, Sun 11 am 2:30 pm*
Price range: Moderately expensive-expensive.
Credit cards: A   C   D   M   V
Reservations: Recommended
Handicap

Critics love to hate some restaurants while others they love to love. Cricket's falls into the latter category. People rave about the food, which always strikes me as solid, but nothing to write raves about.

Modeled after New York's "21"—complete with corporate logos, emblems, product models covering the walls and dangling from the ceiling and patrons with competitive ego—Cricket's knows that its diners care more about the social atmosphere than their food. While none of the food here is offensive, none of it is excellent, either. On balance, the menu is one more reason to focus on the show going on throughout the room. The service is good, though, under maitre d' Jean-Piere Lutz and his talented staff.

Appetizers include good, shelless escargot in an herbed garlic butter with a touch of wine. The lump crabmeat, however, like much of the other seafood here, seems to have been too long out of its natural environment; not spoiled, but strong-tasting and dry. Shrimp cocktail works fine, but at just under $10 seems a tad expensive. A duck terrine is

148

more reasonable at $6, but lacks flavor. A good bet is Gravlax with dill and cucumber sauce—tastes great and it's reasonably priced. One thing Cricket's does consistently is burn the crusty rolls in stripes across the bottom.

Salads are highly recommended. Good are the romaine and watercress, spinach with hot dressing and even the plain, mixed green salad. Asparagus is pricey but perfectly prepared.

The poached salmon with an excellent herb mayonnaise and small cucumber salad looks great under vegetables and a thin layer of aspic, but the fish is slightly dry and somewhat stale. Grilled salmon is fresh and accompanied by a mustard sauce. Lemon sole with shellfish does not fare so well with its mushy texture and iodine-tasting shrimp. In general, meat turns out better than fish. A filet mignon with a credible bearnaise is perfectly cooked. Good, too, is the liver with bacon and avocado, especially when accompanied by creamy raspberry-vinegar sauce to help cut the rich meat. In the mixed grill, the liver is a little overcooked but works well with its mix of kidney and nicely seasoned sausage.

Desserts fare pretty well. The selection of fruit tarts looks and tastes good. Again, nothing tastes awful. But considering the a la carte menu, the price tag is steep. It is nearly impossible for two to eat a four-course meal at Cricket's for under $70, not including wine—and the wine list is tempting but pricey. A high price to pay for people-watching and food of uneven quality, even though the people-watching is good.

★ ★ DA NICOLA
Italian

3114 N. Lincoln Ave.   *935-8000*

Hours: Mon-Thurs 4-11:30 pm, Fri & Sat 4 pm-12:30 am, Sun
4-11:30 pm, closed Tues
Price Range: Moderate
Credit cards: A   V
Reservations: Accepted
Handicap

I heard a kid talking to a friend outside Da Nicola. "Yeah, I walked in there the other day thinking it was still Pepe's," said the disheveled youth. "You should have seen their faces because now it's this fancy Italian restaurant."

Indeed Da Nicola used to be Pepe's, the ersatz Mexican restaurant more fast than good. The ownership of the place hasn't changed, but the food surely has. Owner Nicholas DiBrizzi still operates a Pepe's on Ashland, but decided he wanted to try his hand at a fine Italian restaurant.

Word of the sudden change started moving through all of the right circles almost immediately. Photographer Victor Skrebneski was one of the first to hear. He went and liked and told public relations whiz Margie Korshak, who went and liked and told. . . Da Nicola soon replaced Kelly Mondelli as the "right" place in town for reasonably priced Italian food.

In this case right means more than trendy. The food here is fresh and good.

Da Nicola is called a ristorante and pizzeria with good reason. The thin crust pizzas are a delight. The crisp, wafer-thin crust sports toppings less exotic than at Spiaggia, but the simple fresh chopped tomato, mozzarello pizza is no less pleasing. Small pizzas big enough to be shared by two can be ordered as an appetizer, and larger pizzas are available.

Clearly the chef is committed to seeking fresh and often innovative ingredients for his dishes. Standard black mussels might be ordered sauted in a garlicky wine broth flecked with fresh herbs. Or diners could choose far less common green mussels from Iceland. These large, plump mussels have stronger flavor than the smaller black mussels, but also taste uncommonly rich.

House salads, which come with entrees and full pasta orders, consist of romaine lettuce mixed with red onions and black olives with a few wedges of tomato on the side, covered lightly with a better-than-average Italian vinaigrette.

Pastas are near perfection. Several fresh homemade pastas, including raviolis and noodles, along with a few dried pastas are offered. Sauces tend to be simple, like chopped fresh tomatoes and herbs over fresh spinach noodles. Nevertheless the essence of good ingredients shines through to make the pasta dishes something special. Spaghetti topped with chopped tomato, green onions and pepper, cooked to a perfect al dente, is served on the side with entrees.

A fresh seafood special as well as a good selection of veal dishes is always available. Under a crisp coat of seasoned breading lies a thick veal chop stuffed with four cheeses. Moist and tender, the veal seems a tad grey for the top quality Provimi the waiter promises, but doesn't disappoint with its full flavor.

The Italian-style cheesecake—made with slightly sweetened ricotta—is topped with baked meringue; the crust consists of sponge cake laced with Grand Marnier. A delightful Italian custard has a satiny texture and sweet, light taste.

The funny thing is despite its recent transformation from Mexican to Italian, the place looks and feels as though it's been around forever. The waiters seem at home with the cuisine. Waits between courses can be lengthy, but for the most part the staff are extremely attentive and helpful.

The interior is complete with red and white checked oil cloth table cloths, lots of dark wood that forms eaves over the bar and part of the dining room, fake grape vines that crawl along these eaves, and candles, artificial roses and a bottle of chianti at every table. It's easy to forget that you're not in the heart of the Italian district until you walk outside.

Prices are moderate, including those on the list of Italian wines. Da Nicola offers good value and unexpectedly good Italian food.

★★ DANILO'S
Italian

1235 W. Grand Ave.   421-0218
Hours: Tues-Sat 11 am-11 pm, closed Sun & Mon
Price Range: Moderate
Credit cards: A M V
Reservations: Accepted
Handicap

Danilo's may not be the best north-side Italian restaurant, but it is certainly one of the better ones. Owner Danilo Lenzi moved his place to this location from South Western Avenue in 1983 saying he had so many north-side customers that he should have a north-side restaurant. The owners have shown a lot of restraint in decorating. Done in tones of gray and a color just short of burgundy, with flowered wallpaper, carpeted floors, upholstered chairs, old-fashioned industrial-style hanging lights, ceiling fans and white tablecloths, the dining room is quite pleasing. (A chair hanging upside down from the ceiling in the bar area suggests Danilo's rowdier heritage.)

The food here is consistently good. The pizza bread is an excellent way to begin. The tortellini in brodo soup, with rich broth and light, nutmeg-flavored tortellini pasta is especially good.

Chicken vesuvio at Danilo's is moist and great-tasting, with a light covering of herbs and an unusual, roux-like sauce of olive oil, herbs and garlic that begs to be soaked up with the fresh, crisply crusted Italian bread.

Pastas at Danilo's come cooked al dente. The linguini primavera is served without the popular but in authentic cream sauce but with plenty of fresh vegetables including artichoke hearts, broccoli, cauliflower and mushrooms. It's good, if unexciting. The fettucine Alfredo is classic and wonderful. The spaghetti and mostaccioli come with a thick and rich tomato sauce chock-full of meat.

Meat plays nearly as large a role as pasta on the Danilo menu. In general, the steaks are excellent, especially the pepper steak—a steak rubbed with garlic and peppercorns and sauteed in sherry, garlic, herbs, and peppers. While the meat doesn't match that of the area's best steak houses, the quality isn't bad, the preparation is expert and the taste good, particularly considering the price.

Cappuccino cheesecake is worth a visit in itself—a light, creamy topping with a chocolate-crumb crust. The cannoli also is terrific, with a light, creamy filling and crisp crust dusted with powdered sugar.

DAVIS STREET FISHMARKET
Seafood
Rating: Fair

501 Davis St., Evanston   869-3474
Hours: Mon-Thurs 11:30 am-10 pm, Fri & Sat 11:30 am-
*   11 pm*
Price range: Moderately expensive
Credit cards: A   M   V
Reservations: Accepted
Handicap

This make-over of the Famous Deli takes great pride in its fresh fish and careful preparation. However, it needs to pay more attention to things like sauces and salads before it can rise above run-of-the-mill. It still looks like a cafeteria-style restaurant despite the fish nets draped over the brass rail at the windows and the chalkboards surrounded by rope that bear the night's special. The tables are topped with brown paper. Bread is delivered in plastic baskets.

The servers try to be nice, but they come off as rather obtrusive. One answered "okay" to just about everything, seemed hyper and had a tendency to rush off and fill orders before the ordering was completed.

The calamari should probably come on a smaller plate; it's not really that the portion is small, but it looks dwarfed. The calamari itself tasted tender and fresh, as does all the seafood here, under its crisp, outer coating. There is a somewhat spicy cocktail sauce in the middle of the large plate. As it says at the bottom of the chalkboard, "We serve no fish after its prime."

Cioppino had a single mussel floating in it, a red sauce that had a good, full-bodied flavor but lacked the spiciness of some better versions of this tomato-based stew of fish and shell-fish bits. The broth could have been hotter in every way. Escargot de Jonghe, based on the classic Chicago shrimp de Jonghe, is the strangest version of this dish I've ever tasted. Snail meat is served on mushroom caps; the snails have been breaded, according to the waitress, then served with de Jonghe butter. But this butter tasted of curry powder—not altogether unpleasant, but definitely ugly to look at. Fresh green herbs in the breading help the flavor, but the chef should go curry all the way or just stick with a good shot of garlic.

Salads here are rather mundane affairs: iceberg lettuce with tomatoes and some chopped olives, cabbage and julienne of carrots. Homemade dressing includes French, vinaigrette and thousand island. The Calypso French tastes canned. The dressings are poured on top, not tossed.

Sauteed trout has been filleted and breaded. The fish was a little crusty at the edges, but it was moist and had a fine taste. It was served with steamed broccoli dusted with parmesan and with boiled potatoes, which also came with other entrees. Broiled swordfish also benefited from careful cooking. The generous filet was medium-rare, almost pink at the very center. Despite the freshness, the fish had surprisingly little flavor. A rather thin but good bearnaise sauce came on the side.

Desserts number only three. A lemon cheesecake topped with sour cream and sitting on a graham-cracker crust was surprisingly light, with just enough tartness to be refreshing. The pecan pie was sweet and rich and plenty of pecans, but was overdone so that the crust was too brown and the sugar had begun to caramelize. The wine list is limited, with good California offerings at around $15.

★ DEARBORN STREET OYSTER BAR
Seafood

409 S. Dearborn St.   922-1217
Hours: Mon-Fri 11:30 am-8:30 pm, closed Sat & Sun
Price range: Inexpensive
Credit cards: A C D M V
Reservations: Accepted
Handicap

The South Loop shows signs of rejuvenation, and a growing number of new restaurants have been attracted to the area. The Oyster Bar lives up to its billing. It captures the look of a Cape Cod fish-house with gray-blue-painted wainscoting, booths and a pleasantly casual atmosphere.

Low prices, good food and attentive service make this a good stop for informal dining. The fried clams and oysters here may be the best in the city. Other traditional favorites include fish and chips, burgers, oyster poor boys and pastas, which have a tendency to be somewhat over-cooked.

Unusual offerings also show up on the menu. Bears fans may appreciate the deep-fried alligator. Yes, it does taste like extremely rubbery chicken.

Naturally, there are good, fresh oysters. All of the seafood is fresh and carefully prepared. A few items such as shark, halibut and tuna can be ordered grilled. Most other fish is simply sauteed, served without fancy adornment. Fresh fish entrees run under $15.

The limited wine list features moderately priced whites, mostly from California, with a sprinkling of reds.

★ DEE'S RESTAURANT
Chinese

2010 N. Sheffield St.   477-1500
Hours: Mon-Thurs 4:30-11 pm, Fri & Sat to midnight, Sun 4-
*   10:30 pm*
Price range: Moderately expensive
Credit cards: A M V
Reservations: Accepted

There's always a line at Dee's during peak dining hours—perhaps because it's the only good Chinese restaurant in the neighborhood. Although it isn't Chicago's best Chinese eatery, it attracts trendy, knowledgeable diners.

Tucked into an apartment building just north of Armitage on Sheffield, Dee's is an odd mix of modern and Victorian, with a few tasteful Chinese prints, brick walls, brass rails and padded, bamboo-like swivel chairs. The main dining room is small, with only 12 tables. A second, equally small dining room is adjacent to the main room.

Service is friendly and efficient. The food is decent, not great; but then, great Mandarin restaurants are scarce in the metropolitan area. Dinner for two can easily run $40 if some of the more expensive entrees are chosen. Wine selections can add to the tab: the list is surprisingly wide for a Chinese restaurant.

Among the appetizers, steamed dumplings and pan-fried pot stickers are both good. The dumplings' slightly bland filling is offset by a soy and vinegar sauce spiked with pepper, ginger and green onion. Other appetizers are disappointing to varying degrees: the shrimp toast tastes fishy, the spring roll has more cabbage flavor than anything else, the fried dumplings are as bland as their steamed brethren.

Mongolian beef features tender bits of beef in a rich, dark brown sauce with green onions—pleasing, but nothing special. The garlic chicken with vegetables comes in plain, mild and spicy versions; the latter is too spicy for tender palates. Dee's serves up a good many moo shu dishes, and they are among the best offerings. The whole red snapper is huge, easily enough to serve two. Covered with black mushrooms, julienne of carrot, onion and green onion, the fish looks great but it's somewhat mushy. The spicy but not overwhelmingly hot Szechwan sauce is excellent.

Fried rice with everything includes shrimp, chicken, pork and peppers—it turns out rather bland and soggy, the only dish sampled that diners should avoid.

All in all, Dee's pleases despite a sameness to the dishes and the annoying background music. At the very least, it is a cut above the average neighborhood Chinese restaurant.

★ ★ ★ THE DINING ROOM AT THE RITZ-CARLTON
French

Ritz Carlton Hotel, Water Tower Place, 160 E. Pearson
266-1000
Hours: Lunch Mon-Fri noon-2:30 pm, Dinner Mon-Sat 6-11
pm, Sun 6-10 pm, brunch Sun 10:30 am-2 pm
Price range: Expensive
Credit cards: A C D M V
Reservations: Accepted for dinner only
Handicap

In keeping with the image the name "Ritz" conjures up, the Dining Room exudes comfort and class. Quality cloth drapes tables set with expensive silver and china, the well-padded circular banquettes provide privacy and servers

157

keep attentive but unobtrusive vigil. Like most major hotels that have realized their kitchens cannot live by convention trade alone, the Ritz works hard to woo local patrons. To that end, chef Fernand Gutierrez rejoined the hotel two years ago and the food has steadily improved. Maitre d' Toni Tontini sternly watches over the proceedings in the dining room.

One of the nice touches here is the complimentary appetizer that is served shortly after diners place their orders. It includes a creamy mousse of pheasant dressed in a tart blueberry sauce that works nicely, and game and seafood patés and terrines that are generally well-conceived and prepared.

A special seaweed, saffron and salmon mousse wrapped with a thin layer of turbot delights with its delicate flavor. This appetizer finds a perfect complement in the cucumber sauce with chopped tomato. A salad with some kind of game also usually appears as a special: rare breast of squab or moist duckmeat with walnuts, served over red cabbage and endive. Both provide nice contrasts between warm and cold. A large portion of moist, smoky gravlox comes surrounded with capers, parsley, chopped onions, mayonnaise and an herb sauce. The feuillete of vegetables is disappointingly bland, and the sauteed green and white asparagus and mushrooms aren't any more exciting.

Putting on the Ritz doesn't come cheap. Entree prices hover at more than $20. However, a prix-fixe menu contains several nightly specials at $35 for a complete dinner, a good bargain for a generous sampling of chef Gutierrez's cuisine. The prix-fixe meal includes soup; a particularly good one is the cream of white asparagus with fine herbs and a rich broth. Wild-hare consomme lacks distinctive wild-hare flavor.

No truly bad entree emerges from the kitchen, but some turn out just okay. At these prices, even for the prix-fixe meal, "okay" isn't good enough. Good, though, are the grilled medaillons of veal seared on the outside to seal in moisture and flavor. Served with a terrific cream sauce and perfectly cooked, thin noodles topped with two tender sweetbreads, it's a visual delight, as well. Presentation is part of the experience here. Fricassee of rabbit with snails comes with a little pastry rabbit standing guard over the plate. The moist rabbit is nicely flavored, but the snails lack taste.

Beauty also plays an important role in the braised salmon, but this time the dish is a mere pretty face. Little raspberry-shaped clumps of caviar with parsley top the fish, which swims in a rather bland cream sauce. The salmon is okay, but dull. Although more interesting in concept, the poached sea bass with enoki mushroom and sole paupiette also disappoints. Not so the cassoulet special: sweetbread and foie gras make a perfect couple in a wonderfully flavored creation.

The prix-fixe menu offers a cheese course following the entrees; recently, the offering was a mundane selection of the usual dessert cheeses. The dessert selection changes nightly and the tarts, cakes and mousses taste as good as they look. The wine list is as massive as it is expensive, although there are good wines for about $20. The wine steward is friendly, helpful and knowledgeable.

That can be said of the servers in general.

★ DIXIE BAR & GRILL
American

225 W. Chicago Ave.   642-3336
Hours: Lunch Sun-Sat 11:30 am-2:30 pm, Dinner Sun-Thurs
       5:30-10 pm, Fri & Sat 5:30-11 pm
Price range: Moderately expensive
Credit cards: A D M V

Reservations: Accepted for lunch only
Handicap

Crowds. Expect crowds beyond all reason here. Perhaps the first Chicago restaurant designed to take advantage of "restaurant madness," the Dixie packs in diners, leaving hopefuls lined up outside waiting just to get into the bar. Around town, people complain about the waits but clamor to get in all the same. Madness. Madness that costs Dixie a star.

The facility (more than the food), the elan that owner Roger Greenfield has created, the-see-and-be-seen atmosphere, the jazz—all work together for magnetic appeal. Most of all, Greenfield has created a theater for dining at a time when the city sorely needs such a gathering place.

A mix of old and new, the Dixie has bar stools upholstered with fabric hand-painted in pastel squiggles surrounding the oval bar just inside the front door; the upholstery also covers the banquettes in the dining room. Rustic twig furniture next to a small stage behind the bar forms a snug cocktail lounge perfect for listening to the jazz musicians who hold forth every evening. ($5 minimum when musicians are playing.) The terrific music greatly enhances the dining experience and makes for a relaxed atmosphere.

Located in a former warehouse, the dining room behind the bar and cocktail lounge is a two-storied affair, with skylight and open beams spanning an arched roof. Ceiling, beams, walls and all have been painted white, again lending a contemporary touch to the obviously vintage space. A large rectangular opening at the rear of the room leaves the kitchen open to full view of the diners—a sort of second stage where the chefs cook up a bit of jazz themselves.

As one might expect from a place called Dixie Bar & Grill, Dixie beer from New Orleans is served. The brew tastes a good deal like Beck's and at $1.50 a bottle won't set diners back an arm and a leg. Indeed, one of the attractions of this place is price. Entrees average about $12. Although not exactly cheap eats, a filling dinner for two including a couple of beers apiece costs less than $25 each—with entertainment.

Yes, blackened fish of the day leads the menu. Swordfish got the nod recently and came out juicy, with enough spice to add interest while not searing tastebuds to ashes or overwhelming the fish. And there's beignets made from shrimp and redfish—crisp on the outside, reasonably light inside, with excellent flavor. Jambalaya also makes its appearance, but here it's served with pasta rather than rice and turns out marvelously. One of the more interesting appetizers is fried chicken salad—moist, boned pieces of breast with a crisp coating of breading. Also interesting is Mardi Gras three-colored pasta with earthy, smoky flavor. Other appetizers include a good Carolina crab and corn chowder, fresh oysters, shrimp remoulade, spicy cajun popcorn (although some of the pieces of fish were too large to qualify as popcorn) and tempting morsels of blackened scallops on a bed of lettuce.

Many dishes are breaded and deep-fried southern-style. Panned rabbit comes heavily breaded, but the crisp coating doesn't get in the way of the slightly gamey flavor. A large filet of fresh catfish coated with corn meal comes with a light lemon-mustard sauce. Hush puppies served on the side are dense and heavy, but flavorful.

In general, side dishes add to the meals here. Crisp sweet potato French fries get a dusting of spices that adds interest. Collard greens cooked with vinegar and smoked pork are worth the trip to this restaurant in themselves. A whole meal could easily be made of the red beans and rice cooked with sausage. Grit cakes may please those who love grits, but let's face it: grits is grits. A basket of muffins, corn bread and quick breads comes to the table early on. The baker experiments with different flavors daily.

Desserts further lure you to over indulge. Bread pudding has an exceptionally smooth texture that may disappoint those used to courser, homemade versions. The sweet-potato pie tastes like pumpkin with an interesting difference.

The wine list does not feature any of the wines coming out of such Southern states as Texas, the Carolinas and Florida which, come to think of it, may be just as well. Heavy on California wines with a sprinkling of French vintages, the list is limited, but provides plenty of variety at generally moderate prices.

Much of the service staff, like the cooks in the kitchen, have been imported from New Orleans. They exude a sense of southern hospitality and are knowledgeable, smooth and efficient. Indeed, in the evening the service can be too fast, giving diners a sense of being rushed. Unfortunately, the heavy crowds have had an adverse effect on service.

★ DON'S FISHMARKET AND TAVERN
Seafood

9335 Skokie Blvd., Skokie   677-3424
Hours: Lunch Mon-Fri 11:30 am-2:30 pm, Dinner Mon-Thurs
        5-11 pm, Fri & Sat 5 pm-midnight, Sun 4-10 pm
Price range: Moderately expensive
Credit cards: A C D M V
Reservations: Accepted
Handicap
Other: Smoking and no-smoking sections

A large rambling tavern to the right of the entrance offers simple fare and longer hours than those listed above. However, the more comfortable restaurant to the left is a better bet for dinner.

Don's Fishmarket tries to recreate the feel of a New England seafood house with wainscoting and blue colonial wallpaper. The main dining room has a fireplace ablaze in winter. Seafaring prints and shelves with books and other decorations finish the decor. Wooden tables have no cloths; cotton terry hand towels replace napkins.

Two things favor this restaurant: the fish is unquestionably fresh and the preparation is careful. However, none of the dishes rises above average in flavor.

A large number of fresh-fish specials come baked, broiled sauteed and charcoal-grilled. For starters, there are fresh clams and oysters, steamed mussels or a combination of steamed mussels and clams. Oddly, cherrystone clams are used for steaming instead of the thin, soft-shell variety—unusual but good, in a rich clam broth with drawn butter on the side.

Salad and a fish chowder that would greatly benefit from more fish in the tomato-vegetable broth come with entrees. The salad is a mix of small shrimp and lettuce topped with blue cheese and egg, dressed too heavily with a too-sweet dressing.

Blackened grouper doesn't really get blackened in a skillet here; it has more of a pepper coating than the complex mix of herbs and spices that makes New Orleans blackened red fish a national treasure. Although the fish is moist and tender, the technique and spicing need a lot of work.

Don's Platter, a mix of seabass, salmon and lake whitefish is simply boring. A little paprika gives some color to the fish and lemon adds some zest, but this stuff is plain. Both entrees come with a choice of rice pilaf or red potato and vegetable, which on one visit was overcooked Brussel sprouts.

So while the ingredients that go into dishes here are high in quality and cooking is careful, excitement is low, low, low. At the same time, the friendly service can be slow, slow, slow, even with the restaurant only half-full.

California wines dominate the list, with a monthly special

163

available by the glass in addition to house wines. Desserts are mostly cheesecake and ice cream, with occasional specials.

★★ DON ROTH'S RIVER PLAZA
American

405 N. Wabash Ave.   *527-3100*
Hours: Lunch Mon-Sat 11:30 am-3 pm, Dinner Mon-Thurs
        5-10:30 pm, Fri 5-11 pm, Sat 5-midnight, Sun 5-9:30
        pm
Price range: Moderately expensive
Credit cards: A C D M V
Reservations: Recommended
Handicap

Those who remember Don Roth's as a beef-and-potato restaurant with Boston scrod thrown in for good measure will be surprised at the diversity of the menu. The prime rib and scrod are still here, but they're now augmented by offerings that range from grilled duck to Cajun and Creole specialities.

Serious dining takes place on the second level which offers a good view of the Chicago river and the south skyline. Downstairs is a popular bar and a dining area that features lighter fare. In warm weather, an outdoor patio beside the bar creates a cafe environment.

Blackened dishes highlight the new Cajun/Creole items. The blackened redfish ranks among the best in the area, crisp and spicy on the outside but not so hot that the flavor of the tender fish is obliterated. The same preparation works well for River Plaza's sirloin strip, a good-quality piece of meat cooked precisely to order.

Neither the etouffe nor the pasta jambalaya turns out quite as well as the other Cajun specialities. But the Cajun popcorn appetizer definitely makes addictive eating, as does the rich, thick gumbo.

Unlike many restaurants where the salad can be picked at so as to save room for more interesting courses, Don Roth's salads should be taken seriously. The house salad is almost a Cobb salad, with a myriad of small, chopped vegetables in addition to the lettuce. Of course, there's also the famous spinning salad bowl salad (which unfortunately no longer gets prepared at the table), a mix of greens with creamy dressing.

For dessert, try the hot fudge sundae or bread pudding with whiskey-laced sauce over gloppy sweet-potato pie. The limited wine list offers some good values. Service is young, but well-disciplined and generally attentive.

★ DRAGON PALACE
Chinese

3357 W. Peterson Ave.   588-2726
Hours: Tues-Thurs 11:30 am-10 pm, Fri & Sat 11:30 am-
        midnight, Sun noon-10 pm
Price range: Inexpensive
Credit cards: M   V
Reservations: Accepted
Handicap

This place looks more like a cross between an American diner and a typical storefront Chinese restaurant than it does a Palace. Background music from Chicago's "all love song" radio station doesn't help that image much.

Prefab gold plastic banquettes line three walls of the dining room. Large tables, usually occupied by Chinese families, fill the middle of the room. However, there are white cloths on the tables, silk flowers everywhere, a few golden Chinese lanterns and Chinese art on the walls. Overall the effect is pleasant and comfortable.

The Chinese and some locals in the know come for the food, not the decor. In a city with literally hundreds of Chinese restaurants big and small, this unpretentious little eatery stands out as one of the best.

Getting at some of the better dishes may try the patience of a saint. Many servers have a rudimentary grasp of English at best. Well meaning, they try hard to please, but orders often get bolixed and sometimes forgotten. Forge ahead. The effort is worth it.

Start with pot stickers that, unlike so many in Chicago's Chinese restaurants, actually have a fresh meat filling that tastes like something other than ground cardboard. Splash on some of the soy sauce provided on the side at your own risk. It's loaded with garlic.

Fried scallops, coated in a light, airy batter, deep fried and presented on a bed of lettuce also make a strong beginning. Hot and sour soup is neither too hot nor too sour, but has wonderfully full body nevertheless.

Strangely after the powerful soy with the pot stickers, garlic chicken might use more garlic. Still, the moist, tender chicken with mushrooms, green onions and vegetables tastes great without it.

Hunan spicy shrimp has the look of awful canned sweet and sour sauce. Luckily the sauce over the fresh, medium-sized shrimp, red and green peppers and green onions is spicy rather than sweet.

Many Chinese desserts are better left untried. By all means try the flaming bananas here. Battered and deep fried, they are sprinkled with sugar laced with grenadine and doused with rum at tableside. The waiter turns the bananas on their flaming platter to glaze the outside completely and give the hot interior the texture of a good pudding.

★ ★ ED DEBEVIC'S SHORT ORDERS/DELUXE
American

640 N. Wells St.   664-1707
Hours: Mon–Thurs 11 am–midnight, Fri & Sat 11–1 am, Sun
*   11 am–10 pm*
Price range: Inexpensive
Credit cards: Not accepted
Reservations: Not accepted
Handicap

Perhaps the ultimate greasy-spoon diner of the '80s, Ed Debevic's Short Orders/Deluxe is authentic right down to its gum-chewing, white polyester-uniformed waitresses wearing $3^1/_2$-inch "Eat At Ed's" buttons. Designer Spiros Zakas has recreated the '50s at Ed's complete with custom-designed light fixtures and '50s-style venetian blinds, black-and-white tile floors, stainless steel furniture and, of course, genuine Formica-topped tables. Zakas is said to have wanted to create a diner for years; he has done it on the grandest of scales.

There are a few anomalies, including a full-service bar ("No Premium Beer Here" except Ed Debevic's private label at $1.50 and tap beer for 95 cents) and enough room to sit 200. And Ed's packs them in, from punkers to dowagers to yuppies. A 30-minute wait is normal. It's the sort of place where you go for the waitresses' wise-cracks, '50s music and such vintage signs as: "Buy American, Eat at Ed's," "If you can find a better diner, eat there" and "Famous since 1984." The unmistakable sense of humor of part-owner Richard Melman shines through. He knows Ed's time has come, exemplified by the huge American flag hanging in the main dining room with the slogan, "Love It or Leave It," emblazoned underneath. Sensing the public's yearning for nostalgia or, simply, pig-out food, Melman created Ed's.

Ed's is an important restaurant without important food. It

attracts customers because of the mood it exudes. This very "New York" approach to dining is midwesternized by its no-reservations policy ("If you think you have reservations, you're in the wrong place") and fast food-competitive prices. Melman has worked like a dog to pull all this off. Ed Debevic's, part of a joint venture involving Melman, Phoenix restaurateur Lee Cohn and the West Coast-based Collins Foods, is Melman's first opportunity to go national with the concepts that have worked so well in Chicago.

The food? Thick, juicy burgers and great hand-cut fries, good chili and fabulous chili dogs, too-salty mushroom soup, peppery meat loaf with real mashed potatoes, tuna salad and chicken salad with Jell-O, super malts and crusted-over chocolate pudding like Mom used to make. . . . You get the picture.

★ EDGEWATER BEACH CAFE
Continental

5545 N. Sheridan Rd.   275-4141
Hours: Tues–Sun 5–10 pm, closed Mon
Price range: Moderate
Credit cards: A   M   V
Reservations: Accepted
Handicap
Other: Free parking

The consistency of substance and form from a different era makes the Edgewater Beach Cafe unique on the contemporary dining scene. The moment one pulls into the parking garage (marked by a small sign at the Edgewater apartment building's south end) one is sealed in a sort of time capsule: the friendly parking attendant, the walk upstairs through the old-fashioned lobby, by the beauty shop, dress shop, travel agency and barber shop that lead down the long, dim hallway to the restaurant.

Inside, a small bar area without seating boasts burnt-orange carpet and matching walls. Comfortably large tables sport beige table linens and white cloth napkins. The unusually high chairs are definitely pre-1950s in style—the waiter described them as "antiques." The menu, while updated with morel mushrooms and sauces, matches the period decor. The young waiters provide professional, almost stately service in a pleasantly old-fashioned way.

Bread and butter start the meal. The crusty rolls are white and bland and the substitute croissants aren't much better. Appetizers include escargots bourguignonne, shrimp cocktail, shrimp de Jonghe, coquilles St. Jacques and Welsh rarebit. The shrimp de Jonghe, coquilles St. Jacques and Welsh rarebit. The shrimp cocktail provides four large, properly cooked shrimp in a mild sauce, the coquilles St. Jacques features tender, juicy sea scallops well served by a creamy wine-and-mushroom sauce and the shrimp de Jonghe has a full-flavored sauce. The five large escargots, although highly recommended, arrive too hot, are somewhat mushy and have a mild, uninteresting sauce. Consult the waiter in advance on the availability of menu items. Neither Welsh rarebit nor the mixed grill, although listed, seem to exist.

The large portions of entrees may obviate the need for appetizers altogether, especially since salad or soup is included as is a side of vegetables and choice of potatoes or wild rice. The cream of celery soup is sublime and the cream of spinach quite good. The salad, otherwise fine, is overwhelmed by iceberg lettuce. The side dishes don't fare much better— overcooked wild rice, ratatouille sans tomato, stringy "creamed" spinach and bland cabbage. In general, the tastes are there but the preparation needs more care.

Red meat plays a main role at the Edgewater. Two small tenderloins of high-quality, perfectly cooked beef make the tournedos forestiere well worth ordering. Its '50s-style, heavy, button mushroom-covered sauce works very well.

Chicken maison makes a concession to modernity with three morel mushrooms in a heavy sauce that saves the slightly dry chicken. Again, a flavorful sauce helps the veal scallopini but cannot save the three pieces of tough, gray, breaded veal. Boned duck in calvados sauce, a special, wins the most-contemporary-dish award. Apple wedges alternate with large pieces of crisp-skinned roasted duck that are sauced underneath with a mild applejack sauce and sprinkled with cashews—a moist and richly flavored dish.

The best dessert is the light and smooth creme caramel. A chocolate cake with fudge sauce, the chef's specialty, is a huge wedge smothered in hot sauce and flanked by a scoop of ice cream and whipped cream. An apple tart has a tough, flavorless crust, good pastry cream and perfectly cooked apples. But a maraschino cherry topping? Chef Rudy Leon takes care to prepare good food; despite a few faults, the Edgewater Beach Cafe serves food befitting the "good old days."

★★ ELI'S THE PLACE FOR STEAK
Steak

215 E. Chicago Ave.   642-1393
Hours: Lunch daily 11 am-2:30 pm, Dinner daily 4-11 pm
Price range: Moderately expensive
Credit cards: A   C   D
Reservations: Recommended

Smaller than Morton's, Chicago's other great steakhouse, Eli's is very nearly as good and its menu is more varied, despite the slogan appended to the name. The dinner menu includes four seafood offerings, lamb chops, calves' liver, chicken, veal and barbecued ribs, in addition to Eli's excellent steak.

It's a family affair, with Eli Shulman and his wife present

in the restaurant almost every night. The service is excellent, if a tad pushy.

Diners enter through a hallway into a small but usually bustling piano bar. Walls of the restaurant are plastered with caricatures of Chicago notables. It isn't unusual to see some of those same faces among the customers in the dining room.

A fresh relish plate and basket of breads are served immediately. For appetizers, the French onion soup is quite good, as is the chopped chicken liver with onions. The shrimp de Jonghe has a good topping. Rib lovers can check out an appetizer-sized portion of their favorite—well-cooked with a better-than-average sauce—before trying the entree.

The beef here has been as carefully selected as it is prepared. The New York strip is the definitive good steak, and Eli's perfectly grilled special sirloin topped with cracked peppercorns is a treat. So is the large cut of tender, full-flavored roast prime rib. The filet of whitefish is fresh and expertly cooked but an overpowering topping of onions, pepper and lemon butter masks the excellent fish. Portions are large.

Eli's cheesecake is wonderful: light, slightly tangy, with a good crust and excellent toppings. It is also sold at a growing number of outlets around the country.

★ FATHER & SON PIZZA
Italian

2475 N. Milwaukee Ave.   252-2620
Hours: Sun–Thurs 11–1:15 am, Fri & Sat 11–2:30 am
Price range: Inexpensive
Credit cards: Not accepted
Reservations: Not accepted

It's not difficult to spot this restaurant amidst the second-hand clothing shops and down-at-the-heel stores along Milwaukee Avenue. A big, brightly lit sign of a father and son looms over the traffic and stands out like a sore thumb.

The decor of this bright, cheery restaurant would make a plastic salesman ecstatic. But the restaurant is comfortable, and decor isn't what entices people to go out of their way to come here.

Like most local pizzerias, this one offers thick-crusted Chicago-style pizza. But again, this isn't the calling card. What makes this place special is that it's one of the few in town that offers excellent, thin-crust pizza at prices that don't make one's jaw drop.

The crusts are cracker-thin and exceptionally crisp, even when they're loaded up with the works. Toppings run the gamut, from traditional sausage, mushrooms, peppers, anchovies and the like to some fairly far-out things for pizza, such as pineapple and taco trimmings.

Vegetarians can satisfy their cravings with plain pizzas, cheese pizzas and various veggie numbers, including eggplant. The latter comes on a New York-style pizza that falls halfway between the thick- and the-thin crust varieties. However, New Yorkers will note that the crust is considerably thicker than the run-of-the mill pie in their city.

Other menu items are available—salads, entrees and desserts—but the pizza's the thing. Service is fast and attentive.

★★ FLORENTINE ROOM
Northern Italian

71 W. Monroe St.   332-7005
Hours: Lunch Mon–Fri 11:30 am–2:30 pm, Dinner Mon–Fri
       5–10 pm, Sat 5–midnight
Price range: Expensive
Credit cards: A C D
Reservations: Accepted

The most expensive of the three-restaurant Italian Village complex, The Florentine Room also offers some of the best eating.

Florentine family crests decorate this long, rectangular room upstairs from the entrance. Don't let the worn decor put you off. The room has looked like this for years, and those in the know continue to enjoy the fine food.

Friendly waiters like to joke with customers, which can grate if one isn't in the mood. Simply rebuff the jokes and put them to work at their always-efficient serving.

The creativity of the kitchen is often startling. This place dosen't *look* as if innovative dishes should be expected.

Recommending dishes is difficult since the menu constantly changes with the seasons. A walnut-oil pesto might dress a game dish, an assortment of unusual cheeses might stuff a pasta shell, grilled meat may have a simple sauce of lemon, olive oil and pine nuts.

On the whole, however, sauces here make the dishes, and probably are the most adventurous of any to be found in Chicago's Northern Italian restaurants. Many homemade pastas are worth sampling and can be shared as an appetizer or mid-course, or ordered as the main course.

Portions are large, generally rich, and filling. Desserts also change frequently and are no less creative. The excellent list of Italian wines is tempting; bottles can add considerably to the cost of the meal, although there are plenty of reasonably priced selections.

★★ FOLEY'S FIRST STREET
Eclectic

1732 N. Halsted St.   943-6433
Hours: Lunch Mon–Thurs 11:30 am–2:30 pm, Dinner Mon–
*   Thurs 5:30–11 pm, Fri & Sat 5:30 pm–midnight,*
*   closed Sun*
Price range: Moderate

Credit cards: A D M V
Reservations: For large groups only

"Eclectic" doesn't do justice to the varied menu here which includes French, German, Cajun, Chinese, Italian, American and other ethnic dishes. Combined, this diversity may well make for the ultimate grazing menu.

Named for the original name of Halsted, First Street occupies the space formerly held by Bentley's wine bar. Wine still plays an important role here, with several red, white and sparking wines offered at generally reasonable prices. The bar, which stretches toward the rear of the restaurant, gets loud and crowded, especially on weekends.

The dining rooms behind the bar tend to be a bit quieter, but they're still lively when filled with diners, which is most of the time. The service here, dismally slow and inept at first, has steadily improved, although the wait between courses can still try one's patience. Through it all, the servers never seem to lose their sense of humor or friendliness.

Bright and open, this restaurant seems designed for meeting and greeting friends, right down to the low-priced menu. The best way to appreciate First Street is to go with a group and share the various treats from the kitchen.

For a first course, the group might choose the wholewheat, thin-crust pizza topped with pesto, tomato and cheese; egg rolls; the fiery venison chilli topped with melted cheddar; gazpacho or pasta, to name a few of the offerings. Carefully prepared, the dishes tend toward intense, rather than subtle, flavors.

Most entrees cost about $10 or under. Try the blackened fish of the day or one of the simple but expertly grilled fish offerings. Grilled beef tenderloin or chicken also turn out perfectly. Excellent cream sauces support many of the pastas, which occasionally suffer a tad from overcooking.

A good if uninteresting dinner salad comes with entrees, as does a choice of lightly cooked, mixed vegetables or crisp

French fries. Not surprisingly, desserts are as varied as the rest of the menu, from fresh, light, fresh fruit fritters to incredibly rich banana ice cream.

Portions that are hefty but not so large as to be obscene, seasonings that are intense but not heavy-handed, and careful cooking build value into First Street—incredible value, at that.

★★ FOLEY'S GRAND OHIO
American

211 E. Ohio St.   645-2161
Hours: Lunch Mon–Fri 11:30 am–2:30 pm, Dinner Mon–
            Thurs 5:30–10 pm, Fri & Sat 5:30–11 pm, closed Sun
Price range: Moderately expensive
Credit cards: A C D M V
Reservations: Accepted
Handicap

When Michael Foley and his father first opened this restaurant it didn't win the hearts or palates of many local critics. Part of the problem was one of expectations. The critics and the public had grown to expect innovations from Mike Foley based on the cuisine served at his Printer's Row and First Street restaurants. Indeed as a result of is efforts he was named to the "Who's Who of American Cooking" in 1984.

As the reviews began to come out, each one with a litany of complaints about the menu and the fare, Foley and his dad went to work. The menu has been revised and jazzed up a bit to offset what some thought was a too conventional approach.

By and large the revisions have worked to make Grand Ohio a restaurant worth visiting. Prices are moderate, with entrees ranging from a low of $7.50 for pasta to a high of only $12.50 for a tempting filet of broiled salmon with creme fraiche, mustard and dill and an onion-fennel marmalade.

Some of the original dishes are still on the menu - one is the fabulous grilled duck foie gras. The smoothly textured, rich duck liver is trimmed with leaves of endive filled with a tart Michigan cherry vinaigrette. Also a solid bet is the array of pates, terrines and sausages, the latter often grilled, that changes nightly.

The four soups listed on the menu are usually augmented by special offerings and make some of the best choices. The country vegetable broth with its aromatic complement of fresh herbs gives new meaning to this venerable American classic, especially with the large crouton topped with a thick slice of melted local swiss cheese. Other soups include mussel and clam chowders and an earthy black bean soup.

Five pastas listed on the menu, plus nightly specials, offer plenty of variety to pasta lovers. Spinach ravioli with gorgonzola, pancetta and hazelnuts makes an excellent, if somewhat rich, choice.

Fresh seafood plays an important role on the menu. Carefully prepared, the grilled tuna stays moist under its complement of capers, chopped tomato and lemon-laced olive oil. It is simple and good.

Grilled items are consistently good here, whether meat, fish or poultry. The juicy grilled leg of lamb echoes the tuna with the topping of rosemary, tomato and quality olive oil and is no less pleasing. More complicated preparations tend to be less effective. On one visit a confit of chicken was a limp, greasy disaster.

The last menu entry headed "entertaining flavors" offers an eclectic sampler of oddities from baby vegetables cooked in parchment to chicken mole and blue corn chips. These dishes seem out of step with the rest of the menu.

Dessert offerings change nightly. They range from excellent homemade ice cream to fresh fruits with a few cakes and pastries in between. The wine list is divided about equally between California and French vintages. Prices are moderate, in keeping with the food prices.

In warm weather the restaurant will open out onto Ohio Street dramatically changing its character. The high ceilinged room with walls that have the slightest blush of pink and yellow cloths on the tables has a more formal feeling in cold weather. The atmosphere is just a little stiff despite the warmth and friendliness of the servers. The outdoor cafe should help loosen the place up.

For value in downtown dining, Grand Ohio delivers more than most of its competitors. As the kitchen becomes more consistent the restaurant ought to live up to the standard one expects of a Foley restaurant.

★ LA FONTAINE
French

2442 N. Clark St.   525-1800
Hours: Mon–Thurs 5–10:30 pm, Fri & Sat 5–11 pm, closed Sun
Price Range: Expensive
Credit cards: A C D JCD M V
Reservations: Accepted

Another restaurant where diners must be regulars in order to obtain the best in food and service, La Fontaine enjoys great popularity for its elegant interior and classic French cuisine. On busy nights, both food and service suffer mightily for those who are not members of the "club."

La Fontaine's attempts at formality include a French menu and waiters with French accents. The two rooms upstairs offer French-country charm and a sense of coziness, with fireplaces, weathered wood trim and small, curtained windows. The food is not cheap. A four- or five-course dinner will cost an average of $70 a couple, excluding wine. Dishes served

177

for two—roast duck, rack of lamb, tenderloin and sirloin—are priced reasonably, if two diners care to eat the same entrees.

The menu presents a balanced selection of rather traditional French dishes. Some of the most attractive offerings are specials such as the outstanding smoked slamon with cream sauce and homemade noodles. Another special, salmon mousse, is light and delicate—too delicate to have much flavor, although a sprightly herb mayonnaise with Dijon mustard on the side helped. Vichyssoise with chives has a nice flavor, but the cold soup is thick and pasty. Best bets among menu offerings include the salads, especially the house version—fresh, bite-sized spinach with eggs and a thick mustard vinaigrette—that comes free with entrees. A timbale of seasonal vegetables also accompanies meals. An endive and apple salad with a tart creamy dressing is worth the extra cost. Ditto the Boston lettuce, watercress, mushroom and heart of palm salad.

Among the entrees, sole muscove, a rolled piece of sole with American caviar and smoked oysters, benefits from beautiful presentation; the combination works well. Sauteed tournedos of beef with Roquefort sauce also falls short of expectations, despite the full flavored, creamy sauce; the somewhat tough meat simply doesn't have enough flavor to stand up to the sauce. Grilled swordfish, a special one night, could have been wonderful; the two large, half-inch-thick filets were moist, tender and juicy—a feat—but they were overpowered by cognac and pepper. Veal with morel mushrooms suffers from a chalky, bland cream sauce.

Desserts tend to be losers. The chocolate mousse one night looked and tasted like packaged chocolate pudding, and came topped with a glob of whipped cream that had been sitting around too long. A hazelnut cake was better, but hardly special.

A good French wine list offers a wide selection at prices

that are average $30 a bottle or more. All in all, this French restaurant should be a good deal better considering the price.

★ FOUR FARTHINGS
French

2060 N. Cleveland Ave.   935-2060
Hours: Sun brunch 10 am–3 pm, dinner daily 5:30–11 pm
Price range: Moderately expensive
Credit cards: A C D M V
Reservations: Accepted until 7:45, and for parties of five or more after that time

Four Farthings is equal parts tavern and restaurant. Divided quite literally down the middle, the store front on the right houses a loud neighborhood bar crowded with yuppies. The storefront on the left houses an also fairly loud, but more civilized dining room frequented by slightly older groups of customers.

Service is so conscientious that it borders on the exhausting, with waitresses asking after every course, (could it have been every bite?) how things are. Still they try to make the evening pleasant for diners, more than can be said for many other restaurants.

Although the decorations in the room appear to be new, they accurately recall the old. Dark stained mouldings trim walls and windows. Wallpaper in beige and rust-red lends a country kitchen feeling to the room.

The quality of the food has declined somewhat since the departure of the original chef to run the kitchen at Cafe D'Artagnon. However, some dishes still rise to excellence, and all have potential. At this writing inconsistency plagues the kitchen.

The menu offerings change with some frequency, but tend to be pretty straightforward: grilled meats, poultry, pastas. More interesting items generally show up on the card of specials, which of course is as it should be despite the fact that many restaurants try to dazzle diners with creativity and broad selections everywhere. Seafood items usually make up at least half of the specials.

From the regular menu calamari makes a good beginning. The tiny squid turned out a tad tough one night, but had fine flavor without a hint of fishiness and with a light coating of crisp batter.

Tri-colored pasta spirals with roquefort sauce also please. Cooked just slightly beyond al dente the pasta rests in a rich cream sauce fortified with cheese flavor, but not overwhelmed by it. A good dish.

House salads, a better than average melange of leaf lettuce, strips of carrot and tomato wedge, is perfectly adequate with its light coating of dijon vinaigrette.

Although highly recommended by the waitress, the medallions of duck described as moist and tender disappointed. Moist the skin was with its thick layer of fat wedged between it and the duck meat, but that meat was overcooked and dry. The sauce helped, but better duck can be had elsewhere. Good fresh vegetables with a touch of garlic and the pleasant surprise of ginger come with entrees.

The grilled veal chop, also recommended, turned out far better. The large chop was juicy and well served by its tarragon cream sauce.

Simple desserts predominate here, which is just fine. The lemon meringue pie reminds one very much of what mother used to make except that the meringue has greater height and the crust turns out a bit overcooked and tough. A special profiterole with home-made vanilla ice cream and Giardelli chocolate sauce couldn't be better, the bitter sauce contrasting and augmenting nicely the sweet ice cream and crisp pastry.

While the wine list is limited, the selections are extremely careful with several suggestions listed on a blackboard for sampling by the glass or bottle. Wine prices are quite reasonable.

★★★★ LE FRANCAIS
French

269 S. Milwaukee Ave., Wheeling   541-7470
Hours: Tues–Sun 5:30–9:30 pm, closed Mon
Price range: Expensive
Credit cards: A C D M V
Reservations: Necessary
Handicap

"Too opulent, too ambitious, too dramatic...," complained one French food expert about Le Francais. Indeed, Le Francais is all of these things and more. But it is essential to recognize that this is a *Midwestern* French restaurant.

Sure, it's showy, and, with the wrong waiter, knowledgeable diners can feel they're being treated a bit like hicks. But for all its show, for all its foibles, Le Francais provides a total immersion in fine cuisine unparalleled in this area.

Chef Banchet's creations range in quality from good to super-fantastic. And note, the sauces are no longer too salty, although the portions are still large—but why complain? The display of the evening's offerings—wave after wave of dome-covered dishes and raw ingredients—is overwhelming and might well be left alone.

Selections are enormous and include all kinds of seafood, choice livers, sausage, paté, game, meat, poultry...a list that could go on. The resutling "oohs" and "aahs" from diners create a high noise level, but add to the festive atmosphere. The dining room mixes Midwestern coziness and French-country atmosphere. Copper pots sparkle amid stuffed game and paintings. Doris Banchet greets diners at the door and leads them to their tables. But the generally plain decor plays second fiddle to the food.

Marvelous appetizers include a three-salmon salad—fresh, marinated and smoked salmon with cabbage, French green beans, radicchio, lettuce leaves and mache in a light dill sauce. Veal and duck also make a wonderful salad-like appetizer on a bed of cabbage, lettuce and mushrooms in a delicate sauce. The serious side of Banchet provides French scallops with the coral, a delicacy in France, still attached. These scallops star in the feuillette appetizer with asparagus, filet of sole, mussels and shrimp artfully presented in an exquisite watercress sauce. Also from France, fresh foie gras so smooth, rich and flavorful, you're compelled to fork out the $20 for it. Consider its price in France and skip everything else, if only to taste the huge delicacy served on a bed of cabbage, surrounded with a silken sauce and topped with a large slice of truffle.

Grapefruit sorbet arrives to cleanse the palate but is meritorious in itself. The perfectly cooked entree assortment of breast of mallard duck, quail and squab with morels and rouennaise sauce, requires—and deserves—a massive appetite. Stuffed pheasant here will surprise diners used to the dried-out flavorless birds served in so many other places. Moist and delightful, the pheasant finds a pleasant complement in the mushroom cream sauce. Sweetbreads, topped with truffles on a bed of spinach, seem to melt in the mouth as they release their delicate flavor. But these sweetbreads, served with a creamy sauce, and unsurpassed in quality, seem unspectacular in comparison to some other dishes.

Suffice to say, the dessert trays offer the same bewildering array of possibilities. This citadel of haute cuisine should be welcomed by anyone with a good sense of humor, and a grasp of the absurdity of dropping a few hundred bucks on dinner.

★ FRICANO'S
Italian/seafood

2512 N. Halsted St.   929-7550
Hours: Sun–Thurs 4–10 pm, Fri & Sat 4–11 pm
Price range: Moderate
Credit cards: A C M V
Reservations: Not accepted
Handicap

Inside, Fricano's looks and functions like a neighborhood bar. A few tables on the left and a bar on the right leave just enough space for passage to the back room where the serious eating takes place.

This room isn't fancy, either. Just tables and chairs crowded together in a plain, comfortable room that gets noisy when it's crowded, which is most every night.

Seafood predominates on this vast menu, which also includes lots of pasta dishes and Italian specialties. For starters, calamari is crisp, fresh and good. Arancini, saffron-seasoned rice wrapped around a meatball, also is good. Other appetizers include raw and baked oysters and clams, crab legs, french fried zucchini and artichokes.

Linguini carbonara, marred by the intense flavor of the smoky bacon, pleases nonetheless with its rich, creamy sauce and just slightly overcooked pasta.

Grilled with care, such seafood items as trout, red snapper, swordfish and salmon make excellent choices here. The exquisitely fresh seafood stays juicy and picks up just a hint of flavor from the grill. More complicated preparations may not fare so well.

In addition to the seafood, several veal dishes are offered. Veal limone starts with reasonably good veal, but too much lemon overwhelms the meat—a bit like having a little veal with your lemon.

Friendly servers tend to get overworked as the dining room fills. Their tempers get shorter and waits between

183

courses get longer. In other words, service is inconsistent.

Cheesecake, spumoni and cannoli lead the dessert offerings. Both the Amaretto cheesecake and cannoli are better than average. The wine list is limited, but well priced.

For a neighborhood eatery, Fricano's succeeds better than most. Reasonable prices and reasonably good food make this a good spot for a casual evening out.

★ ★ FROGGY'S
French

306 Green Bay, Highwood   433-7080
Hours: Lunch Mon–Fri 11:30 am–2 pm, Dinner Mon–Thurs
*   5–10 pm, Fri & Sat 5–11 pm, closed Sun*
Price range: Moderate
Credit cards: C D M V
Reservations: Not accepted

With a full-course meal for $20 or less, Froggy's offers good value for French cuisine in a sort of luncheonette chic, non-intimidating atmosphere. A mixed set goes to Froggy's for good food and good times. The casual mood excuses the waiters' service gaffes and some inconsistencies in the food. Otherwise, the waiters are enthusiastic and charming, the ingredients fresh, the preparations careful and the prices moderate. Here is a good-natured French restaurant that provides good food without taking itself too seriously.

The specials are almost always good choices. Among appetizers, a special terrine of scallops underlaid with saffron sauce is outstanding. The scallops, barely cooked, are tender spheres in a silky, mousse-like loaf that floats on rich saffron cream. Equally delightful is quail stuffed with veal mousse and served with a raisin cream sauce. Escargot arrives under a pastry crust left unmentioned on the menu but is good in a rich red wine and cream sauce.

Soups change nightly. A cream of watercress captures full watercress flavor, but is too salty. The salad comes after appetizers unless otherwise requested. A standard house salad mixes leaf lettuce with parboiled carrots and red cabbage under vinaigrette. Special salads can be substituted. A special of fresh, crisp Belgian endive with high-quality prosciutto ham on a bed of leaf lettuce with a nice herbed mayonnaise on the side would have been great but for the additional limp carrots and peas.

A special entree, tips of beef with goat cheese and green onions, pleases despite the overcooked meat. Zucchini and pattypan (a squash-like vegetable) support the dish. Leg of lamb with tomato basil sauce is also overcooked and tough and dry. The effect was an uninteresting lamb stew. Best is the mousse of chive surrounding a two-inch medallion of rich, tender lobster baked en croute with a light sauce. Fresh walleyed pike comes in a white sauce with green and purple grapes and fresh herbs. The creamed wine sauce, though, is too much of a good thing.

Desserts, like the rest of the menu, tend to be inconsistent. A light textured, flavorful chocolate mousse cake came with a weak, watery creme Anglaise instead of the promised raspberry sauce. Baked pears turn out mushy with a too sweet caramel sauce. Creme caramel with a hint of expresso works well. This small wine list offers a careful selection of California and French wines at reasonable prices. A 1982 chablis grand cru at $14.50 recommended by the waiter one night worked well with the pike.

To keep turns of the tables high and prices low, no reservations are taken. At peak dining hours (7:30 to 9) waits can be long.

★ HACKNEY'S
American

Three locations:
1914 E. Lake Ave., Glenview   724-7171
Hours: Mon–Thurs 11:30–11 pm, Fri & Sat 11:30 am–midnight,
*   Sun 11:30 am–10 pm*
Price range: Moderate
Credit cards: A   M   V
Reservations: Accepted
Handicap

241 S. Milwaukee Ave., Wheeling   537-2100
Hours: Mon–Sat 11:15 am–11 pm, Sun noon–11 pm
Price range: Moderate
Credit cards: A   M   V
Reservations: Accepted

880 Old Rand Rd., Lake Zurich   438-2103
Hours: Mon–Thurs 11:30 am–11:15 pm, Fri & Sat 11:30–12:15
*   am, Sun noon–11:15 pm*
Price range: Moderate
Credit cards: A   M   V
Reservations: Accepted

Hackney's packs diners in throughout the suburbs mostly on its reputation for great burgers, reasonable prices and comfortable atmosphere that's a good deal classier than the average. The burgers are pan fried rather than grilled or broiled, the meat is lean, moist and full flavored. They're usually cooked to perfection, served on a bun or black bread with a side plate of onions and small bowl of slaw. Stay away from the french fries—they're limp, unappealing and not worth the effort. Instead choose the onion cake. Make sure the kitchen doesn't overcook the onions and they're excellent.

HAMBURGER HAMLET
American
Rating: Fair

44 E. Walton St.   649-6600
Hours: Mon–Thurs 11:30 am–11 pm, Fri & Sat 11:30 am–
*   midnight, Sun brunch 11:30 am–3 pm, dinner to 11*
*   pm*
Price range: Moderate
Credit cards: A   M   V
Reservations: Not accepted

Step inside the door and you step into a classic example of the brass-and-oak school of gathering-place design. A large bar with a fascinating contraption overhead fanning the air provides a clue to this restaurant's real reason for being.

The menu sports a mind-boggling array of items, at least 10 different varieties of hamburgers alone. Most of the other stuff—nachos, deep fried mushrooms and the like—can be overlooked completely. But the burgers have merit.

Good quality beef goes into the thick, juicy burgers that are cooked to order and served on a fresh bun. And no place offers greater variety. Burgers come with crisp french fries—the real thing.

Service, on the other hand, can be abysmal. Some of the "Hi, my name is..." servers forget orders, disappear for what seems like hours and try to make up for shortcomings with "cute" personalities.

★★ HAPPI SUSHI
Japanese

Three locations:
3346 N. Clark St.   528-1225

Hours: Lunch Mon, Wed–Sun noon–2:30 pm, Dinner Mon,
Wed–Sat 5–10:30 pm

14 N. Vail, Arlington Heights   577-4400
Lunch Mon, Tues, Thurs, Fri 11:30 am–2 pm, Dinner Thurs–
Tues 5–9:30 pm

600 Central, Highland Park   432-1516
Lunch Tues–Sun 11:45 am–2 pm, Dinner Tues–Sun 5–10 pm
Price range: Moderately expensive
Credit cards: A   C   D   M   V
Reservations: Accepted except at Clark St. location
Handicap

   Although the three units of this mini-sushi chain
have different looks and somewhat different menus, the sim-
ilarities outweigh the differences. All produce fine sushi with
impeccably fresh fish, along with enough cooked Japanese
specialties to provide something good for those who cannot
stomach raw fish.

   The Clark St. location is the most cramped and least attractive of the three. The other two are sleeker with more
room between tables and diners. All have sushi bars where
the expert craftsmen ply their trade and provide great theater, wielding their knives and shouting out orders and salu-
tations to one another and to their customers.

   Basic, aromatic miso soup preceeds most orders. So does
a forgettable iceberg lettuce salad with a few bean sprouts
and soy-based dressing.

   Predetermined selections of sushi are available on the
menu or diners can pick and choose their own selections.
The easiest way to make selections is at the sushi bar where
the chefs will offer some guidance and you can watch as
your order is prepared. However, cards printed with color
photos of the various types of sushi available sit on the tables to help diners decide.

188

Shrimp, tuna, yellow tail and salmon make good choices for beginners. All are mild in flavor and fairly firm in texture. More adventurous eaters might head for the sea urchin or salty salmon roe. One word of caution, the green stuff served with the sushi order, called osabi, is hot enough to knock your socks off. Experiment with it, gingerly mixed into the soy sauce also served on the side.

Negi maki, thin slices of cooked beef wrapped around green onions and served with a sweetened soy sauce, makes a good alternative for non-sushi eaters. Tempura provides another. Shrimp or vegetables such as pepper, sweet potato and squash are dipped in the lightest of batter and deep fried to crisp outside and fresh-tasting inside. Traditional teriyaki is safe, but not as good here as it is at other places.

Fish comes cooked here as chawan mushi, a baked fish custard. Presented in an earthenware crock, this somewhat watery custard with pieces of fish takes some getting used to, but ultimately has a pleasing flavor. Grilled salmon at the Highland Park location is a better bet in cooked fish. It's served with a good teriyaki sauce and, oddly, a scoop of potato salad on the side.

Good Japanese beer goes well with all. Desserts include fresh fruit and tempura (fried) ice cream. Friendly, polite servers do a good job, but don't offer much help with sushi selections.

★ **HEIDELBERGER FASS**
German

4300 N. Lincoln Ave.   478-2486
Hours: Mon, Wed, Thurs 11:30 am–10 pm, Fri & Sat 11:30
*   am–11 pm, Sun noon–10 pm, closed Tues*
Price range: Moderate
Credit cards: A   M   V
Reservations: Recommended

Need relief from a bout of excessive trendiness? A visit to Heidelberger Fass might be just what you need.

Step inside the door and up to the bar, where the draft beer comes in quarter-, half- and full-liter portions. Dark wood dominates the two dining rooms which are lined with all sorts of old-world memorabilia. White-clothed tables, German marches or classical music playing in the background and waitresses in costume add to the appeal.

The cheerful young waitress brings good, hearty chopped liver, excellent, mild pickled herring with beets and cottage cheese to the table along with a basket of warm rolls. Dinners include soup, salad, vegetable and choice of potatoes or spaetzle starch with the entrees, so an additional appetizer is unnecessary.

Soups are excellent, especially the clear brothed, liver dumpling soup. Although the dumpling tastes like liver itself, the texture is amazingly light and airy. Also good is the split pea soup, which is not as thick as some, but full-flavored nevertheless.

Only two salad choices are offered, neither of which has much to recommend it. The iceberg lettuce salad with tomato and onion comes with a variety of dressings led by the creamy garlic. Cucumbers in a vinaigrette are fine, but unexciting.

A long list of specials augments the already formidable menu. Roast duck ranks high among the offerings—crisp-skinned, the moist duck meat lies on a good bread dressing. Skip the cherry sauce thoughtfully provided on the side end simply enjoy the slightly gamey, perfectly prepared meat.

Roladen, thin slices of tender beef wrapped around onions and bacon, turns out suprisingly bland, but well-prepared. Veal schnitzels, pork schnitzels and, when in season, venison schnitzels are standouts. Smoked meat lovers should head for the Heidelberger combination of smoked thuringer, bratwurst and smoked pork chop with sauerkraut.

Vegetables include excellent sauerkraut, good if somewhat sweet red cabbage and overcooked vegetables such as broccoli, zucchini or cauliflower.

An excellent apple strudel, delicate pastry chock full of apples, raisins and nuts, underscores the fact that, despite all the awful versions of strudel out there, this dish can be good. A scoop of whipped cream adds richness.

Good food, good service and modest prices make Heidelberger Fass a fine place for dinner and fun.

★★ THE HELMAND
Afghanistan

3201 N. Halsted St.   935-2447
Hours: Mon–Thurs 5-10:30 pm, Fri & Sat 5-11:30 pm, closed
*   Sun*
Price range: Moderate
Credit Cards: A   C   D
Reservations: Recommended
Handicap

The first Afghan restaurant in Chicago, The Helmand shows off this interesting and complex cuisine with aplomb. The interior of this bright, cheery, L-shaped dining room is tastefully decorated in an odd mix of old and new, with beige carpeting, grey patterned wallpaper, and a Victorian pressed- tin ceiling. There are framed prints of Afghan market scenes and generously-sized white-clothed tables flanked by comfortable wooden chairs, which allow diners plenty of room to relax.

Friendly, knowledgable servers, including one of the owners, take time to explain the exotic dishes. Service is generally attentive and efficient.

Five appetizers and three soups head the menu. *Aushak,*

ravioli filled with leeks, comes topped with a tart yogurt sauce with mint and richly seasoned ground beef. Although not as hot as it should be when served, the contrasting tastes add a new dimension to the ordinary notion of ravioli. *Banjan Borawni*, a sort of Afghan ratatouille of eggplant, tomatoes and herbs drizzled with a tangy garlic-yogurt sauce also could be hotter, but it tastes great. Other appetizers include an interesting pan-fried and baked baby pumpkin, and pastry shells filled with leeks and spiced potatoes or with onions and beef.

Aush, a noodle soup with small meatballs and mint yogurt, leads the soup offerings. Also offered are *mashawa*, a hearty mix of beans, chick peas, black-eyed peas, beef and yogurt, and *shorwa*, a vegetable/bean broth with lamb.

Salad includes a mix of sliced potatoes, chick-peas and onions that would be plain if it weren't enlivened with cilantro vinaigrette dressing and spicy Afghan cilanto sauce. The mixed green salad of leaf lettuce, tomatoes, carrots and onions is dressed with a light lemon-mint dressing and garnished with cilantro—a vast improvement over the pre-fab dressings served elsewhere.

Although it sounds off-putting, *geechrai*, a bed of mixed mung beans and rice with meatballs in the middle and yogurt sauce, again provides a pleasing mix of tastes and textures. A terrine of additional meatballs in a rich tomato sauce comes on the side. The only disappointment here is the tenderloin of lamb, which has a gamey, muttony flavor. The dish works despite the quality of the lamb because the sharpness of the vinegar marinade and marinated-onion cuts the gaminess.

Unusual desserts are an apt end to the meal. *Feereny*, homemade ricotta-like cheese topped with raisins and candied carrots in a sweet carrot sauce, sounds unlikely and tastes that way at first, but the dish quickly grows on you. *Kishmish paneer* is a thin pool of custard topped with fragrant cardamom that adds interest to an otherwise plain dish.

The consistent use of yogurt for saucing, and the similarity of other ingredients, creates the illusion of sameness among the dishes. But in fact each tastes surprisingly different. Although some of the mixtures of ingredients look a bit like mud, presentation of the dishes is quite attractive. And with entrees priced at $8.50 and under, The Helmand offers exceptional value as well as a chance to experience something different in pleasant surroundings. The wine list, comprised of just 10 selections, offers equally low prices.

HIBBELER'S
Alsatian
Rating: Fair

917 W. Armitage   883-5050
Hours: Lunch Mon–Fri 10:30 am–3 pm, Sat noon–3 pm,
*   Dinner Mon–Fri 5–10 pm, Sat 5–11 pm, Sun 4–9 pm*
Price range: Moderate to moderately expensive
Credit cards: A   C   D
Reservations: Recommended

Billed as Chicago's only Alsatian restaurant, Hibbeler's enjoys great popularity as a neighborhood place. Unfortunately, while the place is good enough for an inexpensive meal with friends, inconsistency plagues the kitchen and the food rarely soars to great heights.

The bar easily takes up a third of this small storefront restaurant. And the beer selection from an old fashioned cooler at the back of the room is among the best in the city.

Pastel walls have been intricately stenciled. That combined with the high, pressed-tin ceilings give the room a certain old world charm. Tables are close together, but the effect is more intimate than bothersome.

Menu offerings range from sandwiches, salads and sausages, all safe bets, to wienerschnitzle, duck and poultry.

These freshly prepared items can turn out quite well. But avoid items made in advance. They don't fare so well.

When in doubt, ask the servers. They try hard to please and can lead to the better items of the day. A good selection of Alsatian wines also is available.

★★ HOUSE OF HUNAN
Chinese

535 N. Michigan Ave.   329-9494
Hours: Sun–Sat 11:30 am–10:30 pm
Price range: Moderately expensive
Credit Cards: A C D M V
Reservations: Accepted

Although Chicago has a large population of Chinese immigrants, finding truly good Chinese food isn't as easy as it ought to be. On two counts this restaurant ranks high: for food and for comfort.

A long hallway with booths on each side leads to the reception area with a bar behind it and the dining room to the left. Red dominates the color scheme just to let you know you're in a Chinese restaurant. However, with carpeting, large clothed tables, unformed waiters and the complete absence of tacky Chinese decorations, the atmosphere is more classy than ethnic.

Begin a meal with some of the best pot stickers in town or hacked chicken, pieces of chicken breast in a slightly spicy sauce. Pass over the mundane won ton soups for the better hot and sour or the corn soup with crab, even better yet.

The extensive menu includes the usual suspects as well as a few more adventurous items. Generally the chef shows restraint in spicing the dishes. However diners can ask that the heat be turned on or season dishes themselves with hot sauce at the table.

Empress chicken, white meat in a slightly spicy sauce with

fresh vegetables, or orange beef, a hotter dish with pieces of orange peel and vegetables are good choices. Twice-cooked pork turns out moist and tender.

Seafood offerings may be the best choices of all. Scallops, shrimp and whole fish, all pristinely fresh, are offered in a variety of dishes ranging from simple and mild to spicy and complex.

Presentation is as careful as the preparation. Waiters speak English well and can explain dishes fully. Full bar service includes a few wines and Asian beers.

★ HUNAN PALACE
Chinese

1050 N. State St.   642-1800
Hours: Mon–Thurs 11:30 am–10:30 pm, Fri noon–11:30 pm,
*   Sat noon–10:30 pm*
Price range: Moderately expensive
Credit Cards: A D M V
Reservations: Accepted

Hunan Palace produces some of Chicago's best Chinese food, but inconsistencies sometimes take this cuisine from superb to totally blah. At the prices, some of the highest you'll encounter here for Chinese fare, every dish should be perfect.

The interior is done in burgundies with tasteful art. Comfortable seating and private sections made this a fine restaurant for entertaining.

The chef takes as much care in presentation of dishes as owner Austin Koo did with decor. Intricately carved vegetables often adorn the dishes, adding color and beauty.

Service can be excellent or somewhat indifferent. On one visit dishes came all at once, despite repeated requests that the meal be paced. Language problems lead to mystery dishes and substitutions. But if you know how to order, you can taste some good food here.

The shark meat fire pot appetizer is an assortment of seafood, wonton and pot stickers—with ups and downs. Better is a selection of cold fish, steamed and served with cuttlefish, cucumbers and dipping sauces. The best is the sea scallops; tender and moist, with cashew nuts and sauce. Another good bet is golden coins, shrimp paste molded into a pork medaillion, deep fried and deceptively light. The pot stickers with different sauces also work well.

If you can get your entrees delivered one at a time, start with the hottest and work to a cool-down. Yu Hsiang pork is a good start, followed by crispy beef and orange with a luscious sauce. If you don't want to waste the sauce, mix it into your rice. Don't miss the deep-fried soft shell crabs when they're available—incredibly crisp, yet moist. But avoid shrimp with snowpeas, water chestnuts and mushrooms at all costs—bland is the word. Interesting specials often are available.

The ingredients here are unquestionably fresh and the chef is definitely competent, but he seems reluctant to show his stuff for fear of offending unsophisticated tastes. The best strategy is to get the maitre 'd to order for you and insist you be served authentic Chinese dishes—not those tamed for American palates.

HY'S OF CANADA
American/steak
Rating: Poor

100 E. Walton St.   649-9555
Hours: Mon–Sat 11:30 am–11 pm, closed Sun
Price range: Moderately expensive
Credit cards: A   D   M   V
Reservations: Accepted

Hy's of Canada stays in business by catering to the convention trade, and performs two valuable services for Chicagoans. First, it is one of the few places in town with decent food that caters to large groups who want to dine together at the same table. Second, by attracting hordes of conventioneers, Hy's helps keep those poorly behaved, if innocuous, visitors out of our better restaurants.

This is no place for a romantic evening alone—a romantic evening with 80 of your closest friends, perhaps. Hy's does succeed at recreating an "exclusive" men's club atmosphere (only a few female diners seem to infiltrate the fraternity.) Carved dark wood paneling covers the walls; a glass-enclosed grill in the main dining room makes grilling steaks into real theatre; old-looking oil portraits, shelves of books, fireplaces, big plush chairs and a few semi-private alcoves complete the look.

Beware the Hy's "short wait": even diners who honor their reservation on time can be put on hold in the bar for 45 minutes—where they receive efficiently attentive service, of course. Beef remains Hy's specialty, although there's a long list of seafood specials. But while it's good and properly prepared, Hy's New York strip steak can't compare with Morton's or Eli's. And with prices that range from the mid-teens to more than $20 per entree, Hy's can take a hike.

★ IMPERIAL CATHAY
Chinese

2 E. Delaware Pl.   642-0626
Hours: Sun–Thurs 11:30 am–10:30 pm, Fri & Sat 11:30 am–
*   11 pm*
Price range: Moderately expensive
Credit Cards: A D M V
Reservations: Accepted
Handicap

Although popular on the West Coast, Mongolian barbecue did not reach Chicago until former computer programmer David Yang switched from bytes to bites and opened Imperial Cathay in December, 1984. It took nearly a year and a good deal of money to convert two Near North Side store fronts, formerly a drug store and shoe store, into an airy, two-level Chinese restaurant devoid of lanterns and other typical decoration.

The barbecue—a large, steel-topped cylinder under a red ventilation hood—stands in the first-floor dining room with a long expanse of raw ingredients displayed on a stainless steel counter that stretches along one wall. The idea is for customers to mix and match meats, vegetables and sauces to create their own dishes, then hand the plate over to the chef, who deftly sears the concoction on the sizzling hot surface of the cylinder. Watching the cook using long kitchen chop sticks to stir the meat and vegetables, then slide the steaming food off the cooking surface into a plate, makes for great restaurant theatre and, happily, a good meal. The only danger lies in excess. Confronted with choices of chicken, beef and pork, an array of fresh veggies to gladden the heart of any greengrocer and at least 10 sauces, an unwitting diner may wind up with a plate of overwrought mishmash. But seconds are encouraged, as are second tries. The menu says, "Even Genghis Khan had to try several times before it suited his taste."

For those who don't want to bother with participatory dining, an extensive traditional menu features Mandarin and what are said to be Szechwan and Hunan dishes. Some are outstanding, others hopelessly bland. Among the steller offerings is the ginger duck entree, tender duck served in a seductively perfumed, delicately spicy brown sauce with thin slices of ginger, green pepper and silver dollar-sized chunks of bamboo shoots imbued with flavor.

Servers are friendly and attempt to be helpful, although

language barriers occasionally interfere with the flow of information.

★ IRELAND'S
Seafood

500 N. LaSalle St.   337-2020
Hours: Mon–Thurs 11 am–11 pm, Fri 11 am–11:30 pm, Sat
      5–11:30 pm, Sun 5–10 pm
Price range: Moderately expensive
Credit Cards: A C D M V
Reservations: Recommended

Ireland's has grown from the old, stodgy seafood restaurant it used to be into a pretty good, almost contemporary eatery. It still caters to the convention and tourist trade, but its updated menu also has appeal to locals.

The vintage building that houses the restaurant offers many opportunities for sleek, modern, loft-like decor. However, the owners chose hackneyed maritime themes not quite "out" enough to be "in."

In the bar, to the left inside the entrance, ropes tied with mariner's knots and fish nets form room dividers. This old-time sea-faring ambience stands in sharp contrast to the rock and disco music playing in the bar. At one end an oyster bar with exquisitely fresh clams, oysters and crab legs helps drinkers take the edge off their hunger.

To the right of the entrance a stairway leads upstairs to the dining room. Here the maritime theme is carried out by stained glass, including one huge panel which hangs overhead in the main dining room and depicts a massive lobster. Brick walls and large wooden beams give the room a sort of industrial charm. Jazz replaces rock in the dining room.

Appetizers include the same fresh shellfish found in the oyster bar below; steamers, excellent chowders and not so excellent seafood-stuffed mushrooms, among other things.

All but a few items, like Australian lobster tails and shrimp, are fresh daily. A few gloppy, old-fashioned preparations still appear on the menu, but most of the seafood comes broiled, grilled over mesquite, simply sauteed or poached.

Trendy blackened red fish has a seared, spicy, blackened crust outside, but stays moist and flavorsome inside. Unfortunately it sits on a superfluous dijon, garlic butter sauce. Ask that the sauce be held or served on the side.

Grilled salmon comes with no adornment, but tastes just fine. Roasted shrimp in a butter and garlic sauce spiked with healthy amounts of sherry may turn out a tad overcooked, but the dish works well.

Entrees include boiled potato and a visit to one of the better salad bars in the area with head lettuce, spinach, fresh raw vegetables, pasta salads, bean salads, apple salads and all manner of toppings.

Desserts include cheesecake, chocolate cake, carrot cake, ice cream and hot fudge sundaes. Service is attentive and knowledgeable. However the clatter of the computerized cash registers constantly intrudes on conversations and reminds diners that there's no such thing as a free lunch or dinner.

★ J. P.'S EATING PLACE
Eclectic

1800 N. Halsted St.   664-1801
Hours: Lunch Mon–Fri 11:30 am–2:30 pm, Sat 11 am–3 pm,
*   Dinner Sun–Thurs 4–10:30 pm, Fri & Sat 4–11 pm,*
*   Sun 4–10 pm*

122 W. Lake (J. P 's West)   351-3968
Hours: Lunch daily 11:30 am–3 pm, Dinner 5–10 pm
Price range: Moderate

Credit Cards: A C D M V
Reservations: Accepted

A great restaurant J. P. 's is not, but it does offer decent food at a decent price, something increasingly difficult to find along the ever more trendy Halsted strip.

Just inside the entrance, diners are greeted by a host, often owner Jorge Perez, and an array of the fresh seafood offerings for the night. A small bar to the left holds waiting diners. Should you end up at the bar, try one of the world-class margaritas.

To the right the dining room stretches to the front of the building. Brick walls and light-colored wood frame the room, but the focal points are a beautiful red and black wall hanging and a wooden sculpture in the center of the room.

The menu lists a mix ranging from Mexican to American to Italian specialties. Some of these work admirably. Others fall short of excellence.

Appetizers include good nachos, quesadillas and queso fundido, melted Mexican cheese served over sausage, all of which turn out well. Non-Mexican offerings include calamari and ceviche, which also turn out well.

The dinner salad here could easily be dinner instead of coming with it. All manner of chopped greens and vegetables augmented with salami and cheese come tossed with a light-handed vinaigrette.

For some reason, Mexican specialties that do so well as appetizers fail as entrees. Stay with the fresh fish instead. The seafood gets careful handling, especially when it's grilled. Italian specialties such as chicken Vesuvio or veal fare better than the Mexican dishes, but still offer few delights. Barbecued ribs surprise with their quality and flavor.

Most entrees come with a side of pasta. The wine list is limited, but not high priced. Cheesecake, flan and a hot fudge sundae sum up the dessert offerings.

On busy evenings service can be slow and frustrating. However, starting with the owner/host, servers are warm, friendly and well-meaning. They want this eating place to offer a good time to all who come.

★ ★ ★ JACKIE'S
French

2478 N. Lincoln Ave.   880-0003
Hours: Lunch Tues–Sat 11:30 am–2 pm, Dinner Tues–Thurs
        5:45–9 pm, Fri & Sat 5:30–10 pm, closed Sun & Mon
Price range: Expensive
Credit Cards: A C D M V
Reservations: Required
Handicap

Jackie Etcheber, one of the celebrated chefs in the Great Chefs of Chicago series, takes her cuisine seriously. After apprenticing with Jean Banchet at Le Francais and at La Mer, she opened Jackie's to adoring reviews.

Jackie's small, low-keyed, pleasantly appointed room has a small bar at the rear primarily for service purposes, but with a few chairs to hold customers whose tables may not be ready. Large oil paintings hang on the beige walls blushed with pink. White clothed tables sit so closely together it's possible to overhear conversations, but the feeling is intimate.

Whether or not one appreciates this restaurant largely depends on one's approach to dining. Those out for a good, free-wheeling time may find Jackie's stuffy and confining. Those out for a Food Experience, will find it here.

Jackie's cuisine dazzles with a wide array of ingredients. Indeed, waiters who announce the specials sometimes get tangled up in the long list of attractions of a single dish: "Phyllo nest with special scallops with the roe, a selection of seasonal mushrooms, topped with tomato coullis and fresh

Beluga caviar on a bed of lettuce with two sauces, a lemon hollandaise and sauce cherone." Whew!

Unlike many other restaurants where the description entices but the dish disappoints, Jackie's delivers. The carefully thought-out combinations never fail to satisfy. The phyllo nest special delights with its crisp, thin basket brimming with mushrooms and succulent scallops well-served by the tangy sauces.

Other appetizers include a coarse, country-style duck paté a la Jean Banchet, both cold. Hot seafood terrine, hot sea food salad and soup du jour—an exceedingly hot, but excellent cream of watercress broth—recently round out the starters.

Salads come with entrees. The mix of ingredients changes, but generally includes leaf lettuce, jullienne of carrots, red cabbage and often bean sprouts, reflecting Etcheber's Japanese heritage. This simple salad comes with just enough good vinaigrette to flavor the greens without flooding them.

Fresh seafood leads the tempting list of specials. Light moist red snapper marries with tender Florida shrimp for one special. Half a sliced avocado covers one side of the fish and half a sliced papaya covers the other side for an exquisite presentation. The dish includes red pepper slices with a garnish of baby pear tomatoes, baby squash with the flowers attached, olives and nasturtium, all in a cilantro hollandaise.

Seafood also heads the printed menu. The delicate Dover sole wrapped around a light scallop mousse atop a flaky puff pastry shell goes out to many tables here, with good reason. Supported by a lobster sauce on one side and lemon sauce on the other, this dish plays a symphony of textures and flavors on the palate.

At many restaurants, pheasant reminds one of nothing

more than tough, characterless chicken. Here the pheasant has gamey overtones and turns out exceptionally succulent. It came as part of a triumvirate of duck cooked medium rare, boned quail and pheasant, on a bed of wild rice with green peppercorn sauce, a recent special that demands superlatives.

The Oriental influence shows up again with the flavorsome baby chicken accompanied by Oriental sweetened rice, cloud ear mushrooms and julienne of vegetables.

A good wine list allows diners a sufficient selection from moderately priced to fairly expensive to complement dinner selections. However, some wines listed may not be available.

Desserts provide a proper finale for the excellent food here, and tend to be difficult to resist even when one feels totally stuffed. Chocolate lovers should not miss the chocolate, raison, walnut torte, which is nothing short of great. However, many choose Jackie's signature Chocolate Bag, a thin shell of dark chocolate in the shape of a small bag, filled with white chocolate mousse and topped with raspberries. The carrot cake with bits of carrot and orange nearly equals the torte. Both come on a creme Anglaise that tends to be a tad heavy on vanilla. Fruit tarts, pear and recently apple, are simple and delicious.

Waiters, either by design or through inertia, tend to add to the serious tone of the restaurant. Often they seem aloof, if not just a bit bored with their charges and the long recitation of the specials. This is not to say that service is bad, but it does lack warmth, something restaurants such as Le Francais and Carlos demonstrate does not have to be sacrificed, even in high-toned places.

★★ JIMMY'S PLACE
French

3420 N. Elston   539-2999

Hours: Lunch Mon–Fri 11:30 am–2 pm, Dinner Mon–Sat 5–
    9:30 pm, closed Sun
Price range: Expensive
Credit cards: C D M V
Reservations: Accepted

Jimmy's Place has a relaxed and attractive atmosphere with its purple and lime decor, operatic music in the background, opera posters everywhere and a glassed-in kitchen open to view in the main dining room. The effect is bright and cheery even on the grayest Chicago winter days.

No restaurant in Chicago has a more intensely loyal following. Many diners are regulars so there's a sense of community on a busy night.

While servers are polished and friendly, at times non-regulars can feel a bit like intruders on the party. Nevertheless, Jimmy's can be a fun night out.

Jimmy's food is good, very good, in fact. Because the menu changes monthly, the offerings are never boring. Enticing nightly specials often include some of the best bets here with unique, well-conceived marriages of ingredients.

Most dishes are prepared with a minimum of embellishments: for example a perfectly grilled swordfish with an effective mustard sauce or succulent scallops in cream sauce with mushrooms.

The appetizer selections may include such items as tender snails baked in a casserole with a flaky pastry top, a selection of patés—smooth chicken liver, venison and duck—seafood mousse or braised Belgium endive wrapped in ham and broiled with a white wine, cream and cheese sauce.

Skip the house salad in favor of the special salads, creative combinations of ingredients lightly dressed that change nightly.

The entrees here include excellent fresh seafood dishes

with a variety of preparations as well as meat, game and poultry. Attention is paid to the integrity of the featured ingredients, which get supported by excellent, flavorsome sauces.

While most dishes work well, there is a sense of experimentation here. Sometimes the combinations fail, but at least the kitchen attempts to reach for excitement rather than settling for the proven mundane.

Desserts are a mixed bag. Those based on fruits such as poached pear, sliced caramel apple with heavenly ice cream and tart make good choices. Cakes tend to be excessively sweet and uninteresting.

★ JOHN'S RESTAURANT AND PIZZERIA
Italian

121 W. State St., Calumet City   862-8870
Hours: 11–2 am daily.
Price range: Moderate
Credit cards: A   D   V
Reservations: Accepted

If you're ever lost and hungry near the Indiana border, look for John's. A cavernous place with two dining rooms and a large bar area made warmer with red carpeting, black booths and friendly service, John's offers better than average Italian food in huge quantities at a reasonable price.

The menu is overwhelmingly long, indicating the place is more than a pizzeria. But the photos showing the owners standing proudly in front of their new pizza oven mean a pie should be tried. John's turn out to be among the best thin-crust pizza in the Chicago area. Available in three sizes, the pizza has a crust that is not too thin or thick and remains crisp and crunchy under a touch of sauce and huge amounts of cheese and extra ingredients.

If you must have appetizers, stuffed eggplant is good although heavily garlicky. Lightly battered fried calamari is also a nice start and can be ordered as an entree as well. Salads disappoint. The salad that comes with dinner orders is plain. The "fancy" Italian salad" costs $1.50 and is made worthy by its additional tomato, green olive halves and anchovies. A spinach salad " with all the trimmings" uses canned ingredients.

The pasta makes up for the salads. Huge portions, perfectly cooked and with excellent sauces—mostaccioli, spaghetti or linguine with clams are equally good. The sauce in the baked lasagna seems to come from a different pot, ruining an otherwise excellent dish. Some entrees mix meat and pasta; good are pork tenderloin piccata and veal rollatini—especially if prosciutto is used instead of common ham.

Desserts include a variety of ice creams, strudels and an occasional special. A peach cobbler special was just like Mom used to make—a couple of dry drop biscuits in a puddle of overly sweet, thickened peach juice with a hint of cinnamon and peach slices. The wine list inexplicably includes French wines along with Italian but both are reasonably priced. Avoid a 1975 Barbaresco—it seems suitable only for salad dressings.

Although not really cheap by neighborhood restaurant standards and with a few flaws, this restaurant in general is worth a small detour.

★★ KAVKAZ
Georgian

6405 N. Claremont St.   338-1316
Hours: Mon–Thurs noon–10 pm, Fri noon–1 am, Sat noon–2
      pm, Sun noon–midnight.
Price range: Moderate
Credit cards: M   V
Reservations: Accepted

No, this is not the Georgia of America's south, but rather the Georgia of the southwest Soviet Union between the Caspian and Black Seas. The food, the prices and the fun make Kavkaz a great place for an ethnic food outing.

The warehouse-like interior has been softened with dark blue walls and crystal chandeliers. White cloths and dark blue napkins also attempt a look of elegance, but this does not resemble a designer interior.

However, as with Miomir's, people don't come here for the decorations. They come for the food and the fun. It's not unusual for a Russian-speaking group to take a table, order a bottle of vodka and hold forth for an entire evening, their debates growing hotter with each shot of liquor.

That's only part of the show. On weekends, entertainment livens the place even more. And owner Margarita Starobudsky goes from table to table, imparting wisdom seasoned with wit to both English and Russian speaking customers. She makes everyone feel at home.

Start with the eggplant caviar, a dish similar to ratatouille, meant for spreading on the excellent warm bread. Or try the *satsivy*, chicken in a tangy chopped walnut sauce. The chicken, served cold with bone in, comes coated with a mixture of ground walnuts and walnut oil.

A slightly tart sauce of tomato and coriander enlivens chicken tabaka, broiled half chicken with fresh garlic on top.

This dish is served with a good rice pilaf flecked with carrot and a garnish of tomato and cucumber.

The same sort of tart, red, coriander-seasoned dipping sauce comes with shashlik, basically, a shishkebob with big chunks of meat. The lamb was fresh-tasting if a bit gristly and fatty, but still moist and good. Most entrees come with the pilaf, although this one also includes french fries.

Kiev, named for the city of the owner's origin, is a dessert rather than the famous chicken dish. Expensive to produce, this cake is chock full of walnuts and it looks and tastes a bit like a quick bread with layers of a chocolate buttercream frosting—dense, but not sickeningly sweet. Also good is the eclair with a Russian custard filling—although it's unclear what makes it Russian.

The ethnic atmosphere, as well as the unbelievably low prices make this friendly restaurant one of Chicago's dining treasures.

★ KING CRAB TAVERN & SEAFOOD GRILL
Seafood

1816 N. Halsted St.   280-8990
Hours: Lunch Mon–Fri 11:30 am–2:30 pm, Dinner Sun–Thurs
*   5–11 pm, Fri & Sat 5 pm–midnight*
Price range: Moderate
Credit cards: A   M   V
Reservations: Accepted for parties of 6 or more
Handicap
Other: Valet parking

Clean, bright, open and casual, King Crab's decor has been seen hundreds of times before. A bar in the middle of the room separates the two dining areas.

Seafood specials are listed on a blackboard. In general, preparations are basic, solid and in keeping with the feel of the restaurant.

Addictive toasted pita topped with butter, garlic, oregano and sesame seeds tempts diners as soon as they are seated. Seafood chowder or fresh oysters or clams make a good choice of starters here.

A lobster tank teems with the live shellfish waiting to be steamed or broiled. Grilled fish turns out succulent with little adornment so the good natural flavor of the seafood shines through. Seafood and steak kebabs also turn out well.

Don't miss King Crab's Broadway fries: thin slices of potato with skin deep fried in peanut oil and sprinkled with celery powder and salt—super.

Wine offerings, listed on a blackboard at the bar, are limited, but well-priced. Service is casual and unpolished, but gets the job done in a friendly manner.

King Crab is not a fancy place, but the prices aren't fancy either. The seafood is fresh, carefully prepared, presented without much embellishment and is the equal of the fare at many a more expensive seafood restaurant.

★ KO CHI RESTAURANT
Japanese/French

5402 N. Clark St.   784-4030
Hours: Tues–Sun 5–10 pm, closed Mon
Price range: Moderate
Credit cards: Not accepted
Reservations: Accepted
Handicap

Ko Chi is no Lettuce Entertain You or Levy Organization orchestration; chances are, chef Akira Matsushita doesn't know the meaning of the word "marketing," but he sure can cook.

The restaurant is somewhat plain and could use some fixing-up, but it is clean. In the style of true Japanese restaurants, color photographs (long since faded) of the chef's dishes paper the window to the left of the entrance. Inside, is a small bar/staging area where the attendant greets diners. Some beautiful paper cutouts and a few ceremonial masks add warmth there, in contrast to the rather stark dining room with dropped acoustical tile ceilings, grass-papered walls and bare tables.

Ko Chi bills itself as a seafood and steak restaurant that's Japanese/French. Some interesting combinations and good ideas that sometimes surprise with their excellence result from this split identity.

To begin, the all-purpose attendant immediately brings thick slices of dark brown, homemade raisin bread. Next diners choose entrees from an ever-changing selection of fresh fish, steak or chicken on one side of the menu, then make their choice of sauce from the other side. This can be great fun, but diners should ask for sauces to be served on the side in case the combination doesn't please them.

After orders are taken, a little unannounced appetizer in the style of a French restaurant arrives: small chunks of fruit in crême fraiche flavored with honey. It may sound like dessert, but the combination is quite refreshing.

Appetizers from the menu include good sacura shrimp with a super-rich, thick Hollandaise-like sauce on the side. Steamed mussels served in the shell with a thick, herbed cream topping are plump, free of grit and fresh, but a few were undercooked. Escargot in the shell are properly cooked but unexciting. The black mushroom soup did excite, with a dollop of crême fraiche atop a rich, smooth broth that captures the essence of the mushrooms.

Entrees, all an experience in diner participation, excel. The simplicity of the dishes demands top-quality ingredients and care in cooking; Ko Chi provides just that.

Steaks cooked to a perfect medium-rare will rival any in the city. Juicy and tender, the steak must be chewed slowly to fully appreciate the slight tartness of the good beef. The house sauce—chives, tarragon, garlic and cream—complements this excellent cut of meat. For more pizzazz, try the green peppercorn sauce.

Seafood offerings, augmented with daily specials listed on a blackboard, are pristinely fresh, grilled, sauteed or breaded and fried to perfection. Simple dishes turn out better than the complicated ones. Slices of carrots sweetened with what tastes like orange marmalade, coconut shreds and a bit of honey are served on the side, along with zucchini slices topped with slivers of toasted almonds and half a boiled red potato.

Only two good, simple desserts are offered: flan and equally good puff pastry filled with ice cream and topped with hot fudge sauce. The wine list is limited, with most bottles less than $10. In fact, one of the joys of Ko Chi is dining on fresh, well-prepared, simple food at a reasonable price.

LA MEME CHOSE
French
Rating: Fair

5819 W. Dempster St., Morton Grove   965-1645
Hours: Tues–Sun 5-10 pm, closed Mon
Price range: Moderate
Credit cards: A   M   V
Reservations: Accepted
Handicap

The room is unpretentious: booths line the right wall, divided from the rest of the room by a half wall of plastic panelling. Service is good and concerned, although at early seatings diners may feel a bit rushed.

The food varies from very good to not very good at all. For an appetizer, gravlax, cured salmon, turns out too salty, although fresh and with good texture. The extremely thick

212

slice comes served on a lettuce leaf with capers. The mustard mayonnaise was heavy on mustard and mayonnaise, but short on dill flavor.

Salad or soup comes with entrees. The Caesar salad had excellent flavor. Boston lettuce with sherry walnut dressing and homemade croutons could make an evening. Lots of walnuts and fresh lettuce make this salad a winner. The seafood gumbo soup, a rich broth big on the vegetables and stingy on the seafood—mussels and small pieces of fish—doesn't work as well as the asparagus soup.

The best of the entrees sampled was the roast fresh squab stuffed with veal and walnut in a madeira sauce. The squab turns out extremely moist, no mean feat with this tiny bird. The coarse stuffing is a heavenly mix of herbed ground veal with chunks of walnuts. Finished with the rich sauce, this ambitious dish comes off beautifully, served with just-cooked asparagus spears, a cabbage leaf rolled with seaweed and a puree of bright red beets and yellow-orange squash. Swordfish turns out moist, served with a coulis of tomato that adds interest to the pristinely fresh fish. A slice of lemon and a mound of excellent caviar tops the fish. Also fresh, the sea bass a la Japanaise comes topped with shiitake mushrooms and underlaid with a ginger butter low on ginger taste. Although this dish turned out mild and not at all fishy, some nights the fish is less than fresh.

The most surprising, which is not to say the best, entree was the sauted duck breast on Belgium endive with mustard seed akvavit sauce. First of all, the breast isn't on the endive, but surrounded by the sickest-looking endive imaginable. Second, the breast looks and tastes like cube steak. Served in big, three-by-six flat, gray slices, breaded and fried, it is like no other duck breast sampled. Again, the great sauce cannot save this dish.

For dessert, it's hard not to try something called "Cho Cho Cho," which turns out to be a rather dense flourless chocolate cake topped with a large scoop of chocolate chip Haagen Dazs ice cream, topped again with hot fudge sauce, which in turn is topped with whipped cream. Rich-rich-rich, but it should please chocolate and sweet lovers. For those who want something a bit lighter, try the fresh strawberries with brown sugar and sour cream and amaretto.

La Meme Chose gets high marks for creative attempts, but it needs to establish some consistency before it can command respect for excellence.

★★★ LAWRY'S—THE PRIME RIB
American

100 E. Ontario St.   787-5000
Hours: Lunch Mon–Fri 11:30 am–2:30 pm, Dinner Mon–
*   Thurs 5–11 pm, Fri & Sat 5 pm–midnight,*
*   Sun 3–10 pm*
Price range: Moderately expensive
Credit cards: A C D M V
Reservations: Suggested

Roast prime rib of beef—that's the menu for dinner. Oh sure, there are some go-with-its: mashed potatoes and gravy, Yorkshire pudding and some options like creamed spinach and baked potatoes which chives and bacon. But basically, the beef is it.

And the restaurant with Chicago's most limited menu continues to pack in customers. Why? This prime rib is about the best you can come by.

Housed in the former McCormick mansion, the dining room is appropriately plain and down-to-earth. Friendly, professional waitresses wear hideously outdated costumes, but it all adds to the meat-and-potatoes nature of this restaurant.

For variety, the prime rib comes in three sizes and is served from rolling carts. Real gravy tops off the meat and the smooth genuine mashed potatoes.

For lunch, Lawry's actually does have more to offer than rib. Fresh fish and a large number of excellent salads augment the prime rib offering, and daily specials might also include rack of lamb, pasta with seafood, and soups.

Although portions at both lunch and dinner challenge capacity, desserts are well worth sampling. Fresh fruit trifle—alternating layers of custard cake soaked in sherry and topped with whipped cream—leads the list.

★ ★ ★ LEM'S RIBS
Barbecue

5914 S. State St.   684-5007
Hours: Sun, Tues–Thurs 5 pm–3 am, Fri & Sat 5 pm–5 am.
       closed Mon
Price: Full slab, $9.90; half slab, $5.25
Reservations: Get in line
Credit cards: Are you kidding!

When the *Chicago Tribune* rated Lem's ribs the best in the area after an extensive taste test, many readers complained that we were sending people into neighborhoods where they shouldn't go. Maybe so, but in the pursuit of good ribs no distance or danger seems excessive. Anyway, we went to Lem's then and have returned with no difficulty, although common sense and healthy urban caution are well advised.

According to the late Arthur Bryant, whose Kansas City rib house was known as the nation's best before his death in 1984: "You don't get fancy with barbecue. When you get fancy, you get out of line." Lem's fits this description like a glove. Nothing fancy. No tables. Lem's is all business, and that business is ribs.

The small storefront fills with smoke, and not the kind found in the Chicago political back rooms. The ribs cook in all that smoke for hours and had the smokiest flavor of all those tasted by the *Tribune's* panel. The ribs are huge and meaty with very little fat. The meat, which pulls away from the bones nicely, is dry and chewy, but that's where the sauce comes in.

Lem's sauce strikes a not-too-sweet, not-too-tart spicy balance. As one taster commented, "these are ribs with pow"— enough pow to make the mouth tingle but not so much that the senses scream with pain. Fries and plain white bread come with the slab. The wait at Lem's can be long, but the ribs are worth it.

★ LEONA'S
Italian

3215 N. Sheffield Ave.   327-8861
Hours: Sun–Thurs 11–1 am, Fri & Sat 11–2:30 am
Price range: Moderate
Credit cards: A
Reservations: Not accepted
Handicap

Value. Leona's has built a reputation since 1950 on value—good, honest food at a reasonable price in a clean atmosphere with respectful service. And Leona's really packs 'em in.

There's nothing fancy about the place. True, you can watch the activity in the kitchen through a big glass window as you can in some of the most fashionable places in town. There are cloths on the tables, lots of wood and servers who tell you their names. But at its heart this is still a home-spun, attractive family-owned and operated business serving simple fare that starts with good fresh ingredients and, for the most part, is competently prepared.

All of this plus low prices make the place incredibly popular. The dining rooms now cover three floors. At least two of them are usually full and at times there can be substantial waits for tables despite the size of the place.

Appetizers are predictable: mushroom caps, baked clams uniquely priced at 80 cents each, shrimp cocktail, potato skins and the like. Perhaps the best bet in this starchy lot is the garlic bread with a healthy dose of garlic and a unique ricotta cheese spread.

There's a large selection of salads and a dozen variations on the basic burger, which comes with a choice of eight side dishes. Other sandwiches, generally priced under $5, include poorboys, fish, sausage and chicken.

Many love Leona's pizza, which comes in thin-crust, deep-crust, double-deck, stuffed and whole-wheat versions with a bewildering array of more than two dozen toppings. I like other pizzas around town better, but Leona's is no slouch and again, the basic ingredients are fresh and good.

As might be expected, pastas are a good bet. All are priced under $7 and many of them are homemade. Pasta orders include soup or salad. There are good cheese-filled manicotti or meat-filled cannelloni, excellent ravioli and baked lasagna. Sides of pasta come with entree orders.

Each day has its specials: spaghetti and shrimp on Sunday, green cappelletti on Monday, etc. The Wednesday garlic chicken disappoints with too little garlic and too much cooking of the poor chicken. Again, this isn't terrible, just slightly off the mark.

Veal dishes, the expensive items on the menu, start with superior-quality veal and careful preparation keeps the meat moist and tender. Unfortunately, all the veal is breaded, egg-battered or smothered under cheese and sauce—not great if you like veal. A simple marsala or piccata should be added to the menu.

Seafood, ribs, grilled pork chops and fried chicken round out the menu. If this sounds like a lot, it is. The menu runs to eight pages.

Dessert includes a good homemade cannoli with a

smooth ricotta cheese filling, better-than-average cheesecake and a brownie-like flourless chocolate cake.

The list of eight wines, evenly divided between red and white, carries one price, an inexpensive $7.99. If you want something a little more expensive, the management invites you to bring your own. And service is friendly. How could you help but like a place like this?

★ LINO'S
Italian

222 W. Ontario St.   266-6159
Hours: Mon–Fri 11 am–midnight, Sat 5 pm to midnight,
        closed Sun
Price range: Moderately expensive
Credit cards: A D M V
Reservations: Accepted
Other: Valet parking

Lino's has improved steadily since it opened. After some inconsistencies, the kitchen has its act together. Physically it hasn't changed much: a bar that's usually busy, depending on the night of the week and who's performing at the piano. Light-colored oak dividers break the white clothed dining room into three section with banquettes and roomy tables.

Since Lino's owners are former city policemen, it is a hangout for politicos, and you can see moving and shaking going on here.

Lino's continues to offer the best calamari in the area— perfectly done with a praiseworthy sauce. The pastas, which have greatly improved, are cooked al dente and the portions are enough for two, especially if they're preceded by the good Italian bread, and tomato, meat and cream sauces are all above-average. The tortellini still has too much nutmeg.

A good house salad comes with the entree, or one can

choose torn romaine salad with a light coating of vinegar and superior-quality olive oil, topped with plentiful chunks of Gorgonzola and a sprinkling of Parmesan cheese.

Skillful handling and high-quality raw ingredients assure the excellence of grilled fish or meats (veal and steak). Chicken brest stuffed with spinach and topped with a rich wine sauce with mushrooms couldn't taste better. The veal scallopini special is too much of a good thing: three 3-inch medaillons of good quality veal under a slice of eggplant, topped with prosciutto, topped again with melted cheese. The simple pan-dripping sauce is understated, but the whole fails to exceed the sum of its parts.

The wine list is Italian and quite reasonable—$8–$14. Portions are large, so desserts probably won't be desired, which is just as well.

While prices don't compare to a friendly neighborhood Italian eatery they aren't bad for a fancy city restaurant. Thus, Lino's is understandably popular.

★ MALLORY'S ON WELLS
American

1400 N. Wells St.   944-5404
Hours: Tues–Sat 11:30 am–11 pm, closed Sun & Mon
Price range: Moderately expensive
Credit cards: A C D M V
Reservations: Accepted
Other: Free parking north of building

CLOSED AT PRESS TIME

The interior has begun to look a bit weary, its tile floor somewhat worn. Shirred fabric runs three-quarters of the way from the ceiling to meet grey/blue paneling with somewhat uneven coloration. Still, some very good food is served here and at a reasonable price.

The room will seat forty. Friendly, attentive servers make

diners feel comfortable and well cared-for, without intruding on privacy and conversations.

Appetizers include excellent soups such as a cream of sorrel, a tangy broth that accurately captures the sorrel flavor, although it could be served hotter. Another good choice of starters is described as garlic sausage, although it tastes more smoky than garlicky. Prettily presented, the rings of sausage, about 2 inches in diameter and three-eights inch thick, are grilled and decorated with strips of yellow and red banana pepper. With a dollop of mustard on the side and red pepper cut to look like a strawberry with "leaves" of parsley, the dish is quite beautiful.

Somewhat limp lettuce mars both the Roquefort and Caesar salads. The Roquefort version has a walnut oil vinaigrette sprinkled with chunks of walnut and pieces of crumbled Roquefort. Seasoned croutons top the Caesar salad, which has traditional dressing heavy on the anchovies.

Cassoulet, a flavorful mix of beans, sausage, ham, duck, lamb and seasonings, suffer from too much salt, but otherwise tastes good. Breast of lamb stuffed with spinach, garlic and egg was a little bit on the gamey side and was tough, with pieces of gristle. However, the stuffing works well with the meat to make it worth ordering. Vegetables such as spaghetti squash, slices of fried sweet potato and red pepper come on the side.

Desserts include good pasteries and cakes, like the chocolate almond dartois, which is not too sweet and is full-flavored if a bit soggy. Pound cake soaked in rum and topped with walnuts turned out moist and good.

If the quality of some of the food isn't exactly top-notch, the pricing isn't exactly out of range either. Mallory's offers good value for reasonably good, imaginative food in a comfortable environment that seems well-suited to a relaxing evening out with friends.

★★ MAMA DESTA'S RED SEA RESTAURANT
Ethiopian

3216 N. Clark St.   935-7561
Hours: Mon 4:30–11 pm, Tues–Sun 11:30 am–11:30 pm
Price range: Inexpensive
Credit cards: A C D M V
Reservations: Accepted
Handicap

Be prepared to enjoy something different at Chicago's first Ethiopian restaurant. The room is plain with green painted floors, formica tables and chairs that don't match. A few prints of Ethiopian scenes hang on the walls. Tropical fish swim in two aquariums at the rear of the restaurant. The atmosphere comes as close to the feel of sitting in the kitchen of someone's home as anything could.

There's a reason there are no utensils on the table. Ethiopian cuisine is the ultimate in messy finger food. Servers thoughtfully provide each diner with extra paper napkins.

When ordering, note two important distinctions. "Wat" dishes are blazing hot, like intense barbecue. "Alitcha" dishes are mild. To experience the full range of flavors, experiment with both in the two different combination platters.

The waiter presents the dishes in a series of small bowls after placing a platter of injera-large, pancake-like bread-on the table. Made from fermented wheat flour, the spongy injera has a sour flavor. The platter of injera forms a foundation upon which the waiter mounds the various specialities. Now comes the fun. A second plate of folded cold injera comes on the side. One tears off a piece of bread from his plate and uses it between the forefinger and thumb to scoop up a bite-sized amounts of food. Most dishes have the consistency of a coarse puree, so eating can become a rather messy affair.

This may sound unattractive, but once you get into the

spirit of things, it seems quite natural. Beef, lamb, vegetable and chicken dishes are cooked with a mix of flavorings that generally includes onions, peppers, herbs and, at times, lemon. Although limited, the variety of tastes in combination with the sour bread makes for an interesting and filling meal.

Few places on Clark can boast prices of $6.95 and less for a full meal. Given the homey atmosphere, pleasant service and unique dining experience, Mama Desta's is a must for anyone serious about ethnic eating.

★★ MANDAR-INN
Chinese

2249 S. Wentworth Ave.   842-4014
Hours: Tues–Thurs 11:30 am–9:30 pm, Fri & Sat 11:30 am–11
      pm, Sun 2–9:30 pm, closed Mon
Price range: Moderately expensive
Credit cards: A   C   D
Reservations: Accepted

Owned by Sharon Jay, ManDar-Inn is refreshingly contemporary, with gray walls, burgundy floors and modern artwork. Keevan Sadock has created a squeaky-clean design a cut- and-a-half above that of most Chinatown restaurants.

A talented kitchen staff prepares a broad selection of offerings and, given notice, will prepare any dish not on the menu. Unfortunately, while some food is very good indeed, some is tamed for western tastes and comes off flat and undistinguished.

In general, appetizers are excellent. Start with the chicken slices in hot sauce—a large mound of cold meat covered with a dark, spicy—or the drunken chicken, moist and marinated in a sherry sauce. The kwoh-te, pan-fried, filled dumplings, far outshine those at most other Chinese restau-

222

rants. So do the fried won ton. "Flaming appetizers"—barbecued ribs, egg rolls, beef kebabs, shrimp toast and rumaki—are more theatre than fine cuisine. Only the shrimp toast and ribs are notable.

With a day's notice, a group of four or more can get a Mongolian fire pot or bird's nest soup, two items not widely available in Chicago. The firepot is a sort of Chinese fondue with marinated meats and vegetables. A meal can be made of the dish, and it's worth ordering for the fun alone. Sizzling rice soup has its own drama, but the broth in this and the "three delicacies" soup need more oomph.

All the dishes here are beautifully presented. The nest is the best part of beef in a nest, a traditional Mandarin dish. It is made of julienned potatoes woven together and deep fried, then filled with sliced beef, mushrooms, pea pods, bamboo shoots and water chestnuts. The sauce fails to tie the varied flavors together. Moo shu pork is delicately seasoned and good. But there is nothing delicate about the spicy Szechuan pork sauteed with potent dried red peppers—an excellent dish. The shrimp in tomato and ginger sauce absolutely falls flat. Smoked tea duck, duck marinated and smoked with tea leaves, is subtle, crisp-skinned, moist and tender. Peking duck also is available.

There can be communication problems with some of the servers, who could be more attentive. Pacing of meals is erratic.

Although reasonably priced, the food here is more expensive than at most other Chinatown restaurants. It is also better, but the ManDar-Inn needs greater consistency as well as resolve to avoid "cooking down" to American tastes.

★ MANDARIN GARDEN
Chinese/Korean

7242 N. Damen Ave.   743-1800

Hours: Mon–Thurs 11:30 am–10 pm, Fri 11:30 am–11 pm,
       Sat & Sun noon–11 pm
Price range: Moderate
Credit cards: A D M V
Reservations: Accepted
Handicap

Knowing how to order helps tremendously here. Too often the Chinese/Korean menu caters to the uninitiated, so the trick is to tell the waiters that you want authentic dishes; then your meal might be cooked by owner Sam Wang, who comes up with some exciting creations.

The large room has some tacky trappings but it is open, bright and clean. A great way to begin the meal is with a selection of cold dishes, best of which is the jellyfish, followed by the cold, fresh abalone. The jellyfish, which resembles clear noodles, is limp but crunchy—a dish that sounds intimidating, but may well be the most accessible of the "exotic" seafood. All seafood here is fresh and good. The cold shrimp appetizer is least interesting. All these can be ordered as a combination.

By all means, try the excellent soups. Three seas soup is a heady broth chock full of fresh fish and shellfish with a few vegetables.

"Fried and Sugar-Seasoned Red Bream" is a lightly battered and deep-fried whole red snapper in a sweet sauce. This is good, but the yellow corvinat, a delicate Chinese fish perfectly cooked, is even better. Chicken with plum sauce is another good choice. The rich homemade sauce puts ordinary pre-packaged varieties to shame. Other decent but less distinctive entrees include beef with oyster sauce and braised shrimp with garlic; standard dishes, nothing out of the ordinary.

Glazed fruits—apple, bananas and lychee nuts—are the main desserts. The fresh fruit comes hot from the kitchen and cools down at the table, ending up with a crisp, sugar coating.

Servers are friendly and personable although they offer little guidance to the many exciting dishes on the massive menu.

★★ MAPLE STREET PIER
Seafood

1 W. Maple St.   266-4810
Hours: Mon–Thurs 5–10:30 pm, Fri & Sat 5–11 pm, lounge
        open until 12:30 am Mon–Thurs, 1 am Fri & Sat,
        closed Sun
Price range: Moderately expensive
Credit cards: A C D M V
Reservations: Accepted
Other: Validated parking in Newberry Plaza Lot

Finally, Arnie Morton seems to have struck the balance of food and theater to make a go of it in a location where a series of restaurants have failed. Opened without much fanfare, this bright, airy eatery packs in diners with good reason.

Like all of the restaurants that have occupied this spot, Maple Street has an interior that is nothing short of spectacular. While few places can match the Shaw's Blue Crab Lounge for sheer feel-at-home comfort, Maple Street Pier succeeds admirably in creating an atmosphere at once casual and sophisticated, uniquely intimate despite its four-level drama.

Inside the entrance, a moderately-sized bar, crowded with waiting customers at popular dining hours, stretches to the right. At the far end is an oyster bar that offers five or more varieties of pristinely fresh oysters as well as clams, crab legs and shrimp.

A wall of natural-finished maple sweeps up from the raw bar to a balcony dining room overlooking the first level. Tall tables with stools dot the bar area. Banquettes flank the wall to the left of the entrance. Behind the bar, stairs lead to the second dining area, also done in maple. Still another dining room lies behind this one.

Not all of the food equals the spectacular interior but the cooking has improved with each visit. The fare is not fancy. Cold offerings from the fresh seafood bar head the appetizer list. Of the hot appetizers, the plump, steamed clams mounded in their own flavorful broth, flecked with onion, taste as if they were just plucked from the sea. Marty's crab cake, available as an appetizer or entree, also pleases with its delicate texture. Not so the clam chowder—thick and chalky, this broth would be banned in Boston.

Only two salads are offered: the Pier salad of Romaine and iceberg lettuce, pine nuts and tiny shrimp, and a rather lackluster cole slaw.

Chilled poached salmon turned out so watery and mushy on one visit it had to be returned to the kitchen. The accompanying dill sauce was good but it could hardly save the dish.

But the blackened redfish more than makes up for the salmon. One of the best versions in town of this Cajun specialty, the fresh New Orleans fish gets a crusty coating of blackened spices that breaks away to reveal fresh, succulent fish. All entrees come with boiled red potatoes, wedges of lime and a bowl of drawn butter. The house specialty, mesquite wood-grilled fish, generally listed on blackboards placed around the dining rooms can be ordered prepared this way. Grilled salmon and swordfish absorb just a hint of nutty flavor from the wood smoke. Lobster lovers will find Maine lobster that comes with clams, mussels, grilled corn, potatoes and cole slaw. Excellent broiled Australian lobster tail also is available.

Dessert offerings are somewhat limited, but the hot fudge brownie will do just fine. It's a big, chewy, chocolatey brownie that diners can make even more outrageous with a selection of toppings such as hot fudge or chocolate sauce, chocolate chip ice cream and whipped cream. The wine list is short but well-selected, with an emphasis on American wines. An excellent David Bruce chardonnay sells for $15, a mid-range price here.

The service is unpolished, but makes no horrendous gaffes. In the case of the soggy salmon, the waitress not only didn't charge for the entree, but upon presenting the check, informed us that the desserts were complimentary.

Maple Street Pier has a way to go before it can stand up to the consistently high quality of the Chestnut Street Grill and Shaw's. But there's no doubt that Morton has finally found a winning combination for this troublesome location if he sticks with the formula that makes Morton's Steak House the best place in town for red meat—keep it simple.

★ ★ ★ MAPLE TREE INN
Cajun/Creole

10730 S. Western Ave.   239-3688
Hours: Mon–Thurs 5–9:30 pm, Fri & Sat 5–10:30 pm, closed
        Sun
Price range: Moderately expensive
Credit cards: M V
Reservations: Accepted for groups of 3 or more, for couples
on Fri & Sat

For some years this Southside, New Orleans-style restaurant went lazily about its business; then it was "discovered," when the Cajun/Creole craze hit. Now getting a reservation can be difficult. But despite its new tremendous popularity, the Maple Tree keeps its wits about it, consistently offering good Cajun and Creole food at attractive prices.

In the summer there's outdoor dining in a garden under the big maple tree after which the restaurant is named. One enters the restaurant proper through the back door, as if entering a friend's kitchen. Indeed, this is a made-over house, a charming, brick former two-flat with an upstairs dining room and a cavelike basement bar. The brightly lighted dining areas, with yellow-and-white-checked wallpaper and random wide-planked floors, have low ceilings and get noisy when packed with diners. The former library, with only four tables, is more intimate. The walls are papered with sheet music and old dictionary pages. The restaurant seats only 48, which can cause long waits, especially on weekends.

A complimentary starter holds diners while they order: a small pate or pickled okra. The menu changes at the whim of the chef and according to availability of ingredients.

The meal gets off to a good start with French bread, sweet butter and muffins—one night corn with cheese, another, sweet potato. The Cajun turtle soup is a heavenly concoction of vegetables and turtle chunks, chewy but not rubbery, in a rich, gumbo-like sauce. A delightful counterpoint is the light cream of mussel soup, with whole mussels rather than pieces. Don't pass up the plate of six oysters Rockefeller or bienville. The oysters are fresh, plump, tender and covered with finely chopped spinach, butter and seasonings. The oysters bienville are baked, covered with a sauce of cream, mushrooms, cheese, shrimp and spices. The owner eases decision-making by providing a combination platter.

Other good appetizers include a genuine andouille sausage, a spicy smoked sausage made from pork, ham and red peppers, imported from New Orleans. Grilled for an appetizer, it is also found in some of the entrees. Crabmeat and shrimp cardinale is a variation on the classic New Orleans crawfish dish (the restaurant serves fresh crawfish in season). Both crab and shrimp are cooked perfectly in a spicy cream sauce. All entrees come with a salad, served with either vinaigrette or remoulade dressing—the former is excellent, the latter, better served on the shrimp.

Catfish lovers will want to come for the fried catfish meuniere pecandine alone: a platter of five large, perfectly fried fish covered with pecans and sauced with a brown meunière (butter, lemon and roux). A chicken gumbo and andouille is a fiery dish that begs to be tasted. The only disappointment was the fresh Rockfish with pimento beurre blanc sauce.

There are only two desserts on the menu, with specials added occasionally. The pecan pie with fresh whipped cream is one of the best anywhere. The pudding part of a bread pudding with bourbon sauce is excellent, but the sauce could use another hit of bourbon. The small wine list is carefully selected and offers good value with most bottles of $20 or less. Service is unpolished, but friendly and helpful. The chef makes the rounds every evening and will help make selections if diners so desire.

The Maple Tree Inn offers one of the best values in town for interesting, well-prepared food. The atmosphere may not be posh, but go for the food and good times.

★ MARY D'S
American

16232 S. Halsted St., Harvey   339-0075
Hours: Mon–Thurs 11 am–11 pm, Fri to midnight, Sat 4 pm–
*   midnight, closed Sun*
Price range: Moderately expensive
Credit cards: A C D M V
Reservations: Accepted
Handicap

This pleasant restaurant has a sort of 1950's modern look with big tables, pre-formica paneling and uniformed waitresses who hustle and bustle their way efficiently around the room.

The two-page menu covers a wide range from fried chicken to steak and seafood. The cooking is more down-home than gourmet, but the meals are filling and well-prepared.

On weekends this popular place gets incredibly busy and there are long waits for a table. A small bar helps ease the pain. The *Tribune* taste-panel visited to sample Mary D's ribs, which seem to be an afterthought on the lengthy menu but are a popular dish here, with good reason. They are exceptionally good, large and meaty with little fat. They were served very hot and had been cooked properly, although the meat does not pull away from the bone as easily as slow-smoked ribs at some other places. For those who like to gnaw, that can be a plus. They had a good, light hickory flavor. The sauce has a tang, but it doesn't make the mouth tingle. The slab comes with nice extras—a green salad rather than the common slaw, fries and bread.

★ EL MATADOR
Mexican

501 S. Bartlett Rd., Schaumburg   289-0700
Hours: Lunch Mon–Fri 11 am–2 pm, Dinner Tues–Sun 5 pm–
*   12:30 am, closed Mon*
Price range: Moderate
Credit cards: A   C   D   M   V
Reservations: Suggested
Handicap

This friendly Mexican place is not easy to find, but once you get there it's easy to like. Manager Roy Casillas has a broad smile and handshake for everyone, and the waiters and busboys are equally attentive. The dining room seats well over 100, so service can get erractic on busy weekends.

But on slower nights, there's no problem.

The large dining room, festooned with piñatas, is packed with red-clothed tables just far enough apart for the staff to pass between them. Despite the candles on each table, this is no place for privacy. On crowded nights the room is loud.

Frozen margaritas, a house speciality, are an excellent way to quell the fire lit by the complimentary bowl of pickled jalapeños, onions and carrots and spicy picante sauce. A mild salsa made with fresh cilantro and a large basket of corn chips also are brought automatically, followed by complimentary soup on all but Fridays and Saturdays.

It's easy to fill up on freebies, but save room—the best is to come. Among the appetizers, red chili con carne is a must for chili lovers; not too spicy, it is great. Four quesadillas (flour tortillas stuffed with melted cheese) with various stuffings are also good, especially the chorizo version.

Entrees have been tamed to satisfy a wider audience, but diners can request more heat from the kitchen or add their own from the table's picante sauce. For meat lovers, good choices include steak or pork a la Mexicana, a sort of Mexican stew in ranchero sauce good enough for dipping with the warm tortillas provided on the side, and banderillas (shish kebob). There are also 12 varieties of enchiladas with two choices of sauce.

Two desserts are offered: a good flan and a grainy chocolate mousse that tastes like cocoa powder mixed into a carton of Cool Whip.

El Matador may not have the best Mexican food in the Chicago area—problems include trying to do too much with a small kitchen—but it is good, and the prices and atmosphere make the place worthwhile for those who live nearby and have a taste for Mexican food.

★★ MEKONG RESTAURANT
Vietnamese

4953 N. Broadway   271-0206
Hours: Mon, Tues, Thurs 10 am–10 pm, Fri 10 am–11 pm,
*   Sat & Sun 9 am–11 pm, closed Wed*
Price range: Inexpensive
Credit cards: M   V
Reservations: Accepted

This family restaurant was designed for Vietnamese immigrants and enjoyed by many others. The decor is nothing to write home about, but the place is clean and the food, especially the Vietnamese specialities, is excellent.

Topping the list is shrimp wrapped in rice paper—an uncooked egg roll filled with crisp lettuce, chopped bean sprouts, onion tops, lemon grass, fresh shrimp and thinly sliced pork. A mild peanut sauce for dipping comes on the side. The Mekong combo soup is outstanding. This originally Mongolian dish—a melange of pork and beef meatballs, sliced pork, squid, mushrooms, cabbage, pork skin and other vegetables—comes in a fire pot with the soup still bubbling.

The bright red barbecued pork meat comes with lettuce, rice noodles, cucumbers, bean sprouts, lemon grass, mint and a stack of rice pancakes. Diners can design their own creations, rolling the selection up in the pancake like an egg roll. The same peanut paste served with the shrimp accompanies these.

Seek out the Vietnamese dishes on the menu. Fried whole white fish with Vietnamese-style sweet and sour sauce is excellent. Presented whole with a garnish of red peppers, black mushrooms and onion, the fresh fish has crisp skin, stays moist inside, and comes in a mild, slightly sweet sauce.

The best of the Chinese-style entrees sampled was sizzling shrimp with vegetables and a slightly sweet sauce. The beef with broccoli is ordinary and dull.

The service is unfailingly polite. However, often nobody clears off the dishes after they're used and long waits can occur between courses. Occasionally orders are forgotten or substituted without warning because of communication problems. At this writing the restaurant's liquor license is on the verge of approval.

If the owner stops making concessions to please what he perceives to be the American palate (nothing too spicy) and concentrates on authentic Vietnamese cuisine, Mekong will be a great asset to the fledgling Argyle Street "New Chinatown."

★ MIMOSA CAFE
Vietnamese

7180 W. Grand Ave.   237-2029
Hours: Tues–Thurs 5:30–9:30 pm, Fri–Sun 5–10 pm, closed
        Mon
Price range: Inexpensive
Credit cards: Not accepted
Reservations: Accepted

Located on the very edge of the city, this tiny, storefront Vietnamese eatery is a bit off the beaten track but offers authentic food at a modest price. The spartan decor, with prefab wood panelling, Formica-topped tables and an open kitchen, is unexciting, but the place is comfortable and exceptionally clean. Forty diners can be crammed into the room but except for weekends the restaurant usually is not crowded. Menu specials are available only on weekends.

The first thing to accept about Vietnamese food is the unusual smell. It comes from *nuoc mam*, a paste or liquid made from salted, fermented anchovies. It is widely used in Vietnamese cooking, which is influenced by Chinese, Indian and French cuisine but unique in itself. *Nuoc mam* replaces salt and takes some getting used to, after which it is indispensable.

Nuoc mam becomes *nuoc cham* when diluted with lemon juice and water and spiked with garlic, sugar, julienne of carrots and bits of red pepper. It comes on the side with many dishes at Mimosa Cafe and adds interest to the excellent egg rolls or Vietnamese pancakes. Many dishes here come with lettuce and other salad fixings and become do-it-yourself affairs. Diners can create their own mix of salad, rolls or sandwiches. Such is the barbecued beef, juicy and tender on a skewer, presented in a basket with salad and rice paper.

A variety of 10 spring rolls is presented in the same vein. The difference between the most expensive of these offerings, two "royal" spring rolls, and the "country" egg rolls, at less than half the price, is that royalty get crab meat in their rolls. It's worth the price. Either way, the excellent rolls come packed with fresh vegetables, shredded meat and shrimp or crabmeat inside a crisp, not too oily skin. The Mimosa pancakes are made from five Oriental flours and chocked full of shrimp, pork or beef and green onions for flavor.

Ordering too much food is easy. Often, one appetizer, a single bowl of soup and one entree shared by two, will suffice. It might help to order the entree after eating the appetizers.

A coastal country, Vietnam makes heavy use of seafood, but because of the French, it also uses beef and at Mimosa, the beef is of high quality. The stir-fried beef in hot sauce with mushrooms and sweet onion is tame but can be spiced up at the table.

Stir-fried chicken with lemongrass and coriander in hot sauce is even better; the tender, juicy chicken comes with mushrooms and large pieces of bamboo shoot. Chicken nugget in sweet and sour sauce is as ordinary as it sounds but is pretty good. The sizzling fish platter should also please.

Desserts are mundane except for the flan cake Parisian style. Specials are available over weekends. Out of the way, maybe, but worth the trip.

★ MIOMIR'S SERBIAN CLUB
Serbian

2255 W. Lawrence Ave.   784-211
Hours: Sun–Fri 5 pm–2 am, Sat 5 pm–3 am
Price range: Moderate
Credit cards: M   V
Reservations: Necessary

Miomir's is neither exclusively Serbian nor a club. It is Chicago's unique, international supper club, where for more than 10 years the gypsy-inspired cabaret has delighted diners out for an old-fashioned good time. Here, musicians play, guests sing and dance and Jovan Mihaelovich enchants with his violin. The plentiful, reasonably priced food doesn't hurt, but people come here mostly for the fun. Come in jeans or evening dress. Either way Miomir's welcome is warm and charming.

When it is not crowded, the barn-like dining room has little charm. But when the club teams with people, the decor becomes secondary to the revelry, lubricated by **slivovitz**, the Serbian plum brandy. But watch out, the punch sneaks up on you.

Meals begin with complimentary appetizers, a plate of chopped liver, *kajmak*—a fermented milk/cheese spread— and a Russian egg salad. Given the portions to follow, no other appetizer is needed but if you must, sample *ajvar*. Said to be good for long life, this appetizer arrives as a grilled pureed eggplant with sweet pepper and celery in olive oil. It's excellent spread over the good crusty bread. A Serbian salad—a good mix of tomatoes, onions, cucumbers and cheese—is available, but save room for the courses to come.

No seafood dish appears on the menu, but one can be specially ordered with 48 hours' notice. The family-style dinner provides a wide sampling of the heavy Eastern European fare. It includes, besides appetizers, royal moussaka, chicken paprikash, goulash, cevapcici, raznici, noodles and a choice of dessert. The best bet is the royal moussaka, richly flavored layers of eggplant, ground meat, eggs, tomato and onion. The chicken paprikash has a nice flavor but can be dry and overdone. The goulash, however, is as good as any found in the area. Cevapcici, a sausage-shaped meatloaf of veal and beef has a mild flavor, but is a tad dry. Raznici, a shishkebob of pork tenderloin, is perfectly cooked and moist.

Bekca snicla is described as imperial wiener schnitzel. The portion is imperial: two huge pieces of good quality veal shamefully overcooked and dry. Sarma, cabbage stuffed with veal, beef and rice served in its broth, has a wonderfully delicate flavor. Muckalica, big chunks of beef and veal, is touched with too little of the wonderful sauce flecked with fresh coriander.

If anyone has room for dessert, the Serbian crepe, palacinke, is probably the best bet. The baklava has tough puff pastry, but the filling is very rich with lots of honey and chopped nuts. Serbian coffee is thick and strong, a fitting end to a heavy meal.

Waitresses want their customers to have a good time. They may chide if plates aren't cleaned, but greatly add to the enjoyment of the evening here.

★ ★ ★ ★ **MORTON'S**
Steaks

1050 N. State in Newberry Plaza   266-4820
Hours: Mon–Thurs 5:30–11 pm, Fri & Sat 5:30–11:30 pm,
*   closed Sun*
Price range: Expensive
Credit cards: A C D M V
Reservations: Accepted until 7:00 pm

Healthful eating is the trend, but when you crave good old red meat, Morton's delivers. It's expensive, but its steaks are some of the best anywhere. When you find Morton's inside the Newberry Plaza behind an inconspicuous door, the room is large and pleasant with Art Deco appointments. The room is usually busy and can be noisy. The tables are too close together for an intimate evening, but then steak generally isn't the stuff of intimate meals. The service is professional, courteous and efficient.

Waiters roll up carts of raw meat for inspection: samples include porterhouse steak, New York strip, veal chop and fresh vegetables. The cuts are huge, aged, marbled and tempting. Only bread and a choice of potatoes (a highly recommended circle of hash browns, easily shared by two or a big baked potato) come with the entrees. All other choices such as steamed vegetables, salad or occasional specials such as asparagus are a la carte. Again, portions are large.

All salads are good but the Ceasar is outstanding. Fresh oysters on the half shell and snowcrab claws make excellent appetizers.

Steak is the main point at Morton's but an excellent lobster, seafood specials and a quality, thick veal chop are also served. The steaks come cooked precisely as ordered, crisply charred outside, juicy within. They are trimmed of excess fat, tender and flavorful. The kitchen will also divide the nearly two pounds of superb beef (without batting an eye) to be shared by two.

If you still want dessert, there's good but not great cheesecake and a decent souffle. The wine list is extensive and contains several good, reasonably priced wines.

★ MURPHY'S BLEACHERS
All American

3655 N. Sheffield Ave.   *281-5356*
Hours: Mon–Fri 11:30–2 am, Sat 11:30–3 am, Sun 11:30–2
         am
Price range: Inexpensive
Credit cards: A   M   V
Reservations: First come, first serve
Handicap

The Cubs have started selling hamburgers at Wrigley Field, but they'll have to go farther than you would from your center field seat to match Murphy's burgers.

Okay, this is a bar more than a restaurant. A bar across the street from the ballpark packed with fans before and after the games when the Cubs play a home game. Still the burgers ($3.75 with or without cheese) here are pretty darned good.

They're said to be half-pound burgers, but appear to be a little smaller than most of the same billing. Nevertheless the charbroiled flavor is good. They come on a sesame bun with lettuce, onion, pickles and fries that are somewhat mushy, but will help stave off the effects of a victory celebration or attempts to drown the sorrow of defeat. (The drinks are cheap.) Hot dogs, sausage and other grilled items also are offered. But a burger and the libation of your choice are the real order of the day here.

★ ★ ★ NEW ROSEBUD CAFE
Italian

1500 W. Taylor St.   *942-1117*
Hours: Mon–Thurs 11 am–11 pm, Fri & Sat 11 am–12 pm,
         closed Sun
Price range: Moderate
Credit cards: A   C   D   M   V

The Rosebud lived quietly for a while on Taylor Street in the old Southern Italian district. Then it was discovered and packed with diners. When that happens, often the quality of the food served at the new "in" restaurant declines precipitously. In this case, the quality of the food continues to excel. However, getting at that food often takes some doing.

It seems the owners of this restaurant have trouble saying no—so rarely are reservations requests denied. However, when diners arrive they often face waits of an hour or more even with reservations, but this may be one of the few places around where the wait is worth the hassle. The food is terrific.

A bustling bar area holds waiting diners. In the dining rooms wall sconces and chandeliers bounce soft lights off the mirrored and paneled walls. When it is packed, the room gets noisy, but that's really part of the fun in this Italian family-style restaurant.

The plain, straightforward menu doesn't look like much. And while everything on it is expertly prepared, those in the know let the servers guide them to the best of the daily specials. Here lie the real treasures.

Exquisite mussels marinara, plump mussels under a blanket of red sauce made from fresh tomatoes and parsley, might be a special starter. Also worthy of sampling among the appetizers are calamari, baked clams, garlicky scampi, deep fried zucchini, super sausage and peppers or roasted red peppers.

Pastas equal the appetizers for quality and portions are large, so pastas can easily be shared by two. Creamy fettucini Alfredo cooked al dente and richly sauced rises above the average, bland versions of this classic dish. Tomato sauce, flecked with onion and prosciutto with white wine, has great flavor and works well on any of the pasta offerings. Linguine with clams or shrimp, broccoli and garlic in a simple butter sauce will not disappoint.

Dinner salads of leaf lettuce with a peppery, anchovy-based dressing come with entrees. Those entrees live up to the quality of the starters.

Veal, the cornerstone of any Italian restaurant, is high quality here. Chicken Vesuvio turns out well, as do fresh seafood dishes.

Portions are so large that desserts probably won't be necessary. They are a sort of afterthought here anyway and don't live up to the quality of the rest of the meal. The wine list offers a good selection of Italians at moderate prices. Service is attentive, but the preparation from scratch takes time so diners probably will experience pauses between courses. These pauses will be welcome opportunities to relax and digest some of what has gone before. No matter how crowded the place gets, diners already seated can linger over their meals as long as they wish.

★ ★ NICK'S FISHMARKET
Seafood

1 First National Plaza   621-0200
Hours: Mon–Fri 11:30 am–3 pm, Mon–Thurs 5:30–11:30 pm,
*   Fri & Sat 5:30 pm–midnight, closed Sun*
Price range: Expensive
Credit cards: A   C   D   M   V
Reservations: Recommended
Handicap

People call Nick's a seafood restaurant, but I like to call it a service restaurant. It is the service more than the cuisine that makes this place something special. Nowhere in the area are treated diners more like queens and kings. Even those who aren't regulars get royal treatment and regulars get the works.

A place designed for business, with high, private booths and plenty of space between the white-clothed tables, Nick's also has its own sense of romance. Dark burgundy leather upholstery exudes sensual power. And every diner is his or her own boss with dimmers that control the lighting overhead for each booth so the atmosphere can be as bright or as dark as the situation demands. Telephones will be brought to tables if requested.

Nicholas was one of the first to bring fresh seafood to Chicago. He did it when seafood was relatively inexpensive. Customers paid for the service, but paid much less then they do today. Now entrees average more than $20 each. Still, Nick's seafood will match most of the area's best.

Appetizers include excellent shrimp or crab cocktails, fresh oysters and clams and seafood crepes. Preparation is straight-forward and with the freshest of ingredients, so how could you lose?

Main courses include many unusual offerings such as Hawaiian mahi-mahi, sauteed and topped with mushrooms, tomato, zucchini and onions. Abalone, salmon, trout, swordfish... a huge variety of seafood is offered broiled, sauteed and baked. Careful handling of the fish and of the preparation ensures that dishes turn out well. Best bets are dishes with simple saucing such as the good, tangy hollandaise, rather than more complicated dishes where the essential goodness of the fish can be lost under too many "extra" ingredients.

Desserts include fresh fruits, good New York style cheesecake and pastries. The wine list is as expensive as it is extensive.

The food is fine, but the attentive service and atmosphere are what make Nick's a Chicago institution worth visiting.

241

★ NIERMAN'S
Continental

833 E. 158th St., Dolton, IL   841-8980
Hours: Lunch Mon–Fri 11 am–3 pm, Dinner Mon–Thurs 5–
*   10:30 pm, Fri & Sat 5–11:30 pm, Sun 1–6 pm*
Price range: Moderately expensive
Credit cards: A   C   D   M   V
Reservations: Accepted
Other: Valet parking on weekend

Nierman's is one of the brightest, classiest suburban
eateries. The food won't set off any fireworks, but the restaurant does offer good, solid cooking based on fresh ingredients, at fairly reasonable price.

A bar is on the right of the entrance and straight ahead is
the dining room, divided into three sections. The room reflects the chef's Florida background with a pastel theme that
is bright and sunny, yet cozy. Peach-colored tablecloths
grace the large tables, which are flanked by comfortable
padded chairs. A large, back-lit, stained-glass ceiling brightens the middle of the room.

Few outstanding dishes come from this kitchen, but nothing terrible happens either. Appetizers include an ordinary
baked escargot and mushrooms Rockefeller. Better is the
scampi, three butterfield jumbo shrimp baked in white wine,
garlic and herbs with a lemon-onion sauce, which can also
be ordered as a main course. A choice of house salad or
soup comes with entrees. The salad is ordinary: the soup is
better.

Cream of mussel soup and Key West conch soup are always available and good. The clean, plump, fresh mussels
swim in a pleasant broth sweetened with heavy cream and
butter. The conch chowder mixes tiny bits of conch with onions, carrots, peppers and potato in a spicy broth.

Nierman's menu claims its seafood, imported from all

over the world, "will be the best you ever had." The offerings don't quite live up to the boast, but most turn out well and they are surely fresh. Cooked to perfection, grilled salmon is served simply, but effectively, with hollandaise. Lightly cooked carrots and green beans come along with sliced, herbed potatoes. Similar vegetables come with all entrees. The red snapper almondine was moist, fresh and good— although overwhelmed by almonds and hollandaise topping. Sauteed with artichoke bottoms, mushrooms and fresh lime butter, chicken breast Rachel with tender, moist chicken, served on a bed of rice, makes one of the better entree choices. Moullard duck breast doesn't fare so well with its overwhelming sweet sauce. The nearly plate-sized, three-quarter-inch English cut of prime rib is very good. Other a la carte offerings include well-prepared fresh asparagus and a respectable Caesar salad.

Desserts provide an intense hit of sugar to end the meal. Ice cream cake Violet tops layers of vanilla, chocolate and strawberry ice cream—separated by thin chocolate cookie wafers—with "Elmer's gold brick" (A hardened milk-chocolate sauce) and fresh raspberry sauce. One of the best offerings, Gram's cheesecake, is a cross between the dense New York-style and fluffier Chicago-style cakes topped with a good, fresh strawberry sauce.

One of Nierman's great assets is the concerned and personable service, which makes diners feel extremely comfortable and well-cared for in every way.

★★ THE 95TH
American

John Hancock Center, 95th Floor   787-9596
Hours: Lunch Mon–Fri 11:30 am–2:30 pm, Dinner Sun–Thurs
*   5:30–10:15 pm, Fri & Sat 6–11:15 pm, brunch Sat &*
*   Sun 11 am–2:30 pm*
Price range: Expensive

Credit cards: A C D M V
Reservations: Recommended

One of the questions restaurant reviewers are asked most often is where one should go for a romantic evening of wine and food. The answer varies according to what one considers romantic, a highly personal matter. However, for its majestic view of the city, creative cuisine and sheer power setting, The 95th has to be one contender.

In the past only tourists and those hungry for a magnificent view went to the John Hancock Center's 95th. Today, you can also go there for excellent food, although, like the chandeliers on a windy night, the quality can swing precariously away from perfection. For the price (no less than $100 for a full dinner for two with wine), one expects complete excellence. To gain a higher rating, the 95th must consistently deliver.

A prix-fixe dinner for $35 allows diners to sample a wide selection of items on the regular menu and definitely represents the best value. The dinner includes appetizer, seafood course, sorbet, entree, salad, dessert and coffee. Offerings range from creative combinations such as steamed salmon with spinach, grapefruit and orange in parsley sauce to more standard offerings such as beef tenderloin with tarragon mustard sauce. A prix-fixe lunch at $13.50 offers even greater value.

Menu offerings change with the seasons, so some of the dishes mentioned here may no longer be offered.

Among the appetizers, the grilled bratwurst with cabbage and apples is excellent. Other offerings include such temptations as bay scallops, broccoli and celery root mousse; lime dressing, trout and sturgeon caviar; New York foie gras sauteed with chanterelles, red onion and pine nuts with cider sauce. The bib lettuce, warm brie and black walnut salad is simple and elegant.

Entrees include trout sauteed with watercress, broccoli,

cauliflower and red onions with lemon sauce; grilled sword-fish with pine nuts and red pepper butter; medallions of pork sauteed with cabbage, pears and brandied raisins in a gewurztraminer sauce.

The combinations often sound intriguing and most work. However, at times the experimentations fall short of their intended mark. Nothing ever really tastes bad, but sometimes a $20 entree tastes like it ought to cost $7.95.

Desserts include souffles, pastries and ice creams. Meals are complemented by one of the best wine lists to be found in the area. However these wines can add immeasurably to the cost of a meal. Service is careful and attentive, befitting the prices and the setting.

★★ ON THE TAO
Chinese

1218 W. Morse Ave.   743-5955
Hours: Tues–Sun 5–11 pm, closed Mon
Price range: Moderate
Credit cards: M   V
Reservations: Recommended

On the Tao lacks the spicy zing found in Chicago's better Szechwan and Hunan restaurants but it is good at what it does, namely Cantonese cuisine, with the addition of some of the chef's original twists. Its unique brand of cooking is among the best compared to other Cantonese and even Mandarin restaurants in and around the city. Chef K.G. Chan, a Cantonese who has traveled throughout China, approaches cooking with classic clarity that preserves the ingredients' basic characters.

This simple approach to food is reflected in the decor. The restaurant is divided into four rooms. The front door opens to a comfortable bar and to the left are the two main dining rooms. At the rear is a small dining room for private parties.

245

Appetizers are a stunning start to any meal here. There's not a bad choice, from the coop salad—a mix of lettuce, green onions, carrots and cornish hen in a sesame oil dressing that is cool and tastes great—to the crackling skin hen or the skewered lamb, an unusual offering of tender, bite-sized chunks of lamb marinated in curry, sesame, ginger and soy sauce. Also good are the spring rolls—light, full of fresh ingredients, tasty and not greasy—and the soups—chicken or hot and sour.

There are nightly specials, often the most exciting and creative dishes found at this restaurant. The quail in a nest is excellent. The perfectly cooked, slightly gamey quail sits atop an interesting bean thread nest. On the regular menu, one of the best entrees is imperial veal. Good quality veal filets are accompanied by snow peas, bok choy, mushrooms and ginger. The crunchy chicken, diced chicken with vegetables and walnuts, is a perfect example of letting all of the natural flavors mingle and complement each other. The sauce is light too, not heavily thickened. Shrimp in black bean sauce is also good, although unexciting. It is a puree of pork, black beans, eggs, green onions and garlic with fresh shrimp. Shrimp with straw mushrooms and tofu is not as hot as the menu claims. Those who want spicier dishes may ask for a bowl of chili sauce.

The wine list is limited but moderately priced and there's not a bad wine on this carefully selected list. No fortune cookies here, or lychees either. However, there are unbelievably good fruit sorbets (cantaloupe) and cheesecake (blueberries).

It's an eclectic mix, but one that works.

PAGO PAGO

Chinese/Polynesian
Rating: Fair

Three locations:
227 W. Jackson Blvd.   922-6686
Hours: Mon–Fri 11 am–9 pm, Sat 11 am–7 pm, closed Sun

316 S. Wabash Ave.   922-1491
Hours: Mon–Sat 11 am–9 pm, closed Sun

122 N. Wells St.   263-1850
Hours: Mon–Fri 11 am–9 pm, closed Sat & Sun
Price range: Moderate
Credit cards: A M V
Reservations: Accepted
Handicap

Every restaurant must find its audience and define its purpose in order to gain some measure of success. Pago Pago probably wouldn't top anyone's list of places to go and see. On the other hand, it successfully serves its south Loop audience. Its niche: surprisingly good food at low prices for the area, a service to office workers as well as conventioneers on a budget.

Pago Pago doesn't look too promising from the outside with its bamboo-covered windows. The down-at-the-heels decor continues inside and the stained menu with so many items crossed off doesn't inspire confidence.

Surprisingly, however, someone in the kitchen knows what he or she is doing. The ingredients are fresh and the saucing light. Careful preparation ensures that dishes turn out well.

This, plus excellent service and reasonable prices, makes Pago Pago a rare find in the Loop. Not a place worth going out of your way to visit, but a good place to know about in case hunger strikes when you're within shouting distance.

★ THE PALM
Steak

181 E. Lake Shore Dr. in the Mayfair Regent Hotel
944-0135
Hours: Mon–Fri 11:30 am–10:45 pm, Sat 5–10:45 pm, closed
Sun
Price range: Expensive
Credit cards: A C D M V
Reservations: Accepted
Handicap

For its steak or lobster, The Palm probably deserves another star, maybe two. But woe be unto women who choose the dine here on business or for pleasure. Sexual equality hasn't yet reached this restaurant.

One afternoon, although two women were honoring their reservation on time, the maitre d' allowed that he had no tables available. When the women protested, the maitre d' unceremoniously led them and their male companion to a room at the back of the bar where no other diners were seated. All the while, the men in the dining room seemed to be enjoying themselves.

Good steaks and chops hover around $20 in price. Hardly cheap, and while well-prepared, the meat here doesn't rival Morton's, Eli's or even Gene and Georgetti's. Lobster is as good here as anywhere and costs roughly $11 a pound.

Portions are huge, so order accordingly. Vegetables come a la carte, as do excellent french fried onion rings and potatoes. Try the baked clams or raw oysters for starters.

Dessert is simply unnecessary. A good wine list offers no

bargains and more than a few bottles are priced as high as $100.

The atmosphere is clubby, with an open, rather noisy dining room, tin ceilings, sawdust on the floor and caricatures on the walls. Service is warm and friendly, at least for regulars and men. However, we advise women to let The Palm know that men aren't the only ones who spend money dining out these days.

★ PANDA'S
Chinese

3200 N. Lake Shore Dr.   935-0300
Hours: Mon–Thurs 4:30–11 pm, Fri & Sat 4:30 pm–midnight,
    Sun 4:30–10 pm
Price range: Moderate
Credit cards: A C D M V
Reservations: Accepted
Handicap

Although not Chicago's best Chinese restaurant, Panda's is far from the worst; yet customers rarely find their way there.

Location is a big part of Panda's problem. Since it is housed in a room on the mezzanine level of the Harbor House condominium building that has seen at least three previous restaurants come and go (including Chef Alberto's), only the most observant restaurant groupie would note its existence.

If only because it is one of Chicago's few Chinese restaurants with no hint of red paint, Chinese lanterns or black-laquered booths, Panda's deserves a try. Inside, white-clothed tables complete with candles offer views of General Philip Henry Sheridan in Lincoln Park.

Of course, elegance has its price. Two or more diners can save a few bucks by ordering the prix fixe dinner that includes soup, appetizer, choice of entree and dessert.

249

The fact that none of the service staff seems to have a trace of Oriental blood has its advantages and disadvantages. Waiters speak and understand their native tongue—English—but they have little knowledge of the food. The best one waiter could do when asked to describe a dish was to say that the sauce is "light." Indeed, that seemed to be the standard response to questions about any dish offered.

Dumpling devotees have good reason to persevere. The object of their devotion—either steamed or panfried with the traditional seasoned soy and vinegar sauce—is superb. Greaseless egg rolls are a cut above average, and sesame shrimp toast, crisp on the outside and moist on the inside, are noteworthy.

Beware the fried won tons. A magnifying glass would make it easier to find the stingy flecks of dried-out meat.

You know the rest: seafood, beef, pork, poultry, vegetable and tofu entrees. Although the menu warns that "hot" means "fiery," don't believe it. Hong shao, rather strong-flavored sliced fish topped with Chinese vegetables, is billed as hot, but turns out just slightly spicy. Then again, the slightly sweet twice-cooked pork—tender, shredded pork with vegetables—could ignite a four-alarm fire.

Although Panda's chef, David Lee—an alumnus of Lan's and Dee's—doesn't dazzle with creativity, he serves up fresh ingredients well-prepared, with a minimum of bells and whistles.

★ PAPA MILANO
Italian

951 N. State St.   787-3710
Hours: Mon–Thurs 11:30 am–9:15 pm, Fri 11:30 am–10:15
*   pm, Sat noon–10:15 pm, Sun 1–9:15 pm*
Price range: Moderate
Credit cards: A   C   D
Reservations: Accepted for parties of six or more

Papa Milano's is a neighborhood place in one of Chicago's most interesting and diverse neighborhoods. One might see Oprah Winfrey sitting at a table next to a '60s-style street person. This popular, informal Italian eatery attracts all kinds, who come in droves for good home-style cooking at moderate prices. Waits can reach 30 minutes and longer because the restaurant seats only about 40.

The traditional Italian fare is better than most found downtown. Papa's claims to have "famous sauce" and it is good—luckily, because the same sauce is basic in easily half the dishes. Don't look for much help from the servers; though friendly, they tend to be of the "everything here is good" variety. When pressed, they will make a recommendation, but not necessarily a good one. Portions are huge, so if you want a pasta and entree, it's best to share the pasta with another.

Scungille (sea snails or conch) salad stars as the most unusual dish. Slightly tough, the conch is marinated in Italian dressing. Also good are the soups, especially the scarola and a rich chicken broth. The antipasto is boring with its mundane selection of good sausages and typical greens. To get aged provolone on this plate requires a separate order. Don't bother.

Spaghetti, mostaccioli, linguine and ravioli play to a variety of variations on the same theme here, many including the "famous sauce." Nothing stands out nor greatly disappoints. A reasonably good thin crust pizza is very popular with the regulars. The crust remains crisp and flaky under generous toppings.

The quality of the veal is not the city's best, but compares favorably with the average neighborhood Italian restaurant's. Again, nothing is creative, but the chef takes care with the preparations. The lasagna, baked with the "famous sauce," is a bit too cheesy, although the riccota is excellent. Eggplant parmagiana doesn't fare quite so well, with its list-

251

less, soggy texture. Potato gnocchi, made daily, is unusually light, digestible and good. These come under a layer of "the sauce." That traditional standby, chicken Vesuvio, arrives steaming in olive oil and tastes better than it looks. Flavorful wedges of browned potato come with the half chicken. All entrees come with a plain house salad.

The limited dessert offerings—spumoni, cannoli, tortoni—are all good but ordinary. Not that dessert is needed, given the portions. Only five wines are available, none exactly wonderful, but all inexpensive.

★ PARTHENON
Greek

314 S. Halsted St.   726-2407
Hours: Daily 11–1:30 am
Price range: Moderate
Credit cards: A C D M V
Reservations: Recommended
Handicap

Despite a facelift, exceedingly friendly service and reasonable prices, the Parthenon's food cannot command consistent praise. Nevertheless, it still provides fodder to fuel debates about Chicago's best Greek food. The restaurant itself is quieter and classier-looking than it used to be. Greek music no longer blares from a jukebox, tasteful stained-wood trim sets off the dining rooms and old photographs hang on the walls. The formica-topped tables are too close together but they and the chairs are big enough for comfort.

The Parthenon claims to have created saganaki, the breaded and fried kasseri cheese drenched with Metaxa and flamed at tableside, but it's become more show than taste here. After torching, the incinerated cheese comes out rubbery and with a processed taste. Cheese pies, a mixture of Greek cheese wrapped in filo and baked, have a nicely flavored if skimpy filling. However, they turn out soggy and greasy. Skordalia, a potent puree of potatoes with a heady dollop of garlic is listed as a side dish but is good enough to be ordered separately. Tzatziki (cucumber-yogurt salad), also works nicely. Taramosalata, a creamy, almost mousse-like dip of roe, has excellent taste and texture.

The standard Greek salad is just that. The Greek village salad is similar, with onions substituted for lettuce. Both come simply but effectively dressed in quality olive oil with vinegar and oregano.

Whole lambs roasted on spits over an open grill in the front window foreshadow some of the best eating on this menu. The roast loin of lamb is fork-tender and temptingly mild. The broiled red snapper is mushy but otherwise good with its coating of olive oil, lemon and oregano. Chicken kapama—chicken simmered in tomatoes, herbs and wine—tastes fine but is cooked dry with an unsupportive sauce. Much better is the gyros—moist and full bodied—the best of its class. Rice pilaf or roast potatoes or both accompany most of the entrees—neither is great. The dolmades is too dry. The pastitsio lacks the custardlike top layer of bechamel sauce that gives much needed moisture. Best is the moussaka, a perfectly seasoned cake of eggplant, meat sauce and cheese layers.

Galaktobouriko—filo filled with custard and baked in a syrup of sugar and honey—will end a meal well here. The baklava is not bad either. The wine list, typical of most of Greek Town restaurants', is reasonably priced from $6.50-$9.95. Avoid the unlabeled, uncorked bottles of roditis (red) and retsina (resin flavored white) in favor of the more expensive wines opened at the table.

Parthenon remains a fun, reasonably priced place for a decent meal.

★★ PATTAYA
Thai

114 W. Chicago Ave.   944-3753
Hours: Mon–Fri 11:30 am–10 pm, Sat & Sun 4:30–10 pm
Price range: Moderate
Credit cards: A C D M V
Reservations: Accepted
Handicap

Named after a picturesque resort town outside of Bangkok, this comfortable little restaurant offers city dwellers the opportunity to experience Thailand through its complex culinary treasures.

One of the new breed of Thai restaurants with white-clothed tables, clean, uncluttered decor and full bar service, Pattaya probably offers the best-rounded combination of food, service and ambiance of any of the downtown Thai restaurants. Careful preparation and attention to detail assures consistent quality.

Start with good satay or spring rolls. While nothing startling appears on this menu, none of the traditional Thai dishes disappoint. Be sure to ask about specials, which are sometimes available.

Complex soups win raves, especially the chicken and seafood versions. Curries tend to be on the mild side, but should please curry lovers.

Servers usually ask how hot to make the entrees. Hot means fiery here so act accordingly. Unlike many Thai restaurants that also serve mild Chinese dishes, most of the offerings here are truly Thai, but plenty of mild dishes are available.

Although not cheap by Thai restaurant standards, Pattaya offers excellent value for a restaurant so near the central business district and shopping areas. This pleasant restaurant deserves its popularity.

★ PERIWINKLE
American

2511 N. Lincoln Ave.   *883-9797*
*Hours: Mon–Thurs noon–11 pm, Fri noon–1 am, Sat 9:30–1
    am, Sun 9:30–11 pm*
Price range: Moderate
Credit cards: A D M V
Reservations: Accepted for parties of five or more
Handicap

Sometimes location kills a place. Other times it makes it. For example, Periwinkle, always a great coffeehouse with its more than 30 varieties of coffee and tea, casual chic, pleasant decor and moderate prices, survived an initially disastrous attempt to become a good restaurant. Perhaps it was the outdoor summer dining that kept people coming back for dinner as well as for coffee—but until recently, the food definitely was not the attraction. Gradually, the food has improved. However, inconsistency still plagues the kitchen. For example, on one visit the hommos turns out smooth and full flavored, on the next it exudes rivers of oil. Sometimes the puff pastry turns out a gooey, doughy mess, other times it's perfect.

A good bet includes the slightly spicy creole with plentiful bay scallops, shrimp and chunks of fish all properly cooked in a complementary sauce. The pastas, when cooked properly, offered some of the best, most creative alternatives on the menu with unusual sauces that often taste as good as they sound. In addition, the fresh fish specials are generally good. The saucing sometimes needs more flavor but the fish is fresh and well-prepared. The roast Long Island duck is crisp-skinned, moist inside, with a good apricot-ginger sauce and great baked apple and red cabbage alongside.

Several salads can be ordered as entrees. The Periwinkle salad—hearts of palm, avocado, walnuts, artichoke hearts,

leaf lettuce, red peppers, tomato slices, carrots, olives—
works handsomely, as does the sweet curried chicken salad.
A simple house salad comes with entrees. Portions are generous, given the moderate price.

The wine list features a narrow selection of American,
French and Italian wines, priced from under $10 to about
$30. Most of the wines are also available in half-bottles.
Save room for dessert. While the orange truffle cake tastes
like it came from a boxed mix, other cakes provide good reasons to linger with a pot of the gourmet coffee brews. Cho-
cophiles are in luck; good are a moist, rich flourless cake
and a creamy chocolate cheesecake with chocolate crumb
crust. The gooey, sweet macadamia nut tart with its
shortbread-like shell or orange carrot cake should please
others.

The food remains unspectacular but there is hope, and a
great location.

★★★★ LE PERROQUET
French

70 E. Walton St.   944-7990
Hours: Lunch Mon–Fri noon–2 pm, Dinner Mon–Sat 6–10
      pm, closed Sun
Price range: Expensive
Credit cards: A   C   D
Reservations: Necessary
Handicap

Restrained and refined, Le Perroquet continues in the
tradition established by Jovan Treboyevic when he opened
this restaurant/salon. In 1984 Treboyevic sold the restaurant
to Jean-Pierre Nespoux, his maitre d' of 12 years. Nespoux
has maintained the quality of both cuisine and service.

People complain that Le Perroquet servers are condescending and rude. The service is dignified, reserved in a

French sort of way, and opinionated—that is, a waiter may suggest that an appetizer selection may be too heavy to go well with the entree the diner has selected. One can take offense at such suggestions or accept them and see what alternatives the server might recommend instead.

The room has its own dignity. Semi-tropical murals brighten the room with its curtained windows overlooking Walton, white-clothed tables with orange and turquoise stripes and caricatures of parrots. Banquettes line the outer walls of the rooms. Mirrors allow discreet views of who's who among the evening's diners.

Lunch offers a tremendous bargain here, and often the room is not completely booked at lunch time. At night dinners from the fixed price menu cost $42.50, and are worth every penny. Prix fixe lunches cost less than half and offer many of the same dishes.

The printed menu remains constant and contains some great dishes. However, the daily specials usually offer the greatest temptations.

Start with one of the extremely delicate yet full-flavored vegetable mousses with fresh shellfish or a puff pastry with vegetables and seafood. Rich, velvety sauces, usually butter-based, support these dishes with excellence. Or try the steamed mussels in a calvados cream sauce. Lowly mussels seem fit for royalty in this simple but exquisite dish.

Grilled or poached fish, game birds such as pigeon and white, tender veal with creative light sauces will please as entrees. These come with an appropriate starch as well as lightly cooked vegetables on the side.

Salads and a cheese course follow the entrees and precede desserts. If necessary, skip the salad in favor of the desserts here. The floating island is a house tradition and worth saving room for. Diners can select a sampler of several different nightly pastries offered at tableside from a cart. For an extra charge a heavenly souffle can be substituted for the desserts on the cart.

Le Perroquet has many detractors, possibly because it stands for something in a time when most restaurants don't. Whether or not its style is to one's liking, no serious eater should miss the opportunity to visit this restaurant.

★★ PHILANDER'S
American

1120 Pleasant Ave., Oak Park   848-4250
Hours: Mon–Thurs 4 pm–1 am, Fri & Sat 4 pm–2 am, closed
*   Sun*
Price range: Moderately expensive
Credit cards: A C D M V
Reservations: Recommended

Although the construction is modern, Philander's reaches for a turn-of-the-century atmosphere with lots of darkly stained wood, brass and huge reproductions of photographs that depict Oak Park scenes in the early 1900s. Indeed, these fascinating photos, taken by Philander Barclay, lend the restaurant its name.

Healthy portions, reasonable prices and friendly service make this a fine spot for an evening out. To the right of the entrance in the front of the room, live music—generally vintage '30s and '40s swing—sets the tone in the bar and lounge. When the place is busy, which it often is, the noise level can be high.

Seafood dominates the menu, but you may want to come here for the fresh oysters alone. No place offers more variety, with up to 15 different types of oysters available at the peak of the season, from the tiny, quarter-sized Olympias to bluepoints, Chathams, Marylands, Quilcenes and Wellfleets. A selection of one of each can be ordered. All of the oysters are good and cold. Some of them are excellent, especially the minuscule Olympias from Washington State that taste unlike any other oyster.

Oyster lovers easily might make a meal of these alone. However, many other selections tempt as well. Among the hot appetizers, as might be expected, oysters Rockefeller excel. So do the baked clams, garlicky snails and mushrooms stuffed with crab meat.

Like most seafood restaurants these days, New Orleans dishes get top billing here. In general, these preparations, including a crisply coated blackened fish, turn out well. Other good entree choices include fresh Maine lobster, bouillabaisse big enough for two to share, barbecued shrimp (also available as an appetizer) and Dover sole. A changing variety of fresh broiled fish also turns out well.

For non-seafood devotees, steaks and chops round out the menu. Carefully prepared, the red meat almost matches the seafood despite the fact that seafood is this restaurant's real reason for being. A good, fresh house salad and lightly cooked seasonal vegetables come with entrees.

The impressive wine list offers excellent variety, but its allure can rapidly add to the price of a meal. Nightly specials of wine by the glass allow diners to sample. A vast number of unique mixed drinks is offered here as well.

Desserts include a good cheesecake and fresh fruit always available with strawberries served with brown sugar and sour cream.

★★ PIZZERIAS UNO & DUE
Pizza

Uno
Pizza

29 E. Ohio St.   321-1000
Hours: Mon 5:30–11 pm, Tues–Thurs 11:30 am–11 pm, Fri &
Sat 11:30 am–midnight, Sun 1–8 pm

Due
Pizza

619 N. Wabash Ave.   943-2400
Hours: Mon–Fri 11:30–2:30 am, Sat 4 pm–2 am,
*   Sun 4–11:20 pm*
Price range: Inexpensive
Credit cards: A   C   D   M   V
Reservations: Accepted on weekends

Pizzeria Uno is where Chicago-style deep dish pizza got its start. Ike Sewell and his bartender-chef created the dish to give his little basement eatery something "different" in 1943. That difference started a movement that has been imitated many times over in Chicago and throughout the nation.

Pizzeria Due, just a few brisk steps away, is Uno's younger, slicker sister. It has longer hours and a dressier decor. Some complain that the pizza isn't as good at Due, but the recipe and preparation are the same. Still there's something about the crowded original location that makes it seem to have the better pie.

At either place, the deep dish pizzas that started it all still rank among the best the city has to offer. Best bets are the traditional sausage pizza or the vegetarian spinach with its heady hit of garlic.

The crust is thick and heavy, which is my only problem with Ike's pies. The crust tastes more like a biscuit than pizza dough, which is why I give an edge to Gino's East pizza. Still the thick layer of toppings with their chunks of chopped tomato and herby overtones tastes great.

Overdressed salads are uninspired, but help stave off starvation while you are waiting for the pie of your choice. The good minestrone might make a better choice for those who like this Italian vegetable soup. Given the size of the pizza and stomach-expanding properties of the fillings, desserts are unnecessary.

LAS PLUMAS
Mexican
Rating: Fair

875 N. Michigan Ave., John Hancock Center   280-5466
Hours: Lunch Mon–Fri 11:30 am–3 pm, Sat 11:30 am–4 pm,
*   Dinner Mon–Thurs 5–9 pm, Fri & Sat 5–10 pm,*
*   closed Sun*
Price range: Moderate
Credit cards: A C D M V
Reservations: Accepted
Handicap

For a place essentially relegated to a basement, this restaurant achieves the next to impossible. It seems bright, warm and sunny—a very comfortable room. Light, white stucco walls, bright upholstery, lots of booths and Mexican tile provide a welcome oasis on blustery Chicago winter days. The action in the kitchen grill area is open to view, adding to the fun. The '70s pop music seems a tad out of character in this setting, however.

While not terrible, the food doesn't really live up to the decor. Rather than reaching for truly great Mexican, the owners take the safer approach and head for middle-of-the-road food. Careless preparation, such as burning the edges of tortillas under the broiler, flaws many of the dishes. Still, prices are modest for a Michigan Avenue restaurant and portions are large and filling.

For appetizers the chorizo nachos are a good bet. Crisp tortilla chips topped with chorizo sausage, refried beans, jalapeno peppers and cheese arrive at the table nicely on a bed of lettuce. In addition to the complimentary basket of corn chips, unsalted with an average salsa, such "Mexican favorites" as French onion soup, potato skins and New England clam chowder are offered.

The tostada salad, listed under greenhouse salads features lettuce, green onions, black olives, tomato, chorizo, cheddar and monterey jack cheeses, served in a large tostada shell with guacamole, sour cream and salsa. Not bad, not a tostada in the normal sense, but a good and filling salad.

From the grill the beef or chicken fajitas make good choices. Served still sizzling at the table, the marinated meat comes with grilled onions and a stack of hot flour tortillas. One wraps the grilled ingredients in a tortilla for a sort of cross between an egg roll and a sandwich. Other grilled offerings include steak, ribs and fresh seafood on the day.

Desserts—cheesecake; tortilla with fruit, cheese, honey and ice cream; and cakes—fit in with the rest of this eclectic menu. Service is pleasant and reasonably efficient.

While not truly a Mexican restaurant, Las Plumas isn't a bad place for lunch or a drink and quick snack after work for those who work or shop in the area of the John Hancock Center.

★ ★ ★ LES PLUMES
French

2044 N. Halsted St.   525-0121
Hours: Mon–Thurs 5:30–9:30, Fri & Sat 5:30–10 pm,
*   closed Sun*
Price range: Moderately expensive
Credit cards: A   M   V
Reservations: Recommended
Other: No jeans; jackets for men

The best advice anyone could offer to diners headed for Les Plumes: save room for dessert. The menu descriptions sound tempting, and the desserts live up to their billing in looks and taste.

By no means miss the rich, smooth creme brulee. Simple in concept but difficult to execute, this heavenly bowl of brown sugar-glazed custard plays a virtuoso performance on the palate. More flamboyant but no less elegant, the gratin puts layers of lightly browned, hot lemon sabayon over fresh raspberries, vanilla sauce and a sponge cake to create an island in strawberry sauce. The contrasts of hot and cold, sweet and tart sensations of this dish touch every tastebud. Fantaisie au chocolat pleases even non-chocoholics with its flavorsome chocolate macaroon and mint chocolate ice cream supported by two sauces.

Les Plumes' desserts are the creation of Tom Culleeney, who perfected his craft under Le Francais' Jean Banchet for six years, with side trips to learn from famed French chef Roger Verge and to study at Paris's Gaston Lenotre's pastry school. Culleeney owns the restaurant with Greg Mulcahy—also a Le Francais alum—who was Banchet's sous chef, also for six years.

The 26-year-old chef-owners joined forces to open their own restaurant on the site of the ill-fated Cynthia's. As if to underscore the vagaries of the restaurant business, the crowds that swarmed to Cynthia's have been slow to return to sample Les Plumes' cuisine, among the best to join Chicago's restaurant scene in 1985.

Other than the addition of peacock feathers in large cases, the decor has been left largely unchanged from Cynthia's days. A long awning leads diners from the street through a small garden with cafe tables under umbrellas to the main dining room. This room features peachy-pink walls with forest green highlights and light oak trim. The effect is cheerful and comfortable, almost-but-not-quite-casual.

Although a decidedly French restaurant with a nouvelle bent, Les Plumes unabashedly acknowledges Italian influence, especially on its appetizer list. A torte Milannaise features layers of eggs, Swiss cheese, prosciutto, spinach and red peppers baked in a puff pastry, surrounded with a red bell pepper sauce. This dish looks beautiful and tastes fresh and good, if a little flat.

Pastas, made fresh at the restaurant, change daily. Cooked al dente, a pasta primavera special came with a delicate cream sauce and slightly crunchy vegetables.

Any of the four salads will make a fine start to the meal. Especially good is the breast of duck sauteed rare and served atop Belgium endive, radicchio and mushrooms with just enough hazelnut vinaigrette coating. The house salad is a simple but pleasing Boston lettuce, also with hazelnut vinaigrette.

Seafood dishes compose half of the entree offerings, each with different treatments and saucing. A wonderful nantua (crayfish) sauce supports the Dover sole filled with lobster mousse and baked in a pastry. Juicy, fresh salmon alternates with puff dough for the salmon mille feuilles with an earthy watercress sauce. One of the most exciting seafood creations presents three grilled fresh fish with three sauces: salmon, swordfish and tuna, with nantua, mustard and watercress. The combinations work well although the salmon and swordfish turned out a tad overcooked one night.

Sweetbreads mixed with wild mushrooms and rolled in filo dough are perfectly complemented by the accompanying madeira sauce. Even those who cannot stand the thought of sweetbreads may be converted. A thick slice of prosciutto cloaks the medaillons of veal with fresh noodle crepe and basil sauce, which should be wonderful, but the dish fails to excite because the too-salty sauce kills the rest of the ingredients' flavor.

Of course, as with any young restaurant, not all is perfect. First and foremost, the fake French accents and the dropping of French words here and there by the servers must go. Or else give them French lessons. More fundamental, however, Mulcahy and Culleeney try to make too much of a good thing. Culleeney creates a near perfect puff pastry and tends to repeat it on the menu. Diners must order carefully or they can quite easily end up with pastry as part of the appetizer, entree and dessert. Even with great pastry, this becomes tiring.

★ ★ ★ PRINTER'S ROW
American

550 S. Dearborn St.   461-0780
Hours: Lunch Mon–Fri 11:30 am–2:30 pm, Dinner Mon–
       Thurs 5:30–10 pm, Fri & Sat 5:30–11 pm, closed Sun
Price range: Expensive
Credit cards: A C D M V
Reservations: Recommended

This restaurant pioneered fine dining in the south Loop a few years ago and is an excellent example of the direction dining is taking in Chicago. Mike Foley's cuisine is based on fresh, native ingredients and French technique, with a healthy helping of creative twists that can make an evening at Printer's Row a special experience. Food and service are excellent.

Foley says he wants to create a comfortable neighborhood place. The room, in dark wood with large, white-clothed tables, is warm and comfortable, an oddly pleasing mix of formality and clubby atmospheres.

A seductively comfortable bar is to the left of the entrance with a long hallway straight ahead. There's no coat room, simply hooks along the wall where diners can take care of their own wraps.

Refreshingly exotic combinations of ingredients sometimes fail, but most often work far better than conventional wisdom would lead one to expect. Meals might start with a creamy chicken liver paté—nothing too exotic about that, until the gorgonzola cream sauce is added to the mix. Smooth and sweet, the paté gains excitement from the tangy gorgonzola cheese. Or the appetizer might be Illinois brie with vegetables and mushrooms on applesauce. Or try one of the full-bodied soups. Navy bean soup sounds boring, but surprises with an exceptionally smooth cream broth.

Entrees follow in the same manner: interesting combinations expertly prepared. On the menu, which changes with abandon, native game plays an important role.

A good house salad comes with entrees. However, special salads, such as a warm duck breast salad with a walnut vinaigrette, often merit the extra charge.

The dessert list includes many specials. The cakes, fruits and pastries tend to be too sweet at times, but no less creative and attractive than the rest of the fare.

Service can be obnoxiously attentive, although many of the waiters have been at this restaurant for some time and know what they're doing. A good wine list heavy on American vintages supports the meals.

THE PUMP ROOM
American
Rating: Fair

1301 N. State Parkway in the Ambassador East
Hotel   266-0360
Hours: Lunch Mon–Fri 11:30 am–2:30 pm, Sat noon–2:30,
        Sun brunch 10 am–2:30 pm, dinner Mon–Thurs 6–
        11:45 pm, Fri & Sat 6 pm–12:45 am, Sun 6–9:45 pm
Price range: Expensive
Credit cards: A C D M V
Reservations: Recommended
Handicap

This landmark restaurant poses problems for me when it comes to rating. On the one hand, The Pump Room is not bad. On the other, neither is it particularly good. But it does serve a useful function. The Pump Room is one of the few upscale restaurants willing and able to accommodate large groups of diners. This is both blessing and curse. It's a blessing for locals since it keeps large groups from ruining Chicago's smaller fine restaurants. But it's a curse when you happen to be dining at The Pump Room and several large parties tie up all the servers. This is the kind of place people go to impress others when they don't know what else to do.

With all of its failings, the Pump Room is still a great place for a drink. Up a few stairs and down a hall lined with photos of celebs, the bustling bar lies just beyond the hostess's desk. Music and a small dance floor try to recapture the heyday of the room during the big band era.

The hulking dining room stretches back from the bar toward the rear of the hotel. The famous Booth One where scores of very important personalities have held court, is the first booth on the right. A quick check is always in order as the star-studded tradition of dining here still lives on to a certain extent.

The two-story high ceilings, dark stained wood, large white-clothed tables, tuxedoed servers and all still impress. The food can impress as well, but too often it disappoints.

For starters the specials often offer the best bets. Or try the grilled oysters on a bed of spinach, paté or shrimp. The spinach and Ceasar salads also are good.

Entrees include the flaming brochettes that helped make The Pump Room famous. Skip the beef in favor of the seafood version which features fresh seafood cooked just right. Indeed, the seafood offerings, such as sole with champagne sauce, generally turn out well, but sometimes suffer from overcooking.

Desserts highlight the menu. Try the homemade ice creams, flourless chocolate cake or fresh fruit pastries. An extensive, and expensive, wine list can add greatly to the cost of an evening.

As good as some of the food can be, too often it does not live up to the reputation of the room. Moreover, servers lack knowledge and seem to be over-burdened when the room is full.

★ RAGIN' CAJUN
Creole/Cajun

3048 W. Diversey Ave.   342-6457
Hours: Lunch Mon–Fri 11 am–2 pm, Dinner daily 5 pm–
        midnight
Price range: Moderate
Credit cards: A C D M V
Reservations: Accepted

Ragin' Cajun is operated by former high school teacher Bob Collins, who runs the front of the house as maitre d', captain, waiter and bartender, and chef Harvey Durrson, a New Orleans native who cooked at Sage's Artists and Writers and Le Pub. One senses that Collins and Durrson have invested heart and soul in this restaurant, as well as every available penny.

Ragin' Cajun gives a new lease on life to the location that was formerly the Cajun House-the biggest problem with the place, since the location is obscure. However, this is ameliorated by the owners' dedication to New Orleans style cuisine, and the second-floor lounge by itself is worth the visit the building is more than 100 years old. Stairs lead up to the lounge from a long, narrow hallway entrance. Stepping into the lounge, you enter a time warp. Massive mirrors and antique furniture reproductions upholstered in garish, if cushy, red velvet and framed in dark-toned wood, give the appearance of an authentic New Orleans brothel.

The atmosphere downstairs is much more subdued with

its original Victorian wood trim and carved spindlework, large fireplace and stained glass over the bay window. There's plenty of space between tables but overcrowding is rarely a problem.

Don't come here expecting a jambalaya or blackened red-fish that will bring tears a la New Orleans' K. Paul's. Ragin' Cajun's reasonable jambalya lacks richness and spicy kick. The Creole-baked catfish tastes good but is overcooked and dry. Nicely flavored barbecued prawns also suffer from overcooking. The food here is not the best example of the genre in the area but the value is terrific. A complete five-course meal is included in the cost of the entrees, which ranges from $10.95 to under $20. It is quite possible to have a great time at this restaurant inexpensively.

The wine list is limited. But the warmth and friendliness of this place makes up for any of its shortcomings.

★★ RANDALL'S
American

41 E. Superior St.   280-2790
Hours: Lunch Mon–Fri 11:30 am–3 pm, Dinner Mon–Thurs–
      10 pm, Fri & Sat 5–11 pm, Sun 4–9 pm
Price range: Expensive for ribs
Credit cards: A C D M V
Reservations: Accepted
Handicap

Randall's started as a classy alternative to Carson's for ribs. Classy it continues to be with tons of marble, white-clothed tables and slick, sophisticated decor. However, Randall's is more than just the most expensive place in town to get a slab of excellent ribs. The menu now emphasizes steaks and seafood as well as its original reason for being: ribs.

Randall's pork ribs rank among the best in the city: meaty, chewy, heavily smoked with a tangy, but not very spicy barbecue sauce. The beef ribs, while not as flavorful as the pork, also turn out well. Provimi veal ribs, while unique and interesting, don't.barbecue as successfully as pork ribs do.

Appetizers include bite-sized chunks of crisply-coated fried catfish, chicken wings and barbecued shrimp. However, given the size of the portions, appetizers might be skipped, saving room for dessert—maybe.

Owned by the Levy Organization—which operates the Chestnut Street Grill, among other area restaurants—Randall's serves grilled seafood as good as it should be. Grilled trout turns out moist and just slightly smoky from the grilling. Or try the breaded and fried catfish with barbecue sauce—a good version of the Cajun classic. Steaks and prime rib also are available, all properly cooked to order.

House salad, a mix of greens with tomato, bacon and egg, comes with the entrees, as do excellent french fried onions. A good wine list dominated by American vintages offers some reasonably priced bottles.

Rich, sweet and filling desserts round out the menu. Try the whistky-laced bread pudding if you have the capacity. But the best bets probably are the homemade ice creams and ices.

Attentive servers know what they're talking about. They can lead diners willing to listen to the right choices, as well as help with wine selections.

★ R. D. CLUCKER'S
American

2350 N. Clark St.   929-5200
Hours: Lunch Mon–Fri 11:30 am–2:30 pm, Dinner 5–10 pm,
*   Sat 10 am–2:30 pm, 5–11:30 pm, Sun 4–10 pm*
Price range: Moderate
Credit cards: A C D M V

Reservations: Accepted for parties of six or more
Handicap

R. D. Clucker's sounds like another attempt to take on the likes of McDonald's, Kentucky Fried Chicken and maybe even R. J. Grunts. On the inside it looks a little bit as if it belongs in a suburban shopping mall rather than in the midst of Clark Street.

The staff approaches diners with all the fervor of recent converts to a religious cult. Every dish seems to be the server's favorite—if not, then it's simply great. It's all a little much. Still, Clark Street needs a reasonably priced joint with decent food and a sense of humor. Clucker's definitely has all three things going for it.

The humor begins with the valet who wears a chicken-head cap and greets diners with a smile. Inside, the warmth continues with greetings from the host or hostess. The place seems brighter and less oppressive than in the Zacharys' days. Inside the door to the left of the hostess' station, a narrow bar area stretches to the rear of the restaurant where waiting diners or those out for a light meal can order appetizers as well as drinks.

Although the name and various prints that hang throughout the restaurant suggest an all-chicken theme, a few meat and seafood dishes round out the predominantly chicken menu. For starters, the eggplant caviar wins raves from servers and gets billing as "our signature" on the menu. Such a signature dish could send a good many diners packing before they sampled any of the rest of the fare, however. Luckily, the redfish beignets promise better things to come. Crisply deep-fried to golden on the outside, the spicy coating gives way to moist, bite-size pieces of fresh fish on the inside. Chicken beignets are almost as good. Chicken on a skewer also works well with its somewhat spicy honey/peanut butter sauce.

The main dining room has two levels, several comfortable

271

banquettes, white-clothed tables and cheery decor. Large clear glass windows and doors give diners a view of the Clark Street bustle. At the rear of the room, another window opens to the activity in the kitchen, the newest theatrical effect in trendy restaurants.

In keeping with this tad of trendiness, the menu includes a few status dishes. New Orleans blackened redfish being in, blackened fish of the day appears on this menu. The fish one night tasted pristinely fresh, but the charred outer coating, like many attempted at local restaurants these days, came off too salty and too spicy to allow for full enjoyment of the fish itself.

Again, hardwood grilling being in, Clucker's boasts a hardwood grill. Either a half or whole bird is available as Clucker's special grilled chicken. The half portion of the large chickens served here will satisfy all but the heartiest of appetites. Grilled chicken comes with a choice of sauces, including good pesto and excellent house honey-mustard-curry sauce, also lauded by the servers. This sauce was ordered with some trepidation, but it proved to be excellent. The chicken itself has just enough smoky flavor from the coals to flavor the exceptionally tender meat.

The variation on chicken pot pie has a wonderfully flaky crust flavored with parmesan cheese which tops a stew packed with chunks of white meat mingled with bits of zucchini, potato and other vegetables in a full-bodied chicken gravy. Peasant chicken tastes like something Grandmother used to make. A large portion of chicken in clear chicken broth with matzo balls, this hearty meal in a bowl should cure a cold in no time.

Potatoes come with most entrees along with a better-than-average house salad. A choice of three good home-made salad dressings—tomato, pesto and sesame seed (the best)—is presented in old-fashioned corked bottles brought to the table in a basket.

For dessert, diners can choose the frozen custard bar where they can top a bowl of custard from a machine with all manner of sundae makings, from nuts to hot fudge. Calorie counters will have to fight with all their power to avoid the chocolate brownie flecked with bits of chocolate, frozen vanilla custard on the side and topped with thick hot fudge sauce. Bread pudding, which looks suspiciously like stuffing for one of the chickens, also packs a lot of caloric punch; its too-sweet sauce seems a bit much.

Limited to 15 wines, the list concentrates quite logically on California whites offered at prices from $8 to $17.50. Indeed, price combined with good food in a pleasant, casual atmosphere makes Clucker's an attractive addition to the Clark Street dining scene.

★ RICCARDO
Italian

437 N. Rush St.   944-8815
Hours: Mon-Fri 11:30 am–10 pm, closed Sat & Sun
Price range: Moderate
Credit cards: A   C   D
Reservations: Accepted

The first corner of the famed Bermuda triangle (Billy Goat and O'Rourke's compose the other two corners, so called because some who make the trek to all three disappear afterward for days), Riccardo's palette-shaped bar backed by huge paintings of questionable merit is *the* watering hole for many journalists and advertising agency types. Here *Chicago Sun-Times* and *Tribune* staffers peacefully co-exist, arguing the news of the day and each newspaper's play of the stories.

Many of these journalists make the Riccardo bar the first stop of a Friday night of serious drinking. On Fridays it's not unusual to hear *Tribune* writer Clarence Peterson on clarinet joining the roaming guitar and accordian players.

273

The after-effects of much drinking might be avoided with dinner in Riccardo's white-clothed dining room. Most of the advertising people and journalists go no farther than an order of pizza bread (not bad) or complimentary deep-fried fish sticks (not good) in the bar. But Riccardo serves decent Italian food at a reasonable price.

Pastas are a good bet from Riccardo's extensive menu. The carbonara here rivals any in the city with its rich, creamy sauce flecked with pancetta. Fettuccine also works well, as do the pastas with red sauce.

Although nine veal dishes are offered, indicating a specialty here, inconsistency in preparation makes ordering these a bit dicey. Veal piccante with lemon, anchovies and capers does not turn out heavy-handed here as it does so often elsewhere. Marsala also turns out well except when the flour coating the veal is gummy and undercooked. Poultry, steak and chops round out the menu.

Good bread and an ordinary iceberg lettuce salad come with dinners. So do vegetables on the side, but they hardly merit mentioning.

Unremarkable desserts fall into the standard Italian mold. The wine list is limited, but not overpriced. Servers may not be the warmest humans in the world, but are extremely efficient and well-meaning.

★ ★ RIGGIO'S CAFFE PRANZO
Italian

4100 N. Western Ave.   588-6161
Hours: Mon–Thurs 11 am–midnight, Fri 11–1 am, Sat 4 pm–1
     am, Sun 4–11 pm
Price range: Moderate
Credit cards: A   M   V
Reservations: Accepted

A step up from the average neighborhood joint, Riggio's attempts an ambitious menu and often succeeds. There's nothing fancy about the dining room: light-colored wood paneling and etched glass dress the place up a bit more than the average storefront.

Inside the front door is a bar with a dining area to the right. Behind these lies another dining area where large groups often hold forth. A high-tech blackboard hung on the wall lists the nightly specials, often among the best of the offerings.

For starters don't miss the formaggio all' Argentera, Italian cheese sauteed and dressed in a somewhat spicy vinaigrette. An average antipasto and above-average calamari also are available.

Pastas can be ordered in appetizer portions or full orders. Many of the pastas are homemade. Try the excellent pasta primavera al pesto or spicy arrabbiata, penne with a coarse tomato sauce flecked with prosciutto. Also good is the fettuccine all' Artuno, like Alfredo with the addition of pancetta (uncured Italian bacon) and lemon.

Veal dishes start with quality veal. The carefully prepared piccata and marsala versions are better than the heavy-handed parmigiana. Fresh seafood specials generally turn out well. Thin crust pizzas also are offered.

Desserts include a good homemade cannoli and excellent espresso chocolate sundae. However, portions are large and included with the entree is soup or salad as well as a side dish of pasta and vegetable.

The limited wine list of about five reds and five whites offers some excellent choices at less than $10 per bottle. Friendly servers help diners relax and enjoy the neighborhood comfort of this restaurant.

RIO'S
Portuguese-Brazilian
Rating: Fair

4611 N. Kedzie St.   588-7800
Hours: Lunch Tues-Sun 11-2:30, Dinner Tues-Thurs 4-11
*   pm, Fri & Sat 4-midnight, closed Mon*
Price range: Moderate
Credit cards: A C D M V
Reservations: Accepted

Several of the well-known restaurant guides highly recommend this place, perhaps because it is the only Brazilian-Portuguese restaurant in town. However, uniqueness doesn't justify recommendation.

True, the interior with its white-clothed tables and booths, fresh flowers and comfortable chairs is a cut above most storefront restaurants. But the service can be a cut below and the food is inconsistent at best.

Fresh fish may or may not be very fresh when it gets to one's table. Whitefish smelled fishy one night when it was delivered to the table, and had dry texture from too much time on the stove. Caldeirada, a seafood stew, suffered too from suspect ingredients. Dry, overcooked meat also spoils the churrasco, a mixed grill of beef, pork, chicken and sausage. The black beans on the side were disappointingly bland.

No salads come with entrees. A few interesting Portuguese wines at low prices help diners through the meals, service of which can take inordinate amounts of time even when the restaurant isn't crowded.

Rio's may be proof that competition does in fact make businesses do a better job. At times the kitchen rises to better than-average, but one gets the feeling that most of the time this restaurant doesn't believe it has to bother.

★ R. J. GRUNTS
American

2056 N. Lincoln Park West   929-5363
Hours: Mon-Thurs 11:30 am–11 pm, Fri & Sat 11:30–1 am,
*   Sun 10 am–11 pm*
Price range: Moderate
Credit cards: A D M V
Reservations: Accepted for parties of six or more
Handicap

This is the burger joint that bankrolled Richard Melman's Lettuce Entertain You empire. A throwback to the '60s when it opened, Grunts still features pretty, T-shirted waitresses, lots of stuff to look at on the walls and a down-home atmosphere. The menu still has all of the puns that probably started the trend toward cutesiness and now seem a bit tired. In short, Grunts has become its own period piece, locked in the time when it started Melman out on his career as Chicago's acknowledged restaurant genius.

There are many items on the menu. But the burger remains one of the best items on the menu of any of Melman's restaurants. The regular half-pound burger, broiled crusty on the outside and juicy on the inside, costs $4.75.

Melman reportedly likes to have a chocolate malt with his burger, but it can be pretty bland unless he's watching the store. Opt for the plain old vanilla or peanut butter shakes.

Unfortunately, the cottage fries that come with the burgers are oily, flaccid, unworthy companions. Still, for an inexpensive evening and good times, Grunts is pretty hard to beat.

RODITYS
Greek
Rating: Fair

222 S. Halsted St.   454-0800

Hours: Sun–Thurs 11–1:00 am, Fri & Sat 11–2:00 am
Price range: Moderate
Credit cards: A   M   V
Reservations: Accepted

Clean, bright and usually packed with diners, Roditys enjoys popularity that equals that of its competitors along this stretch of Halsted in old Greektown. The murals of Greek waterfront scenes look like paintings, but closer examination reveals that they are fashioned from inlaid pieces of colored wood. These may be worth the visit in and of themselves.

Indifferent servers waste no time getting the food to the table. However, that food is inconsistent. Some dishes can be quite good while others fall short. Although a card affixed to the menu lists nightly specials, most of the dishes can be found on the regular menu.

For starters head for the tzatsiki, cucumbers dressed with garlic-charged yogurt or spanakotiropita, spinach wrapped in a crisp, flaky filo dough. The fish roe salad, taramosalata, is too salty. Skip the disappointing saganaki (flamed cheese). Garlic lovers might choose instead the skordalia, garlic infused mashed potatoes, listed as garlic sauce at the very bottom of the menu—powerful but terrific.

Lamb, braised, roast or barbecued, has an old, gamey flavor, common in Greek restaurants, but not greatly appealing. The roasted lamb turned out overly dry one night.

Standard Greek dishes such as moussaka, made here with exceptionally thick slices of eggplant, fare better. Dolmades also turn out well. The broiled red snapper has good flavor, but is dry from overcooking.

The worst dish sampled, Greek sausages, had fine flavor, but were grossly overcooked and dried-out. Indeed much of the food here suffers from overcooking that ruins good ingredients and balanced use of spices and herbs. That is, balanced use on everything but the bland, flavorless Grecian style chicken.

Roditys' low prices win its fair share of fans, but better food can be found in Greektown just a few steps a way.

★★ RON OF JAPAN
Japanese steak house

230 E. Ontario St.   644-6500
Hours: Daily 5–10 pm
Price range: Expensive
Credit cards: A D M V
Reservations: Accepted
Handicap

Benihana of Tokyo made popular the communal dining and cooking theatrics of Japanese steak houses. Not as well-known, nor as flashy as Benihana of Tokyo, Ron of Japan offers great steak in a classy environment, with more attention paid to the decor and quality ingredients than most other Japanese steak houses. Nevertheless, don't expect a romantic evening alone. Four to eight people are seated around the circular cooking area where the waiter-chef performs.

Dinner includes appetizer, soup, salad, main course and dessert. Choices are minimal: only one soup and salad with a few appetizer options. All of the dishes sampled were cooked to perfection, but the simplicity of the preparations—the epitome of Japanese cooking—can lead to some boredom. Ron's breaks the monotony with more seasoning and an egg yolk batter similar to a thick, orange-eggy mayonnaise that somehow works.

Of course, a steak house depends on its steak. Ron's beef is superb: rich, tender and flavorful. Although it costs more than at other Japanese steak houses, portions are generally larger. In fact, portions are large enough and the beef good enough that diners should be wary of the tempting combination dinners that test one's capacity.

Desserts are offered, but given what goes before, they are largely unnecessary. The waiter-cooks at Ron's don't have the theatrical flair of Benihana's, but somehow seem more genuine and do enough chopping and flipping with their knives to make Ron's a fun evening out.

RUE SAINT CLAIR
American
Rating: Poor

640 N. St. Clair St.   787-6907
Hours: Lunch Mon–Sat 11:30 am–2:30 pm, brunch Sun 10:30
*   am–2 pm, dinner Sun–Thurs 6–10 pm, Fri & Sat 6–11*
*   pm*
Price range: Moderately expensive
Credit cards: A C D M V
Reservations: Accepted

Testimony to the fact that location and a pretty face *do* matter mightily in the restaurant business, Rue Saint Clair does a brisk business. Particularly in summer when the side doors open to create a nifty little sidewalk cafe, people seem to love to congregate at this place.

The room with dark wood, tile floors, big glass doors and brass trim, is attractive. If only the food were better. And it should be noted that I was recognized in this restaurant so it must be assumed that the kitchen did its best. Its best isn't good enough.

Not that all dishes fail. Some turn out very well indeed. Roast baby chicken was moist and flavorful with a sprinkling of fresh herbs. Patés, on the other hand, while good on one visit, were stale-tasting and dry on another. A grilled swordfish special was woefully overcooked and dry. A special seafood pasta suffered the same fate and turned out gummy and starchy. Often the ill-concieved sauces make matters worse.

Well-meaning servers, many of whom seem to practice at being inept, try their best to make diners comfortable, but their lack of knowledge and polish is comical at best and frustrating at worst.

The best strategy may be to come here for a glass of wine or two to enjoy the atmosphere. Have a paté or another appetizer for a snack, then move on to somewhere else for a better dinner.

It's not that the restaurant can't produce good food. It's just that it doesn't seem to have the commitment to excellence at this writing. So sample at your own risk.

★ SAGE'S EAST (NOW SAGE'S ON STATE)
American

1225 N. State   944-1557
Hours: Mon-Thurs 5-midnight, Fri & Sat 5 pm-1 am, closed
        Sun
Price range: Moderately expensive
Credit cards: A C D M V
Reservations: Recommended
Handicap

★ SAGE'S SAGES
American

75 W. Algonquin Rd, Arlington Heights   593-6200
Hours: Breakfast Mon-Fri 6-10 am, lunch Mon-Fri 11:30 am-
        5 pm, dinner Mon-Thurs 5-11 pm, Fri & Sat 5-
        midnight, brunch Sun 11:30 am-3 pm, dinner 3-10
        pm
Price range: Moderately expensive

281

Credit cards: A   C   D   M   V
Reservations: Recommended
Handicap

★ **SAGE'S WEST**
  American

2900 S. Highland Avenue, Downers Grove   964-0550
Hours: Brunch Sun 11 am–3 pm, dinner noon–7:45 pm, lunch
  Mon-Fri 11 am–3:45 pm, dinner Mon 4–10:45 pm,
  dinner Tues-Fri 4–11:45 pm, Sat 4–12:45 am
Price range: Moderately expensive
Credit cards: A   C   D   M   V
Reservations: Recommended

Gene Sage likes to say that he's a saloon keeper and, indeed, his restaurants perform that function extremely well. In the traditional sense of saloon—that is, a comfortable place where folks can meet over a drink—Sage is at the top of a rapidly disappearing class in Chicago.

His three restaurants differ according to their locations, clientele and various experiments in new food and marketing. However, there's a sense of humor common to his establishments—a sense of humor and a sense of comfort. That all of his saloons happen to serve food is almost incidental, would be incidental if he and his customers didn't take it all so seriously.

It should be mentioned, too, that in the tradition of the saloon, regulars at any of the Sage's restaurants get preferential treatment. In an age when service is impersonal and ersatz equality the law of the land, people find it difficult to understand why one customer gets different treatment from another. Still, doesn't it make sense that regulars who are a restaurant's bread-and-butter should get better tables and service than the one-shot customer?

Sage's menus feature items ranging from grilled fish to steaks and chops, with a sprinkling of French preparations. These are augmented by a card of specials that change with the seasons. On top of that the server presents still another card of "chef's specials, which he highly recommends." The waiter or waitress thoughtfully gives diners the option of hearing the specials read or reading the card for themselves. Bravo.

Clearly Sage intends the specials to give the chef a chance to flex his creative muscles and diners the choice of sticking to traditional menu offerings or embarking on an adventure. Unfortunately the chef seems to define creative adventure as an experiment in how many ingredients can be put together without ruining a dish. Stick to the steaks and chops and you'll fare well.

Take one of the autumn specials: "Proovimi veal with shiitake, porcini and chantrelle mushrooms, basil, chevre, shallots; hazelnut bread crumbs and port wine sauce." Where's the kitchen sink?

Another autumn special, called range-free chicken on the card, fares far better. (What the chef means by "free-range chicken" is not uncooked chicken, but chicken that have not been confined to a cramped pen.) Baked with fresh rosemary, the small fowl is moist and tender served with a calvados beurre blanc sauce that compliments without overwhelming.

At least these entrees have flavor. Forget the fried brie. The breaded cheese, still hard and cold at the center, is nearly tasteless, a loser. Not much better is the special sea scallops. What makes this dish special may be unusual presence of grit in the scallops. Even without grit this dish would still be flat, served in a lackluster red pepper mayonnaise.

Sage must like chocolate: plenty of chocolate appears on the dessert menu. A chocolate espresso cake—two layers of moist chocolate cake with a layer of vanilla cake in between, all separated by a layer of velvety espresso butter cream—send most diners away happy.

In addition to the friendly atmosphere of Sage's, two other things work in the restaurant's favor. First, there is no pretense that this is a grand temple of haute cuisine. Second, an effort is made to make the food interesting and challenge the kitchen staff to rise above darned good steaks and boring, but expertly prepared lobster tails.

★ SALVADOR'S
Mexican

Five locations:
30 E. Randolph   346-8457
Hours: Mon–Wed 11 am–9 pm, Thurs 11 am–11 pm, Fri &
*   Sat 11 am–midnight*
Price range: Inexpensive
Credit cards: A   M   V
Reservations: Accepted for parties of 6 or more

661 N. Clark   642-5016
Hours: Sun–Thurs 11 am–11 pm, Fri & Sat 11–1 am
Price range: Inexpensive
Credit cards: A   C   D   M   V
Reservations: Accepted

625 W North Ave., Villa Park   833-5337
Hours: Sun–Thurs 11 am–11 pm, Fri & Sat 11–2 am
Price range: Inexpensive
Credit cards: A   C   D   M   V
Reservations: Accepted

134 N. Ridgeland, Oak Park   848-1781

Hours: Mon–Thurs 11 am–11 pm, Fri 11–1 am, Sat noon–1
     am, Sun noon–11 pm
Price range: Inexpensive
Credit cards: A C D M V
Reservations: Accepted for parties of 6 or more only.
Handicap

1816 W. Irving Park Rd., Hanover Park   830-5930
Hours: Mon–Thurs 11 am–11 pm, Fri & Sat 11–1 am, Sun
     noon–10 pm
Price range: Inexpensive
Credit cards: A C D M V
Reservations: Accepted
Handicap

One of the newest locations for this four-unit chain, the Randolph St. store is typical of the others. Salvador's burrito may not be Chicago's best—as the menu claims—but it certainly is one of the biggest. The decor is typically stuccoed Mexican, with lots of arches, wood, tile and hanging plants. The atmosphere is bright, clean and cheery. A guitarist strolls among the diners.

Nothing distinguishes Salvador's from the run-of-the-mill Mexican restaurants around town. The menu isn't startling in its creativity and the food is average, not exceptional. Appetizers include garnachas, known as nachos most other places, guacamole, potato skins and quesadillas. The large taco salad or avocado salad betters any of the above.

Among the entrees except the "reg.": tacos, tostadas, enchiladas and, of course, the giant burritos. Steaks, red snapper, shrimp and chicken round out the menu offerings. Desserts include sopapillas, flan and rice pudding.

Service is good, prices reasonable, and the margaritas won't kill you. The loop location offers a particularly good value for the area.

★ SANTA FE CAFE
American

800 N. Dearborn St.   944-5722
Hours: Mon–Sat 11 am–midnight, Sun 4–10 pm
Price range: Moderate
Credit cards: A C D M V
Reservations: Not accepted

Less a restaurant than a bar with take-out food service, Santa Fe does have a few tall tables in front for those who wish to eat there.

Billed as a southwestern restaurant, Santa Fe's offerings are limited to barbecues ribs, chicken and beef, home-made bread and sandwiches. But for the price it's hard to beat it for a quick bite to eat.

Ribs here are meaty, smoky and come with a tangy sauce that has just a bit of spiciness. The same sauce comes with the slightly smoky, moist chicken. Good fries accompany these.

The only dessert is cookies, which have always gone unsampled because the main course is so filling. A good selection of beers is available at the bar to help wash down the smoked meats.

★ SAYAT NOVA
Armenian

Two locations:
157 E. Ohio St.   644-9159
Hours: Mon–Thurs 11 am–11 pm, Fri & Sat 11–midnight,
*   Sun 3–10 pm*
Price range: Moderate
Credit cards: A C D M V
Reservations: Accepted

20 Golf Rd., Des Plaines   296-1776
Hours: Lunch, Tues-Fri 11:30 am-2 pm, Dinner Tues-Thurs
4:30-10:30 pm, Fri & Sat 4:30-11:30 pm, Sun 4-10 pm
Price range: Moderate
Credit cards: A C D M V
Reservations: Accepted
Handicap

The newer Des Plaines branch of this downtown standard has a classier dining room with stained glass, stucco walls and circular booths, but somehow the two locations emit the same feeling of warmth. The downtown location has long been popular for its good food and moderate prices.

Some of the best dishes come from the appetizer offerings. Taboule, cracked wheat salad, raw or cooked kibbeh, ground lamb and cracked wheat, and boereg, cheese or spinach-filled puffs of filo dough all make excellent beginnings. Or order a selection and make a meal of just appetizers.

Grilled lamb chops or steaks, sauteed chicken and moist, tender shishkebabs with either lamb or chicken lead the list of entrees. Lulia kebabs, ground lamb and beef molded on a stick and grilled, also turn out well.

For dessert choose the quality baklava. There are a few wines priced in keeping with the rest of the menu. Servers are friendly, well-informed and helpful.

★ SCHULIEN'S
German-American

2100 W. Irving Park Rd.   478-2100
Hours: Mon-Thurs 11:30 am-midnight, Fri & Sat 11:30-1
*   am, closed Sun*
Price Range: Moderately expensive
Credit cards: A C D M V

Reservations: Accepted on weekdays
Other: Free parking

Walls lined with paintings, photographs and an odd collection of fire hats, picks and equipment, Schulien's looks like an old-time saloon. The long wooden bar that dominates the front room could have come out of a Western. In fact, lots of old wood, leaded glass lamp shades, leaded glass windows and a refreshing measure of good old-fashioned hospitality add up to a great time.

Established in 1886, Schulien's is reputedly the oldest continuously-operated restaurant and saloon in Chicago. Charlie Schulien carries on the tradition of his father, Matt, who amazed customers with his card tricks for better than 30 years. No serious card playing goes on here as it did in the old days, but there are some serious sleight-of-hand tricks nevertheless.

American food—steaks, chops and the like—lead the menu, but there's more than a sprinkling of German specialties, most of them quite good. There are several decent sandwiches built around various mounds of meat. The food is filling and portions are large.

An iced-dish of fresh vegetables automatically arrives at the table before the meal, along with a basket of bread sticks and rolls. Other appetizers include escargot, shrimp de Jonghe, shrimp cocktail and oysters in season. Soup or chilled tomato juice, a house salad, potato and vegetable are included in the price of the entree. The onion soup is tasty, although salty. The split pea soup is not very thick but is flavorful with plenty of ham. Salads are large—the mix of lettuce, spinach, red onion, carrots and tomato would shame many a more expensive restaurant.

Broiled whitefish covered with paprika is fresh, cooked to perfection, juicy and flavorful. Just watch for bones. Steaks here start with a good quality meat and end with proper preparation. Thick and juicy, full of flavor without too much fat, they can compete with the city's best. The excellent prime rib is a treat. Schulien's weiner schnitzel is a large piece of good quality, fork-tender veal topped with anchovy fillets, capers and a fried egg. The only disappointment is the roast duck, served with red cabbage and orange sauce. The duck doesn't taste bad and almost finds salvation through the great homemade dressing, but the skin is flaccid and the meat dry.

Peppermint ice hot fudge sundae—a scoop of excellent peppermint ice cream with a good fudge sauce and a load of whipped cream on top—delights those who like that sort of thing. The apple strudel wins praise with its light pastry covering a good, cinnamony, apple filling. Good quality ice-cream can be ordered on the side.

There's nothing creative about Schulien's ordinary fare—it's not the greatest in Chicago. Still this may be one of the city's truly great places, a restaurant from another era, when dining out meant having a good, relaxing time.

★★ SESSIONS PULLMAN PUB
American

605 E. 111th St.   785-7578
Hours: Lunch Mon–Fri 11 am–2 pm, Dinner Wed–Sat 5–10
*   pm, Sun brunch 11 am–3 pm, dinner 3–7 pm*
Price range: Moderately expensive
Credit cards: M   V
Reservations: Accepted

Situated in the Pullman district which is undergoing an urban renaissance, Sessions is housed in a charming three-story house that was the restaurant for executives of the Pullman Palace Car Co. To enter Sessions from the large front porch is to step back in time. A small reception area sports display cases with some Pullman memorabilia and a board with the night's menu. Study the menu carefully: it's the only chance you'll have to look at it, although the waiters will gladly review the listings. Behind and to the right of the entrance, the tastefully decorated dining room blends turn-of-the-century formality with a relaxed contemporary atmosphere. Even when crowded, the room exudes comfort and privacy.

While Sessions suffers from some inconsistencies, the ribs are a constant, among the best in the city. The remainder of the menu offerings, which usually include several fresh seafood varieties, steaks, chops and fowl, frequently change. Simple preparations dominate.

Some dishes turn out marvelously, such as the thick, well trimmed, perfectly-cooked lamb chops, a regular offering. Roast pheasant is rich and full-flavored. Disappointingly dry veal and trout with unimaginative saucing underscore the inconsistencies of the kitchen.

Still, because Sessions offers a full meal, including a nice homemade soup or reasonably good salad, for the price of the entrees, the value is great. Homemade desserts change nightly. Pleasant, polished waiters add to an enjoyable dining experience. There is a limited but well-selected wine list at very reasonable prices.

The lunch menu offers sandwiches and entrees from $3.95 to $6.95—a good way to sample Session's fare at a bargain price. Pullman's is a great place to take a break from a walking tour of the many impressive historic buildings in the nine-square block Pullman district.

★ ★ ★ SHAW'S CRAB & BLUE CRAB LOUNGE
Seafood

21 E. Hubbard St.   527-2722
Hours: Lunch Mon–Fri 11:30 am–2 pm, Dinner Mon–Thurs
*   5:30–10 pm, Fri & Sat 5:30–11 pm, Sun 4–9:30 pm*
Blue Crab hours: Mon–Thurs 11:30 am–10 pm,
*   Fri & Sat 11:30 am–11 pm, closed Sun*

Price range: Moderately expensive to expensive
Credit cards: A C D M V
Reservations: Accepted for lunch only in Shaw's. No reservations for the Blue Crab Lounge

When the Blue Crab Lounge first opened, people thought they had discovered this secret little place from 40 years ago with a great raw bar, a few hot entrees and some excellent salads at a moderate price. Booths painted dark brown, high tables surrounded by bar stools and old fashioned fans on the wall gave the place an intimate, casual atmosphere, helped along by the personable manager, Kevin Brown, who owns part of the restaurant with Richard Melman.

The sprawling Crab House opened next door. Overnight the restaurant was packed. The Blue Crab Lounge handled the overflow from Shaw's own large bar. The secret was out, and some of the charm was gone as well.

Nevertheless, walking into Shaw's Crab House and the Blue Crab Lounge next door still seems like stepping into a New England seafood house plopped down in the middle of the Midwest. Despite the fact that everything is new, the place feels old and well-worn. The incredibly fresh seafood here often excels. However, Shaw's success puts strain on the busy kitchen that cause some inconsistencies.

The menu's array of fresh seafood is vast. Appetizers include decent steamed clams; good, if somewhat eggy, crab cakes; seafood stews and pan roasts, as well as a selection of fresh oysters, clams, blue crab fingers and shrimp from the raw bar.

As the name suggests, Shaw's takes pride in its crab. By all means try the spicy Maryland blue crab when available—messy, but excellent. Good Florida stone crabs fill out the year from May through September with simple preparations that show these delicate crab to the best advantage.

The Cajun and Creole offerings such as gumbo, jambalaya, barbecued shrimp and the like don't really measure up to the best the area has to offer. Indeed more complicated preparations, such as sauteed lump crabmeat with Virginia ham and shiitake mushrooms, tend to fall flat. Opt instead for the simple dishes that let the natural goodness of the excellent ingredients shine through. A number of simply grilled fish appear as specials each evening. Sauteed frog legs or bay scallops never disappoint.

Those who don't care for seafood can order steak and poultry, simply cooked and good. Desserts range from an excellent crème brulee and decent key lime pie to rich ice creams and refreshing fruit ices.

On the good wine list, heavy on domestic whites as one might expect, are a large number of bottles for $20 or less.

Attentive servers generally know their stuff. They seem to enjoy working here, which helps diners relax and enjoy themselves as well. And no matter how busy Shaw's gets—and it does get busy—waiters and waitresses do not hurry their customers through meals in order to turn the table and increase tips.

SHI HU
Chinese
Rating: Fair

6740 N. California Ave.   338-3636
Hours: Mon–Thurs 11:30 am–10 pm, Fri & Sat 11:30 am–
      midnight
Price range: Inexpensive
Credit cards: Not accepted
Reservations: Accepted
Handicap

The owners of Shi Hu put plenty of time, effort and tender loving care into their modest neighborhood restaurant, but it is hardly ever crowded. The service is pleasant, the prices reasonable and while some dishes fail utterly, many dishes are good. For $8 to $10 you can stuff yourself on a selection of appetizers, a couple of entrees and dessert.

Among the appetizers, best bets include good, greaseless egg rolls and light, puffy shrimp toast. The steamed pot stickers, however, suffer from rubbery texture and stale-tasting filling. Big groups, or those with really big appetites, might choose the Confucius Concoction, a selection of an egg roll, two shrimp toasts, two tasty chicken legs (one of the best in this selection), tiny fish cakes heavy on onion, two skewers of nearly fatless beef and—the only bad thing on the platter—dried out tasteless fried wontons. Odd Job's bowler soup mixes sea cucumber, winter melon, chicken and shrimp. Although overly thickened with corn starch, the soup delights with its rich mix of flavors and textures.

Garlic beef will disappoint garlic lovers: the lean, tender meat in a sweet brown sauce lacks hearty garlic flavor. Hot sauce twice-cooked pork comes with bamboo shoots, celery and cabbage, in a heavy, black bean sauce that isn't particularly hot but surrounding it around the dish are fierce dried iridescent red peppers. Half smoked tea duck is almost as large as the whole duck served in some places. Crisp-skinned and lean, the duck has a sweet sauce that adds to the meat. On the other hand, moo shoo pork tastes more like egg foo young. The four pancakes are tough and skimpily-filled. More interesting are the golden shrimp balls with an excellent sauce matched by the airy puffs of shrimp.

Desserts are typical: complimentary fortune cookies, glazed fruits and almond cookies. No alcohol is served but there's a convenience store nearby.

★★ SHILLA RESTAURANT
Korean

5930 N. Lincoln Ave.   *275-5930*

Hours: Daily 11:30 am–10:30 pm
Price range: Moderate
Credit cards: A C D M V
Reservations: Accepted
Handicap

Shilla must be the classiest Korean restaurant in town. It's also one of the best.

The room is huge, and usually filled with more Korean immigrants than American yuppies, a neat trick in these days of restaurant madness. A large aquarium next to the hostess' stand holds some of the largest goldfish in captivity. Just beyond, a short sushi and sashimi bar stretches towards the middle of the dining room. Light wood, bright lighting, plants, good art work on the walls, red chairs and green-trimmed formica tables give the room a clean, sophisticated, contemporary look. Private tea rooms line three walls behind sliding wood and paper panels.

While waiting for your food, you can watch the sushi chef toil over his elaborate arrangements of exquisitely fresh fish. Presentation of cooked Korean dishes almost matches that of the sushi.

Appetizers include some soggy Korean tempura carrots and zucchini that should be bypassed in favor of the Korean stuffed mushroom cap or ground, seasoned, sausage-like beef. Or skip the appetizers altogether for the incendiary soups or hearty casseroles. There's no shame in asking the waitress to have the chef tone down the spicy beef soup. Even in its toned-downstate the stuff has enough spice to make humans feel like dragons.

For entrees try the mild barbecued beef or chap chae, small bits of beef with vegetables on cellophane noodles with a full flavored sauce. In summer sample cold specialities such as raw beef with hot sauce and egg yolk, crunchy cold jellyfish that most people will like if they get past the idea of what it is, and bibim naeng myum, cold noodles topped with a hard boiled egg, beef and vegetables.

All seafood items are extremely fresh and well-prepared. Yellowtail comes sauteed in a light sauce. Shrimp tempura turns our far more crisp than the vegetable version served as an appetizer.

Portions are quite large so desserts are unnecessary. Beer, wine and mixed drinks are available.

The only problem with this restaurant is that waitresses tend to stereotype round-eyed races. It's difficult for non-Orientals to get the same food as the Koreans sitting next door. Service is friendly, attentive and well-meaning, but the servers are reluctant to recommend anything out of the ordinary.

SHOWBOAT SARI-S II
American
Rating: Fair

500 W. Ontario St.   787-8650
Hours: Mon–Fri 11–2 am, Sat 5 pm–2 am, closed Sun
Price range: Inexpensive
Credit cards: A   M   V
Reservations: Accepted

Showboat Sari-S II has only two claims to fame. One: moored on the Chicago River at the foot of Ontario St., the bow deck of this former river boat and yacht club restaurant makes a great place for people to congregate on a clear, warm spring or summer night. It's a place to take in the stars and the skyline and argue the problems of the world over drinks until both the constellations and the issues begin to blur.

Two: the place has excellent ribs. Nothing else is really worth eating, but the ribs are good. Prepared from the "secret recipe of a former Royko Rib Contest winner, Cleo Williams, the barbecued ribs, and sometimes the chicken, turn out delightfully smoky with a pungent spicy sauce.

Other menu offerings, such as the tough, stale-tasting steaks and similarly stale-tasting and over-cooked fish, should be avoided. Also forget the mass produced cheesecake offered for dessert.

Accept the fact that this is a place to look at the urban side of the City of Chicago with little expectation of great food and you'll do just fine.

★★ SIAM SQUARE
Thai

622 Davis St., Evanston   475-0860
Hours: Daily 11 am–10 pm
Price range: Inexpensive
Credit cards: A C D M V
Reservations: Accepted

This restaurant started life in a little storefront on Western Avenue, done in pink and purple and with cheap Thai prints on the walls. The food equalled the best Thai cuisine the city had to offer. Despite communication problems that often frustrated diners, it was a lovely little place with incredibly low prices.

In 1985 it moved to Evanston to bigger, somewhat classier environs although the grass hut and bamboo interior decorations inherited from the former occupant of this space, a Hawaiian restaurant, seem distinctly un-Thai.

Often when a restaurant moves and expands two things happen: prices go up and quality goes down. Not so here.

Friendly deferential waiters continue to serve with markedly improved, if not perfect, English. Ninety-nine percent of the dishes cost less than $6. Most important, Siam Square still serves some of the best Thai food around.

Granted, nothing startles on this menu, it is all pretty standard Thai fare. However, with about 100 dishes from which to choose, there's enough variety to satisfy even finicky eaters. And, making a bad choice is next to impossible.

Try the good fresh spring rolls with a sweet, but light, plum sauce. Moist pork and chicken satay with a mild peanut sauce and fiery cucumber salad also make a good beginning. Or try the fired, seasoned corn with sweet and sour clear vinegar sauce—kernels of corn held together like fritter, but with a crispy fried batter that seems light as air.

In Siam Square's old location, spicy dishes like the soups and curries were powerful enough to set off a nuclear reaction without warning. They still can if you so desire, but now the waiter asks if you want dishes mild, medium or hot. Medium will be plenty hot for most folks, with hot or extra hot reserved for those with asbestos palates. Sour chicken soup in a coconut milk broth with kha, a pungent Thai dried root, is excellent and one order will serve at least two diners.

Panfried beef, pork or chicken with garlic and pepper has a rich, deep brown sauce, but not as much garlic as one might expect. Beef sauteed with vegetables—green onions, cabbage, peppers, tiny pickled corn ears and mushrooms—looks and tastes more Chinese than Thai. Hot sour salad of minced meat—again chicken, beef or pork—served on a large lettuce leaf has wonderful aroma and spicy, slightly tart flavor—a must.

One thing did suffer a bit in the transition. Presentation used to be more decorative and enticing.

A caveat: Siam Square serves a large number of drinks ranging from soda to delicious Thai iced sweetened coffee, but alcohol is not one of them. So if beer or wine is desired, come prepared.

To fully appreciate this restaurant come with a group of people, order a variety of dishes—soups and curries, sautes and salads—and share. The variety of flavor sensations and textures is amazing. Moreover, several people can eat to capacity and beyond on excellent food for less than $10 each.

★★ SINCLAIR'S
American

Forest and Westminster Avenues, Lake Forest   295-8300
Hours: Tues–Thurs 5:30–10 pm, Fri & Sat 5:30–11 pm, Sun
        5–9 pm
Price range: Expensive
Credit cards: A C D M V
Reservations: Recommended
Handicap

Simplicity characterizes the cuisine here, which fits in with owner Gordon Sinclair's concept for the restaurant: a comfortable but classy alternative to the country club dining rooms in the area. By most measures, the place succeeds. A mixture of New Orleans Creole-Cajun and Florida Latin-Island influences many of the culinary creations.

A great deal of thought and effort went into the restaurant's interior design. Rubenesque murals cover the ceiling over the bar and back wall (painted by Fred Sperry of the Pilsen East Guild). There are dark tile floors, brass fixtures, dark-stained wood. However, the atmosphere seems a bit cold, almost sterile.

The extensive menu changes nightly. Specials are exactly that, items the chef finds particularly appealing and fresh that day, prepared according to his whim. There are two columns of first courses, divided between hot and cold appetizers, which provide some of the best eating on the menu.

The perfectly poached oysters are incredibly fresh, lightly sauced in their shells, it's tempting to make an entire meal of them. The shrimp with chorizo is nearly as good, fresh shrimp and pieces of authentically spiced sausage skewered and grilled to perfection. The artichoke fritters, served with a bearnaise sauce, have excellent flavor, but a somewhat soggy coating.

Salads can be passed up at Sinclair's but the soups are to die for. The black bean soup is a classic, topped with a lemon slice, full-bodied, rich with subtle seasoning and the beans perfectly cooked. The "Bahamian" conch chowder is based on a tomato broth with fresh vegetables, flavorful bits of conch and a kick of Tabasco. In a rich, creamy mushroom soup, pureed mushrooms thicken the broth which captures intense mushroom flavor.

The calves' liver when available with country bacon and green onions is worth sampling. Six or more fresh fish entrees are offered grilled or sauteed. The grilling adds little flavor but the sea bass one night was moist and well-served by its basil sauce. A mixed seafood grill—lobster, Florida crab, Alaskian salmon and haddock—is also good. Portions of both are huge. A small portion of fresh vegetables accompanies most entrees.

Led by the flourless chocolate cake, desserts are good at Sinclair's. Apple and pecan pies are excellent, as are the sauces served with them. A Boston creme pie special is moist with a good chocolate frosting but needs more custard.

Service, slow and forgetful at first, has improved. If the kitchen maintains its high standards, Sinclair's should be worth the trip to Lake Forest for city dwellers.

★★ SOGNI DORATI
Italian

660 N. Wells St.   337-6500
Hours: Lunch Mon–Fri 11:30 am–1:45 pm, Dinner Mon–Fri
*   5:30–9:30 pm, Sat 5:30–9:30 pm, closed Sun*
Price range: Expensive

Credit cards: A C D M V
Reservations: Recommended
Handicap

Sogni Dorati plays to outrageously disparate reviews. One local reviewer calls it the best Italian restaurant in the Midwest, "if not in the United States." While he raves, another review rails that both kitchen and service are inept.

In this case, both writers could be correct. As the nursery rhyme goes, when it is good, it is very, very good. But when it is bad it is horrid. Sogni Dorati varies from night to night, sometimes even within the evening. When the kitchen and serving staff are on the mark they do indeed produce some of the best Italian food around and serve it with aplomb in an elegant environment.

Nondescript outside, Sogni Dorati is warm and comfortable inside, free of tacky trappings too often found in Italian restaurants. But try to avoid being seated in the small raised dining room next to the usually deserted bar.

This area, intended to be a cocktail lounge which never caught on, is too crowded for comfortable dining, so narrow that waiters and bus boys often kick the chair of the person facing the wall each time they pass.

The main dining room on two levels beyond the bar area is a different story entirely. It is roomy, comfortable and private. Comfy striped banquettes, forest green carpeting, dark wood and white clothed tables with lamps give this room sophisticated elegance.

Service can be smooth and professional or woefully unpolished. One night it took 25 minutes simply to get the menus, 45 minutes before the first course was served...too long even with the excellent breads and eggplant dip placed on the table as a starter. Although a drink order was taken, no one offered a wine list. No mention was made of the pre-set, pre-fixed piatti della casa special dinner. We experienced gaps of 15–20 minutes between courses. And it was clear no one really knew when to remove finished dishes (only when everyone in the party is finished) or present the next course (only when everyone in the party is present).

Sogni Dorati is the outgrowth of Mama DiPinto's, a modest pizza joint with great food. The crusty light Italian breads baked around herbed Italian sausage, escarole and cheeses are hers, as are many of the dishes. Her son Silvio is the intense young chef.

When this restaurant first opened, Silvio's creations often featured wild combinations of ingredients that surprised and delighted when they worked, and were accepted for experiments when they did not. The menu and list of specials was overwhelmingly long.

The cuisine has settled down. While unusual combinations still exist, they're now the exception rather than the norm. A long list of specials still supplements the printed menu. And the food is rich, rich, rich.

Appetizers include such items as seafood salad, clams with pesto, tomato artichoke salad and duck breast with honey tarragon dressing. By all means, try the apple stuffed with ground veal, raisins and pine nuts with subtle seasoning all on a honey-apple brandy sauce. A special dill and ricotta cheese tart with greens captures the essence of fresh dill, but essentially falls flat—a bland, lifeless appetizer.

Pastas as a mid-course at $5 also are available as a main course for roughly double the price. Due to the large portions and richness of the food, I recommend sharing a pasta as a mid-course. The duck-stuffed ravioli one night had terrific flavor. The fine duck filling in an al dente pasta pillow was supported by an exceedingly buttery sauce that begged to be polished off even as you felt your arteries closing.

A special entree, quail with pesto, comes wrapped around a cooked tomato. Again, the contrast of tastes and textures works marvelously to create a well-rounded dish. Thin slices of veal wrapped around an herbed riccota filling lack the intensity of flavor that characterizes most of DiPinto's cuisine and raises him above the average. Entrees come with a large portion of lightly cooked vegetables such as snow peas, zucchini and carrots.

Excellent moist cakes lead the dessert list. A triple chocolate cake will satisfy any chocoholic. The white cake with layers of sweetened whipped creme and slices of fresh strawberries on strawberry-laced vanilla sauce also pleases.

No one can question the chef's talent or ability. He turns out some exquisite dishes and no true failures. However, greatly flawed service and inconsistencies in the kitchen prevent this restaurant from attaining a higher rating, or ranking among the best Italian restaurants in the U.S.

★★ SONG HUONG
Vietnamese

5424 N. Broadway   271-6702
Hours: Mon, Wed–Fri 10:30 am–11 pm, Sat 9 am–10:30 pm,
         Sun 9 am–10 pm, closed Tues
Price range: Inexpensive
Credit cards: M   Sears   V
Reservations: Accepted

Carved from adjacent storefronts, Song Huong's dimly lighted exterior belies the good things inside, where there are two bright cheery rooms containing generous white-clothed tables and clean decor with no hokey Oriental decorations.

Named for the river that flows through Hue, the former capital of Vietnam, Song Huong serves Vietnamese and Chinese food. The customers tend to be Vietnamese families or students who flock there on weekends for inexpensive home cooking.

The food merits their support. The dishes sampled were

either good or outstanding. The owner's wife, Khen, cooks the Vietnamese dishes, assisted by a Chinese chef who prepares everything from crisp-skinned roast duck in a tantalizingly-complex, herb sauce to chop suey.

If you cannot distinguish between Chinese and Vietnamese dishes on the menu, the servers gladly help. Anything with fish sauce is Vietnamese. Among appetizers, try the sound pancake, a cross between egg foo yong and a stuffed pancake, filled with pork, shrimp and vegetables. Diners wrap pieces of the pancake in leaf lettuce and dip it in fish sauce. Some dishes come pre-wrapped ready for dipping, among them shrimp rice paper—rice paper stuffed with leaf lettuce, fresh coriander (cilantro), rice noodles, pork and shrimp. Others, such as broiled beef in rice paper, are do-it-yourself affairs. A plate of rice paper arrives with a plate of beef, sprouts and other fillings to be rolled inside. All of these are great fun and great-tasting as well.

The textures of some Vietnamese dishes may not appeal to the Western palate-the shrimp paste on sugar cane, for example. A paste of crushed shrimp is molded around sugar cane, then steamed and grilled before serving. The paste is sliced off the cane at the table, wrapped in lettuce and dipped before eating. The flavor, barbecue-like on the outside and slightly sweet from the cane on the inside, could hardly be surpassed but the texture is like rubber. Likewise, the Vietnamese paté that comes with the steamed rolls, ground pork and mushrooms in rice paper, also has a rubbery texture and in this case, little taste. Better appetizers include egg rolls and deep-fried quail.

Nightly specials appear in Vietnamese—ask for a translation. Game, like the venison with lemon grass, is a regular. Fish specialties include a wondrously sauced and seasoned deep-fried red snapper, simmered fish in a clay pot and steamed fish with noodles and mushrooms, made recently with catfish. All fresh fish is carefully prepared with an aromatic array of complimentary seasonings and sauces. Also excellent is the beef on a sizzling platter. The only disappointing dish was the sweet-and-sour spare ribs: plain with dried out stringy pork.

Desserts are limited to five unlikely-sounding sweet drinks based on green beans, red beans or loganberries— depending on the diner's taste—in iced sweetened coconut milk. These desserts take some getting used to, but are refreshing. Song Huong has no liquor license but welcomes customers who bring their own.

★ ★ ★ SPIAGGIA
   Italian

One Magnificent Mile, Oak St. and Michigan Ave.
280-2750
Hours: Mon–Thurs 11:30 am–11 pm, Fri & Sat 11:30 am–
         11:30 pm, Sun 11:30 am–8 pm; dining room hours:
         Mon–Sat lunch 11:30 am–2:30 pm, Mon–Thurs dinner
         5:30–10:30 pm, Fri & Sat dinner 5:30–11:30 pm, Sun
         5:30–9 pm
Price range: Expensive
Credit cards: A C D M V
Reservations: Necessary

From his glass-encased kitchen-stage, chef Tony Mantuano orchestrates his cuisine like a maestro conducting a symphony. Nothing turns out short of good and many dishes are extraordinary. If only the maitre d' could do the same for his crew. Sloppy, inattentive, unprofessional... their performance, while improved since the restaurant opened, is inexcusable in this beautiful expensive restaurant with its talented chef.

Spiaggia is a place to see and be seen. On the second floor of One Magnificent Mile, a marble hallway leads into a large vestibule flanked by wood and glass panels. Beyond the maitre d's station, lies the three-tiered dining room with its floor-to-ceiling windows which allow almost every diner—there's room for 125—a view of Oak Street Beach and the Lake, albeit with a bit of neck-craning. A bar wraps around the wall opposite the windows to the left. To the right, one can watch the kitchen activity through etched glass. Pastel walls, warm-toned marble floors, stained wood banquettes, glass globes, a piano...the look, created by Chicago architect Joseph Meisel, is subdued, sophisticated Postmodern.

Atmosphere alone does not a great restaurant make. Luckily, Mantuano's cuisine shows tremendous promise. The menu offers an impressive array of ambitious dishes. Some smashing successes include the perfect ravioli stuffed with a thin but tasty layer of seasoned, ground lobster and covered with a rich aromatic sauce of cream and cheese with mushrooms. The famed thin-crust pizza topped with duck sausage and goat cheese or sun-dried tomatoes and wild mushrooms is in a league by itself.

The assortment of seafood in the insalata di mare varies daily, revolving around squid, bay scallops and shrimp. In the classic Northern Italian vitello tonnato, thin slices of veal wrapped with tuna-caper mayonnaise are moist, tender and hold up nicely against the light, smooth sauce. Equally classic carpaccio wins raves as well with its thin slices of raw sirloin topped with excellent imported parmesan and capers, dressed with olive oil and lemon juice.

Other commendable dishes include tomato pasta butterflies with asparagus, veal chop with fresh sage, grilled boned quail, soft-shell crab and a changing array of fish specials. Filet of red snapper grilled and topped with garlic butter turns out beautifully. Tagliata, sliced sirloin grilled rare and topped with fresh rosemary, exemplifies the simplicity of Mantuano's cuisine. Underlaid with fine olive oil and lemon, the exceptionally tender meat will satisfy the most demanding carnivore.

A wide range of desserts lures most diners to expand their capacity a notch or two more. The flavors change but the quality of the sorbetti (ices) and gelati (ice-cream) never varies. Particularly good are fresh raspberries and blackberries topped with zabaglione, poached pear in zabaglione and tiramisu, a cross between pudding and cheesecake. The wine list features nothing but Italian wines at moderate prices. The knowledgeable wine steward willingly helps with wine selections.

An Italian-style meal for two will cost at least $100. So go when your plastic isn't closing in on the maximum credit line. A choice bottle of wine or two will push the tariff quickly higher. A good bet for those who want to sample the cuisine without paying the dinner price is the lunch menu with many of the same dishes at about 20 percent less.

★ ★ SRI UTHAI
Thai

4323 W. Addison   725-6751
Hours: Tues–Thurs 11 am–9 pm, Fri–Sun 11 am–11 pm
Price range: Inexpensive
Credit cards: A   V
Reservations: Accepted
Handicap

Sri means "sun" or "bright" in the Thai language and with walls paneled of light-colored wood, forest green clothed-tables topped with glass, black high-tech chairs and bright lighting, Sri Uthai manages to capture the spirit of sunlight despite its storefront location.

There can be some problems of communication. For example, though squid with mint leaves was ordered one night, shrimp with mint leaves was delivered to the table instead. Exquisitely prepared with a wonderful light pan sauce, mint leaves, onion and green jalapeño pepper, the dish looked and tasted so good we didn't bother to change it. The food at this little Thai restaurant is worth the occasional frustrations.

Satay hardly ever tastes bad. On the other hand it is rarely spectacular. Here it is delivered to the table sizzling and flaming. This showiness could be disasterous if the satay didn't turn out well. Luckily it tastes great. A little bowl of somewhat chunky, slightly spicy peanut sauce accompanies the tender, juicy, marinated meat.

Mee krob, sweet crispy noodles with shrimp, egg and bean sprouts, also works well as an appetizer. Shrimp Uthai mixes to good effect shrimp, ground pork, onion and pepper on a bed of cellophane noodles. The tod mun, fish cake, has a light texture and good, slightly spicy curried flavor that may be too fishy for some tastes.

One asterisk next to a dish supposedly means "spicy dish for adventure," according to the menu and two means "very spicy hot." Despite these warnings, those used to fiery hot Thai dishes may be disappointed in the lack of seasoning here. Just ask and the chef will turn on the heat for you if you wish.

Excellent soups include the spicy chicken coconut soup, a delightful mixture of chicken chunks, fresh coriander, onions, red peppers, green peppers and ka, an aromatic Thai root, in an extremely smooth coconut sauce. Poo-tak, the seafood soup, also pleases. Both are served in a fire pot which adds theater as well as keeping the soup hot. Panaeng beef, basically a red curry beef, features moist, tender slices of beef in a rich, spicy red gravy meant to be eaten over rice. The dish seems simple at first, but blossoms on the palate to reveal complex spicing. Like most of the entrees, this one came with a decorative garnish of carved tomato-half with parsley on a bed of lettuce.

Although a number of desserts are listed, most seem to be unavailable. Thai coffee with a plate of lychee nuts and carved orange sections made a fine finale one night, even though it wasn't what we ordered.

The owner-waiter tries hard to please customers despite the occasional difficulties with communication. And he seems genuinely pleased when his customers enjoy their meals, which must be always. For the price, the food is excellent and demonstrates more creative flair than most other neighborhood Thai restaurants.

★ STALEY'S OF CHICAGO
American

505 S. Wells St.   939-4824
Hours: Mon–Fri 11 am–8 pm, closed Sat & Sun
Price range: Moderate
Credit cards: A C D M V
Reservations: Accepted
Handicap

If you thought that all of the old-fashioned places downtown which provided an honest meal at a fair price had been replaced by trendy eateries where combinations of ingredients sounded like something out of a Fellini movie, someone should introduce you to Staley's, the restaurant with a dining car grafted on to its side. It has served the south Loop since 1929.

Owners Pat and Bob are proud of their heritage and say so at some length on their menu. Staley's is a haunt for many regulars, but first-time visitors may wonder what they've gotten themselves into as they navigate their way from the front door through a dark, foreboding hallway to the real entrance. Once inside this door, however, a slightly brighter, considerably warmer bar lined with those who would rather drink lunch or dinner than eat it, stretches toward the dining room to the right with dark wooden tables and chairs. This room is fine, but the real fun is off to the right again: the dining car. Darkly stained oak planks line the entire interior with its square windows open to not-so-beautiful Congress Parkway and a few old buildings beyond. Still, the effect has its charms.

Basically Staley's is a steak and chop house. However a sprinkling of seafood gives a nod to lighter fare. Chef Peter Pappas has cooked at Staley's for more than 36 years. While most everything turns out well, especially the broiled calves' liver with bacon and sauteed onions, Pete may not be quite as careful as he once was. For example, on one visit an otherwise terrific corned beef hash came burned to charcoal on the bottom.

Baked shrimps a la Staley's has a charge of garlic that will send most patrons diving for their Certs when they leave. Nevertheless the breaded shrimp are fresh and taste great.

The seafood chowder has surprisingly full flavor given its somewhat watery broth. A mundane mix of lettuce comes drenched in dressing, but then Staley's never claimed to specialize in light nouvelle fare.

Friendly waitresses generally attend to diners' needs efficiently but occasionally disappear without warning. Still, this is a down home restaurant that more than deserves to thrive downtown for the next fifty years and beyond.

★ **STANDARD INDIA**
Indian

871 N. Rush St.   943-1050
Hours: Lunch daily 11:30 am–3 pm, Dinner 5–10:30 pm
Price range: Moderate
Credit cards: A D V
Reservations: Accepted

This new branch of a long-time Devon Avenue favorite, now occupies the old Doro's space on Rush Street. The new restaurant looks much the same as Doro's did with gold wallpaper, gold-tinged banquettes, red carpet and crystal chandeliers. Only the old sabers and shields hung on the walls and new aromas in the air hint at the transformation that took place.

While not as sophisticated and polished as Gandhara before it burned, Standard India does produce some excellent tandoori oven dishes as well as other good, if not sensational standards. A lunch buffet allows sampling a wide range of Indian curries and tandoori dishes at a very reasonable price.

Among the appetizers try the somosa—two golden-brown fried patties filled with spiced potatos and peas or the kabob, minced lamb patties blended with lentils, onions and fresh herbs. Samosa, mashed potato patties filled with spiced lentils, peas and herbs, is also highly recommended.

Dips come on the side with appetizers and entrees. Be sure to order some of the good tandoori-baked Indian breads. Nan, the Indian staple, is made from leavened white flour. Roti is the leavened, whole wheat version. These also come with such ingredients as ground lamb, onion and spices or potatoes.

The tandoori chicken and lamb dishes are some of the best choices here. However, at times, these selections turn out to be drier than they should. Merg, boneless tandoori chicken cooked with chopped tomatoes and butter, tastes fine, but even the moist toppings fail to mask the chicken's dryness.

Rogan josah, a red lamb curry, doesn't live up to the elegant environs. The pieces of bony lamb are messy to eat, taste too gamey and dry and are gristly.

Portions are quite large and the prices reasonable. However, the food in general seems more down-home than sophisticated Indian fare.

Desserts include kheer, a pudding made from rice, milk, and sugar, garnished with almonds, pistachio nuts and a maraschino cherry. It looks like cottage cheese and except for the sweetness, doesn't taste significantly different, either. Rasmalai is cottage cheese served with sweetened milk topped with pistachios and somehow works better for me.

Two can dine quite handsomely on well under $50. Service is attentive and good. The wine list amounts to several bottles presented at the table on a cart.

★ STAR OF CHICAGO
American

Navy Pier   800-782-7827 or 644-5914
Hours: Warm weather months dinner cruises last 3 hours and
       depart at 7 pm Sat–Thurs, 9 pm Fri, closed Wed
Price range: Cruise and dinner about $40.
Credit cards: A M V
Reservations: Strongly suggested

The Star of Chicago dining and entertainment cruise ship has improved greatly since its 1983 debut. It now provides excellent service. The young servers are pleasant, helpful and fun. The food, now cooked aboard by two chefs, tastes better than the average buffet fare. Of course the real reason to go on the Star of Chicago isn't the food; it's the fun and romance of cruising past the beautiful skyline all a-twinkle at night.

Designed to seat 350 on two dining decks, the ship is reasonably comfortable despite the fairly tight packed tables and chairs. On the first deck, diners are seated at a sort of counter in front of the large windows. On the second deck, a band plays before a small, romantic dance floor. Both decks are air conditioned.

The buffet is served downstairs. A hostess comes around to each party to announce when it is their turn to approach the salad, entree and dessert bars. Waitresses take drink orders and fill them promptly. The dishes emphasize fresh ingredients; however, because of the limitations of buffet serving, some dishes inevitably end up dry and crusted-over. Still, there's a wide enough selection to ensure that some offerings are always fresh and have enough variety to please most tastes.

Entrees include two fish dishes, two fowl and roast beef. The chicken tastes overbaked, the turkey breast wrapped around a slice of ham is nicely flavored, the fish is pretty good and the meat, though not prime rib, is juicy and tender. Scalloped potatoes, new potatoes and rice turn out pretty well, as does the vegetable medley. The salad bar is huge; good are chicken and watercress salad, marinated mushrooms with broccoli and cold tortellini and cucumbers with fresh dill. The Caesar salad is fair, the Waldorf pretty good.

Desserts include four cakes, which are moist, buttery and well-prepared. A limited, but carefully selected list of American wines at moderate prices complement the food.

For a special evening out, the trip is probably worth the price. There are cheaper lunch and Sunday brunch cruises and Friday evening and Saturday night cocktail cruises.

★ STAR OF SIAM
Thai

11 E. Illinois St.   670-0100
Hours: Mon–Thurs 11 am–9:30 pm, Fri & Sat 11 am–10:30
        pm, closed Sun.
Price range: Moderate
Credit cards: A C D M V
Reservations: Accepted

The Star of Siam's sleek interior and large portions at reasonable prices make it one of the most popular downtown Thai restaurants. Like Ananda and Pattaya, Star of Siam is among the new breed of Thai restaurants that have abandoned storefront stoicism for contemporary design. Situated in a clean, loft-like room, the Star makes the most of its stripped-down decor. Huge sand-blasted beams rise from the floor to equally large timbers stretching overhead. The light-colored wood contrasts with red brick walls and red-orange painted accents. Gray industrial carpeting spreads across the floors and up over benches where diners sit on red pillows.

The decor suggest informality and fun, which is just what this bustling restaurant delivers. A friendly knowledgeable staff makes this a great place for newcomers to Thai food, and the food, while not the best Thai cuisine around, isn't bad. Hot spicing typifies Thai cuisine. Here a moderate hand rules the kitchen but bowls of red pepper sauce, green peppers and a deadly dried pepper mixture sits on each table for those who like it (very) hot.

Start with a shared order of some of the best satay in the area. Six skewers of chicken or beef chunks have a pleasant curry flavor and come with a smooth, slightly spicy peanut sauce. Fresh spring rolls fail to show up with the crab meat topping billed in the menu, but otherwise win praise with their mix of crisp, fresh vegetables, tofu and egg. Mee krob—crunchy spaghetti-sized noodles with egg, bean sprouts and sweet tomato sauce—might suit those who like to play it safe. Tod mun koong—fried, spongy-textured shrimp cakes with enough red pepper to get a diner's attention—will please the more adventurous. Both spicy soups—ton kha kai and tom yum —are great.

Thai salads range from vegetarian with fried tofu to meat-based. The fermented fish sauce on the nam tok may assault the nostrils, but the lemon-doused slices of tender beef bloom with flavor when sampled with a bit of cool, crisp lettuce that helps put out the fire from the red peppers. Nothing could taste fresher than naem sod, chicken salad with juicy steamed chicken doused with lemon and ginger.

The entrees include a few conventional Oriental-American dishes, but those playing it safe should try Star's chicken delight, a full-flavored mix of chicken, cashews, and vegetables. Also good are the several complex green and yellow curries, fried spicy basil leaves with meat—not that spicy and terrific tasting—and the super Star snapper, most expensive at $14 but worth every cent.

For desserts there are soothing homemade coconut ice cream or iced tropical fruits or the banana cooked in coconut milk, a hot dessert wonderful in its simplicity.

★★ STAR TOP CAFE
American-Continental

2748 N. Lincoln Ave.   281-0997
Hours: Tues–Sat 5:30–10 pm, closed Sun & Mon
Price range: Moderate
Credit cards: A D M V
Reservations: Recommended

The Star Top Cafe looks like an unassuming neighborhood place with its taupe walls whose plainness is broken by artwork—some of it chef Aydin Dincer's, some by co-owner and waiter Bill Ammon's wife and other local artists. The room is home—and homemade—as if not much money went into finishing touches. Nevertheless, the result is a comfortable and pleasantly casual storefront restaurant.

What the Star Top lacks in interior decoration, it makes up for in spades with good food. In fact, Dincer and Ammons would rather turn away customers than compromise their good food. The 45-seat restaurant allows them to turn out quality.

The menu changes regularly so dishes mentioned here may not be available. Among the appetizers, the homemade spinach-filled raviolis arrive perfectly cooked with an earthy filling. A huge slab of course country-style paté also makes a nice beginning, with its rich flavor, mustard and vegetables. A half dozen fried smelt come perfectly crisp and fresh with a smooth herb mayonnaise. Soups change nightly.

Dincer understands pastas and handles them well, especially the raviolis which frequently show up as entrees as well as appetizers. A ravioli stuffed with mussels, shrimp and lobster served one night was great. The lake trout with the spinach ravioli and mussels on a bed of angel hair pasta is a good, if filling, combination. A salad of chicken, mussels and shrimp offered as an entree one evening was a study in contrasting tastes and textures. If the tuna with lemon basil is available, by all means order it. The sauce is the perfect complement to the fish. A supporting cracked wheat salad served on the side also seems the right match for this entree. Meat lovers will like leg of lamb or scallopini of pork.

Desserts disappoint far more frequently than other courses. The best offering probably is the mocha daquois—a rich, mocha buttercream between crisp layers of airy meringue flecked with nuts. Although limited, the wine list is moderately priced, from $11–$20 a bottle, and all are offered by the glass.

Service can be problematic when the restaurant gets busy, but in general Ammons handles the front of the house with aplomb.

As hard as the owners want this place to remain an unpretentious hangout, the food is simply too good to keep it a secret for long. The Star Top is a jewel in Chicago's restaurant galaxy.

★ STATS
Eclectic

2 E. Ontario St.   943-4854
Hours: Lunch Mon–Sat 11 am–3 pm, Sun 11 am–3 pm, Dinner Sun–Thurs 5–11 pm, Sat 5–midnight.

Price range: Moderately expensive
Credit cards: A   M   V
Reservations: Accepted
Handicapped

An amalgam of everything that's trendy, Stats' interior is slick as the dickens. Polished marble and mirrors seem to be everywhere. The subdued beige-pastel color scheme seems customized for yuppies. Even the little touches are in place. For example, there's no pay telephone, but "guests" can use the high-tech house telephone.

Stats does go the other trendy places one better. Of course, there's the kitchen open to the view of diners. Of course, there's a sprinkling of Cajun and Creole dishes on the lengthy, highly diverse "grazing-style" menu. Of course there's a wood grill. But Stats doesn't go in for just any wood. It uses Hawaiian kiawe wood charcoal for its grill—designer wood for a designer place.

Friendly servers do a good job but don't have a lot of knowledge about what they're serving. The wine list includes some interesting bottles from some unexpected American wineries. Wines by the glass are also available for sampling and prices are attractively moderate. As a hint of what's truly important here, the back page of the menu is devoted to beers, scotches, bourbons and liqueurs—an impressive list.

The food neither delights nor greatly disappoints. It falls somewhere in between. The tempting descriptions of the many dishes on the large menu, with a long list of fresh seafood offerings, sound great. But the food rarely lives up to its advanced billing.

Among the appetizers such items as steamed clams and coco shrimp start with fresh ingredients, but the competently prepared dishes are just that: competent but unexciting. Carpaccio, which even good Italian restaurants often fail to do well, has little flavor here.

A long list of soups and salads offers an alternative to the appetizers. Salads like, romaine or spinach turn out fine. Again, nothing startles, but aside from a bit too much dressing, nothing disasterous happens with these salads either.

The entrees are divided among poultry, pasta, seafood and meat dishes. Pastas turn out on the overcooked side of al dente, but have fresh-tasting sauces. The meaty bolognese surprises with its full flavor.

Fresh seafood is offered with a variety of preparations and saucing. For example, Hawiian ahi might be available kiawe-grilled with ginger and lime butter, grilled with kal bi marinade or baked with simple lemon butter. Grilled rockfish remains moist inside with just a hint of smokiness from the grill.

Although not quite so trendy, and relegated to a lesser position on the menu, grilled steaks and roast leg of lamb are good bets.

Desserts like everything else here are pleasing, but not spectacular. The New Orleans pear bread pudding is interesting. Or try the rich, homemade Irish coffee cheesecake.

Stats will win no awards for culinary sophistication. Still, its trendy interior, trendy menu and trendy clientele probably work as well as any restaurant of the genre in the area.

★★ LA STRADA RISTORANTE
Northern Italian

155 N. Michigan Ave.   565-2200
Hours: Lunch Mon–Fri 11:30 am–2:30 pm, Dinner Mon–
        Thurs 5–10 pm, Sat 5–11 pm, closed Sun
Price range: Expensive
Credit cards: A C D M V
Reservations: Required
Handicap

Its gold banquettes, salmon-colored walls, crystal

chandeliers and white-clothed tables, are intended to create an elegant ambiance, but decor actually falls awkwardly somewhere between baroque and modern. Even so the room is comfortable, its atmosphere is at least pleasing enough. The food more than makes up for any shortcomings in decor.

One enters either down a set of stairs or via a glass-enclosed elevator to the lower level of Doral Plaza. A large bar and cocktail area holds waiting diners at the front of the restaurant. The large dining room is to the rear. At busy times diners may encounter waits despite reservations.

Part of the reason things get tangled up is that diners like to linger over the excellent food here.

Start with steamed mussels or clams in a light, herby tomato wine sauce, wafer-thin dried beef drizzled with premium olive oil and lemon, carpaccio or sauteed shrimp. Then move on to the pastas, some of the best around. Half-orders can be shared as a mid-course.

How the kitchen manages to cook such wire-thin vermicelli to a perfect al dente remains a mystery. But most of the dishes here are prepared with extreme care. This thin spaghetti comes tossed with tomatoes, bits of proscuitto and wild mushrooms, light and flavorful. Homemade noodles under a rich, cheesy Alfredo sauce also turn out perfectly. Strangely, risotto is hard to find in Chicago. Here it is well-prepared with a generous amount of saffron—rich and filling, but delightful.

The house salad of limestone lettuce with endive, hearts of palm, artichoke hearts and tomato dressing with lemon and superb olive oil ranks far above the average. This and three other salads must be ordered a la carte.

Based on high quality veal, such dishes as the simple piccata and the restrained saltimbocca cooked with fresh sage, proscuitto and wine lead the entree offerings. Large gulf shrimp sauteed in wine with mushrooms may be a tad overcooked, but taste terrific in their buttery wine sauce.

Daily specials augment the menu offerings. Portions are large, mitigating the need for desserts, which don't measure up to the rest of the cuisine. However the smooth custard and fresh fruit are good bets.

Generally professional servers get a bit short-tempered when the room is full. By and large however, service is attentive and efficient. The excellent wine list tempts many to add greatly to their bills and their enjoyment.

★ SU CASA
Mexican

49 E. Ontario St.   943-4041
Hours: Mon–Fri 11:30–1 am, Sat 5 pm–1 am, closed Sun
Price range: Moderately expensive
Credit cards: A C D M V
Reservations: Accepted
Handicap

What Ike Sewell (see Pizzerio Uno) did for pizza he didn't even try to do for Mexican cuisine when he opened this restaurant. There are no great innovations on this menu. Indeed most is pretty standard stuff. Nevertheless, the arched stucco walls, Mexican tiles, and large, heavy imported wooden tables and chairs give the feel of a genuine hacienda. Also, on some nights a guitarist strolls through the room, adding to the atmosphere and the fun. The food, while toned down for the gringos, is consistent and good.

One thing has slipped in recent years, costing this restaurant a star: the service. Regulars once received royal treatment. Now the maitre d' doesn't seem to know many people by sight and too many of the servers don't seem to do anything more than get by with minimum effort.

Be sure to sip a margarita or two. Su Casa's potent tequila elixir may be the best in the city.

Among the best of the entrees are the chiles rellenos. Made from real poblano peppers stuffed with cheese or ground meat, then lightly battered and fried, this is a world-class version of the classic Mexican dish.

Other menu offerings run the gamut of usual offerings. Carne asada disappoints with a well-cooked, but poor-quality steak. Burritos are good bets, as are enchiladas, the above-average tacos and tostadas.

A few seafood offerings round out the menu. While not bad, these don't live up to similar dishes at some other restaurants in the area that specialize in Mexican seafood.

Portions are large, with good refried beans, rice and usually shredded lettuce served with the order The low prices for the location attract large crowds so the place gets quite noisy most evenings. Waits, even with advance reservations, are not unusual on extremely busy nights.

Su Casa may have slipped a notch in recent years, but it still offers the best Mexican food close to downtown, and more consistent quality than many of the more authentic Mexican eateries in the ethnic neighborhoods.

SWEETWATER
American
Rating: Fair

1028 Rush St. 787-5552
Hours: Sun–Thurs Lunch 11:30 am–3 pm, Dinner 5–11 pm,
*   Fri & Sat Lunch 11:30 am–3 pm, dinner 5 pm–12:30*
*   am, Sun brunch 11 am–4 pm.*
Price range: Moderately expensive
Credit cards: A C D M V
Reservations: Accepted
Handicap

Once upon a time, Rush Street was so hot that all a restaurant had to do was open its doors, have a large bar and passable food, and it would almost automatically make money. Today things are tougher. Many of the original restaurants no longer exist. Others, like Sweetwater, hang on, but they seem to have lost their focus.

Sweetwater follows part of the original formula. Inside the door to the right is a sort of cafe with large windows that offer a view of the Rush Street action. Beside this, there is seating on both sides of the large bar to encourage mingling. Behind the bar and up a short flight of stairs, the dining area sweeps from the left wall to the right side of the room, so that diners can look down on that action if they desire. The Art Nouveau decor with birds and tulips and mirrors on the walls, candles on the white clothed tables and subdued lighting seems to be an attempt at romantic ambiance. Yet somehow it seems the place should have a big dance floor and throbbing disco music. . .an odd mix.

Service is indifferent at best. The sort of "get 'em in and get 'em out" attitude that prevails when a waitress has been hit on by too many boozed-up conventioneers.

Appetizers are a mixed bag: oysters on the half shell, calamari, escargot, French onion soup, stuffed mushrooms and the like. If all these things were superior one would characterize the menu as eclectic. But when they don't work the characterization becomes less generous.

The escargot-stuffed mushrooms fail miserably. Calamari fares better, but the fresh squid turns rubbery from overcooking and suffers under the too-salty batter. French onion soup rates a "C" for its average broth covered with good, toasted cheese.

Entrees again feature an eclectic mix. Some dishes, such as the broiled chicken breast with avocado and Monterey Jack cheese, show a California influence. Others, such as sea scallops with champagne sauce, are solidly French. A number of seafood specials are offered each evening.

In general, meat dishes better the seafood here. And simple items such as steak and broiled veal chops fare far better than those with complicated preparations and saucing. This restaurant is an unusual case where the quality of the raw ingredients seems to exceed the skill of the cooks or the care they take in preparation.

Sweetwater will have to find itself before it can once again become the darling of Rush St. In the meantime, the place is okay, but far from great.

SZECHWAN KITCHEN
Chinese
Rating: Fair

2660 N. Halsted St.   *348-5652*
Hours: Daily 11 am–11 pm
Price range: Moderate
Credit cards: A   D   M   V
Reservations: Accepted

Although a laborious explanation of Chinese food accompanying the menu shows a certain lack of faith in the sophistication of the Northside diner, the message does underscore the desire to please their patrons.

Divided into two sides (smoking and non-smoking) separated by a plant-filled room divider, the dining room is free of tacky Chinese lanterns and the like. Tables topped with white cloths and candles are flanked by comfortable chairs. Even the ever-present Kikkoman's bottle has been replaced with a pretty china pitcher that holds soy sauce.

Pot stickers disappoint with their rather thick, gummy pastry and bland pork filling. Hunan beef sticks make a better choice. Thin slices of beef on a long wooden skewer look like Thai satay, but have been marinated in a hot pepper sauce before broiling. Tender and flavorsome this boneless barbecued beef makes a great beginning.

Four moo shu pancakes come with the mix of shredded pork, cabbage, green onions, mushrooms and egg for the Moo Shu Pork. The waitress demonstrates the art of wrapping the ingredients in the skin-thin pancakes, then allows she'll let her customers "have some fun" with the next set. Many restaurants serve a sickeningly sweet plum sauce with their moo shu. Here the plum sauce has a tart, slightly vinegary taste that lightens this dish considerably.

The menu warns that garlic chicken is hot. It really isn't unless you happen to bite into one of the dried peppers mixed in with the other ingredients. Luckily those incendiary peppers are bright red and easy to avoid for those with less than iron clad palates. Again this dish proves to be exceedingly light with slightly vinegary overtones.

Steamed rice comes with entrees. Prices are reasonable, about $25 for two with a couple of beers. However, Szechwan Kitchen does not equal the area's great Chinese restaurants.

★ ★ ★ TALLGRASS
French

1006 S. State, Lockport, IL   815-838-556
Hours: Thurs–Sun 6–11 pm, brunch Sun 12:30 am–1 pm,
      closed Mon–Wed
Price range: Expensive
Credit cards: A
Reservations: Necessary

Lockport seems an unlikely location for a fine, creative French restaurant, but here it is. The equally unlikely owners, two former schoolteachers who loved food and decided to try their hand at a restaurant, do a terrific job.

One enters the restaurant by heading down a set of front stairs, through the basement where a bar, apparently intended to hold waiting customers, usually stands vacant and unattended. Diners go upstairs to enter the dining room proper.

This tiny dining room, which seats perhaps forty, has the comfortable feel of an elegant Victorian sitting room, with high ceilings, dark wood, patterned wallpaper and forest green linen. Behind the small bar at the rear antique glassware is displayed. Indeed all of the cut glass and crystal goblets used at the tables are unmatched, but beautiful.

Bread and a small complimentary appetizer start meals off. Entree prices include a second appetizer, salad and dessert. The menu changes regularly to feature the best fresh ingredients the chef finds in the markets.

Appetizer choices include fresh seafood and excellent pastas. Sea scallops with the roe and shrimp in a delicate cream sauce work wonders after the long drive from the city. The same mix of seafood might find its way into a seafood salad. Soups are rich and full-bodied. Pastas have just the slightest resistance to the bite, indicating precise preparation.

A good, simple house salad of leaf lettuce and mustard vinaigrette tastes great. Tempting special salads also are available, such as a warm salad with poached scallops and sweetbreads on a bed of watercress.

As good as the appetizers are, the entrees often exceed them in quality. Duck breast cooked rare has gamey overtones, but is surprisingly tender. The rich sauce based on a reduction of juices brings the dish together gracefully.

Other entrees might include rack of lamb with gorgonzola sauce, sole with rich, creamy lobster sauce, twin filets of veal and beef, or simple lobster with butter sauce and kiwi.

Desserts also excel. For an extra charge of $3.50 diners may select their own assortment of cakes, sherbets and pastries from the nightly offerings of the diner's choosing and is highly recommended.

The wine list, while not as extensive as those at many other restaurants of equal caliber, features some unexpected vintages. The prices are surprisingly reasonable.

Service has improved steadily after a shaky start, and is now by-and-large professional.

★ TAMBORINE
Eclectic

200 E. Chestnut St.   944-4000
Hours: Mon–Thurs 11:30 am–10 pm, Fri & Sat 11:30–2 am,
*   Sun 4:30–10 pm*
Price range: Moderate
Credit cards: A   C   D   M   V
Reservations: Accepted

Located behind Water Tower Place and the Hancock building, this average restaurant should charge an arm and a leg for its average food. Instead it keeps the lid on pricing. Good for it!

One suspects the real profit in the place comes from the bar, which bustles almost every night and really hops on weekends when there's entertainment. Part of that entertainment can be an open microphone where customers can come up and do their thing. Depending on the level of inebriation and talent, this can be a lot of fun or a disaster.

Up a short flight of steps from the coat room, a bar stretches toward the two-level dining room, where the decor makes a run at glitz, but falls short of its goal. At noon, the clientele is a mix of secretaries, business types and little old ladies. The evening crowd tends to be far livelier.

Service is good, although servers can get harried on crowded nights.

Appetizers are predictable: deep-fried mushrooms, crab Louis, good French-fried onion ring loaf and so on. Two of the most interesting appetizers are also probably the best—crisp sesame-coated chicken chunks with a sweet mustard sauce, and hot artichoke heart cocktail.

One entree you can't go wrong with is the hamburger. Big, juicy, made with quality meat and cooked to perfection, it's both filling and good.

Good, fresh-tasting calves liver sauteed with mushrooms, onions and green pepper also works well. Lime chicken stays moist and tender under a tart lime sauce. Steak, one of the highest priced items on the menu, starts with good quality beef and comes cooked precisely as ordered.

Desserts are of the too gooey and too sweet variety and can be passed up. Why not save the calories for another drink? One more might give you enough courage to try your hand at the open mike.

★ **TANGO**
Seafood

Hotel Belmont, 3172 N. Sheridan Rd.   935-0350
Hours: Lunch Tues–Sat 11:30 am–2:30 pm, Dinner Sun–
*   Thurs 5–10:30 pm, Fri & Sat 5–11:30 pm, brunch*
*   Sun 11 am–2:30 pm*
Price range: Expensive
Credit cards: A   M   V
Reservations: Recommended

Tango's crisp and clean decor, considered on the cutting edge a dozen years ago, could use a bit of updating today. Still, the place has interesting Pop art on the walls and somehow manages to impart a sense of romance. The mood starts with the dark womb-like bar area done in tones of black and grey, and carries through to the room next door where high, peach-colored, fabric-covered walls jut out at angles to form private booths. The main dining rooms are open and can get noisy when filled, but generous amounts of space between tables help maintain some sense of privacy.

Tango started out as a place for culinary adventure, then

tired somewhat. Indeed, a succession of chefs has brought highs and lows in the quality of the food. Now the sense of adventure returns, with an eclectic menu that ranges from French-inspired nouvelle dishes to Cajun blackened fish.

Through all of the kitchen regimes the quality of the ingredients remained high, and it remains high today.

Although not adventurous, the oysters copa—pristinely fresh oysters on the half shell, with a dollop of caviar and horseradish sauce—remains a favorite. In general here, the simpler the appetizer the better.

There is a large selection of fish from all over the country, including local sources. A few of the menu offerings plus some specials are routinely grilled over wood, and other selections may be grilled on request. Grilled salmon, tuna and swordfish all turn out just slightly smoky, moist and mild.

The blackened fish is crusty, with enough spice to add interest without overwhelming the flavor of the fish, as it does in so many other restaurants.

Good steaks and chops, poultry and game augment the seafood. Entrees come with soup, salad and fresh vegetables.

The wine list is far better than average, with a good selection of wines in all price ranges. Fresh fruit and pastries lead the dessert offerings.

The quality of the service depends on who does the serving. Most often service is attentive, pleasant and professional, but an occasional waiter is aloof and sloppy.

★ TANIA'S
Cuban

2659 N. Milwaukee Ave.   235-7120
Hours: Daily 11:30 am–midnight
Price range: Moderate
Credit cards: A   C   D   M   V
Reservations: Accepted
Other: Valet parking

My Cuban friends say this isn't really Cuban food. So be it. But at this cozy old Spanish-Cuban-Mexican restaurant, expect the unexpected and lots of fun. Some of the waiters are a bit off-beat and the decor is disappointingly suburban—a packed but comfortable dining room with a small working fountain, beige walls, tiled floors and light wood trim.

To begin, slightly sweet, puffy disks of excellent white bread is served in a basket. The menu lists only four appetizers: nachos, croquette of ham and chicken, guacamole and shrimp cocktail. The croquettes (hot and crisp outside, a smooth puree of seasoned chicken flecked with ham inside, with a slightly spicy sauce) and shrimp (four of them, large, tender and steamed) are the best bets.

The bean soups are excellent. A clean-tasting and wonderful black bean soup balances seasonings that make this Cuban specialty sing with flavor. White bean soup contains ham and chorizo (spicy sausage), onion and greens that work wonderfully together. Tempting shrimp or seafood soups both require 30-minute waits. The salad is the usual melange of lettuce, carrots and peppers.

Entree prices vary greatly: Spanish seafood specialities cost roughly twice as much as the Mexican and Cuban dishes. However, it may be worth it for seafood lovers. Enough to satisfy two or more, the paella Valenciana takes 50 minutes to prepare but the casserole of yellow rice, chicken, clams, shrimp, scallops, red snapper and stone crab is fresh and excellent. Zarzuela mixes similar seafood in a much heavier-handed tomato and wine sauce.

Those with smaller appetites might choose the garlic shrimp: six large, grilled shrimp perfectly prepared with a heady complement of garlic and lemon. Tomatoes, lettuce and orange slices come on the side. Skip the Mexican specialities for the Cuban. While the Mexican dishes here are fine, the Cuban specialities are more exciting and incredibly cheap. One of the best is boliche, eye of round steak wrapped around chorizo and cooked in a spicy tomato sauce with rice and red and green peppers. Slow cooked, the beef absorbs the nicely spiced flavor of the sauce and the excellent chorizo.

A creamy flan would be too sweet if it weren't for the bitter caramel sauce—great stuff. Pudding diplomatico, also good, is a flan set on anisette-soaked sponge cake. Fresh fruits, including guava and papaya, come with cream cheese.

Tania's may not serve great cuisine, but it's a great place for relaxation, fun and Latino culinary treats.

TAP ROOT PUB
Seafood
Rating: Fair

636 W. Willow St.   642-5235
Hours: Daily 11–2 am
Price range: Moderate
Credit cards: A M V
Reservations: Accepted

The original Tap Root was lost to progress. Owner Harley Budd made headlines with his fight to save the 100-year-old building that used to house this tavern. He made headlines a few other times, as well: when someone charged the place was dirty and was operating without a license, when it caught fire and when old Harley was said to have pumped the walls full of bullets. Recently things have settled down. The Tap Root remains a good old working-class pub with some pretty good, if uneven, food at some very low prices. Service can be good or awful but for a casual evening out this neighborhood restaurant is not bad, especially in the outdoor garden on a warm summer evening.

Through all its travails, the Pub has managed to retain most of its charm. There's something comfortable and honest about this pub, from the pleasant outdoor beer garden to the dark, warm interior with logs ablaze in the fireplaces during the cooler months. Friendly cats roam through the garden mooching off patrons.

There's some kind of all-you-can-eat promotion here every night. The best known are the stuff-yourself-to-capacity clambake on Sundays and the fish fry on Fridays. The clambake includes an all-you-can-eat salad bar, crab legs or lobster or sirloin steak, plus all the clams, barbecued chicken and corn-on-the-cob you can eat. The fish fry is a similar eating orgy—only this time with clam chowder, perch, trout, scrod, smelt and shrimp salad. There are also all the crab legs you can eat Monday through Thursday, including soup, salad and corn-on-the-cob, although not all of these items are always available.

The fish here is frozen; the simpler dishes are okay, but forget anything complex. On one visit a flounder stuffed with crabmeat was dry and very fishy. The lobster billed as fresh, is simple and good. Another good selection is the half chicken that is simply broiled. Steak, while somewhat fatty and certainly not the best quality cut of beef, is nevertheless a safe bet. Dinners come with brown bread and cottage fries.

Several of the entrees are available as appetizers for half the price. The shrimp stuffed with crab is surprisingly good. The New England clam chowder is watery and salty but has a generous amount of vegetables and clams

Desserts aren't so good.

★ **TASTE OF ITALY**
   Italian

1235¹/₂ Burnham Ave., Calumet City   868-4440
Hours: Tues–Sat 4–11 pm, Sun 3–10 pm, closed Mon
Price range: Moderate
Credit cards: A   M   V
Reservations: Accepted

The Taste of Italy may not appeal to all tastes, but its pretty good home-style cooking has many fans. Even with a reservation there's often a wait.

A U-shaped bar area holds the overflow from two small adjacent dining rooms that seat about 60. Booths with banquette seating line the stucco walls. A dimmer on the wall at each table controls the individual hanging light. Service is slow so order your drinks and appetizers at the same time, to be safe.

To begin, plump, tender mussels are excellent, in a great fresh slightly tangy red sauce with small pieces of bread for sopping extra sauce. The onion fried zucchini, antipasto (prosciutto, head cheese, cappacola, Fontinella cheese, salami, peperoni, lettuce, roasted and marinated peppers) and deep-fried calamari are all good. Shrimp DeJonghe doesn't quite make it as an appetizer or an entree—not bad, but not great either. A good, hearty minestrone soup and salad or pasta come with entrees.

In general, the first courses are much better than the entrees. Filled shells, supposedly a house specialty, have little to recommend them besides the size of the portion. It's not that they're bad, just that they're not more exciting than what Mom used to make. The most expensive item is shrimp, chopped clams and linguini with white sauce, but the skimpy helping doesn't merit the high tariff. Veal rollatini has an off-taste from overcooking, is dried out and its sauce is too sweet. Another house specialty, chicken Vesuvio, isn't on a par with this dish at other places.

Desserts will lift spirits dampened by the mediocre entrees. A dense, rich cheesecake topped with cherries vies for accolades with a cannoli that, despite its apparently prefab shell contains an excellent homemade filling.

The food here is good solid home cooking, the kind you can do yourself. Taste of Italy has a large and loyal following—I'm simply not one of them.

★ T. COLOMBO'S AND OSCAR'S
Italian, Argentine, French

5207 N. Harlem Ave.   631-5600
Hours: Tues–Fri, Sun 4:30–11 pm, Sat 4:30–midnight
Price range: Moderate
Credit cards: A   M   V
Reservations: Accepted on weekends only

This restaurant is located between the Shear Class hair salon and the Alagna Travel Agency, an unlikely spot for a fine dining experience. It is a former pizzeria, and looks just like dozens of inexpensive southern Italian restaurants found in American cities. But it turns out to be a pretty good restaurant. If the food were more consistent and the service more polished, it would be a very good restaurant.

The Italian chef, Tony Colombo, was chef on the QE2 for seven years. Oscar runs the front of the house. Together they serve up an odd mix of Italian, French and Argentine food. It can take some time to get served here but, in general, the food is worth the wait. The ingredients are fresh and, with the exception of the paté de foie gras, which turned out to be coarsely chopped liver, and the very salty French onion soup, all of the dishes work reasonably well. The portions are huge and should be shared.

One of the best appetizers is the Argentinian matambre, two big portions of white veal rolled around a stuffing of hard-boiled egg, red pepper, carrots and herbs. The antipasto Don Vito is unexceptional. The salad bar, which comes with all entrees, is a Heinz 57 Variety selection that could easily be a meal in itself. It's a mostly excellent eclectic mix.

Four of even the most voracious pasta fans can share one pasta dish here. Fettucine alla Toni is freshly made at the restaurant and perfectly cooked with a rich cream sauce. T. Colombo's and Oscar's has fresh Dover sole, a must for fish lovers. A veal steak with rosemary is incredibly good. Other good meats are the churrasco, a 14-ounce center cut tender-loin served with two fried eggs, and the parrillada, a selection of short ribs, sweetbreads, black blood sausage, skirt steak and Argentinian sausage.

From the Italian selections, breast of chicken al scarpiello is one of the best. The veal pizzarolla could be one of the best "pizzas" in town.

For dessert, the freshly made cannoli is one of the best ever. The Amaretto cheesecake is also creamy and good, but the flan is tasteless. Pass up the weak American coffee for good espresso. The wine list is as eclectic as everything else. Prices range from $8.50-$17 per bottle.

Service is friendly and casual. Occasionally, diners waiting for their meals will notice the chef chatting up some customers at another table. It's best just to relax and enjoy.

★ ★ THAI ROOM
Thai

4022 N. Western Ave.   539-6250
Hours: Tues–Sun 11 am–10 pm, closed Mon
Price range: Inexpensive
Credit cards: D   M   V
Reservations: Accepted

Recently renovated and expanded, the Thai Room joins a growing number of Thai restaurants that have dressed up their dining rooms. The brightly lit room with light-colored wood and simple decorations, is clean and comfortable.

The menu is more limited than some at other Thai eateries. Perhaps this helps the kitchen, which consistently produces excellent food.

Appetizers include the usual satay, fish cakes and the like. The fresh spring rolls outshine the fried egg rolls.

Entrees include more interesting items. The fried squid stuffed with seasoned ground pork makes a great choice. So does the fried red snapper topped with either a fiery chili sauce or seasoned pork similar to the stuffing in the squid. Stir-fried shrimp with garlic is forcefully spiced—definitely not a dish for the timid.

Shrimp lemon cress soup has fine aroma and heats up the palate. So do the various curries.

The refreshing salads use crisp, cool lettuce to balance the spicy ground meat and poultry toppings. The result is a study in contrasts that delights the tastebuds.

The servers are reliable guides to the quality and specimens of the evening's offerings. The chef will tone down or heat up dishes on request.

★★ TIMBERS CHARHOUSE
American

295 Skokie Highway, Highland Park   831-1400
Hours: Mon–Thurs 11:30 am–10 pm, Fri 11:30 am–11:30 pm,
*   Sat noon–11:30 pm, Sun 4:30–8:30 pm*
Price range: Moderate
Credit cards: A M V
Reservations: Accepted
Handicap

The first thing you notice when you walk into Timbers is the tantalizing fragrance of smoke. The second thing you notice is a feeling of having stepped into an old-time wilderness lodge. A warm, clubby atmosphere permeates Timber's dining room as tangibly as the smoky aroma. Closer inspection reveals a strange mix of high and low tech in this cavernous room.

Rustic warmth prevails: twig furniture, a huge stone fireplace, sturdy, properly "aged," oak tables, a panoramic mural of a lake surrounded by mountains and trees. The wooden floors have a light stain, green ducks fly across the buff wallpaper. Comfortable booths and Windsor chairs are upholstered in forest green. Modern accents: high-tech air-conditioning vents, red neon outlining skylights and the open, stainless steel kitchen. Almost magically, hard-edged modern and old-fashioned warmth peacefully co-exist.

There are no menus, just printed placemats and a black-board hung from the ceiling that lists the available fresh fish, their origin and price. Bread is delivered as soon as diners are seated, a tempting loaf of different flavors. Luckily, there are no appetizers to tempt further excess. Bread, choice of soup or salad and fries, pasta, brown rice or baked potato come with entrees. The seafood chowder, one of two soups, is surprisingly bland. Three simple salads—wedge of lettuce, romaine and house—are all good.

The rib and chicken combo is a pleasant surprise: two meaty pieces of chicken, a generous half-slab of ribs and an oversized basket of French fries. The baby back ribs are good—smoky and meaty with only a hint of fat. The pleas-antly tart sauce may not have won *The Tribune*'s last rib taste-off but it would have made the finals. The same smoky sauce covers the hickory-grilled chicken, which is charred without being burnt; moist and tender with a hint of hick-ory flavor. Customers can choose light or dark meat at no extra charge.

Most fish is grilled over mesquite. The swordfish looks terrific and arrives moist, no mean feat. Grilled salmon is plain but good. The grilled veal chop does not have flavor from the wood grill.

There's a dessert tray for anyone who still feels the need to test endurance. Unfortunately, the offerings looked sadly straggly at the end of one evening's meal. A double choco-late cake is huge; the cherry pie seems a saner choice.

Service is slow when the place gets crowded, which is of-ten. Otherwise, it's a perfect restaurant for decent, inexpen-sive family dining.

★ ★ ★ LE TITI DE PARIS
French

2275 Rand Rd., Palatine   359-4434
Hours: Lunch Tues–Fri 11:30 am–2 pm, Dinner Tues–Thurs
*   5:30–9:30 pm, Fri & Sat 5:30–10:30 pm, closed Sun &*
*   Mon*
Price range: Expensive
Credit cards: A C D M V
Reservations: Recommended
Handicap

Probably one of the most underrated of Chicago's French restaurants, Le Titi turns out consistently good food in a pleasant environment at less-than-average prices.

This small restaurant is located on an unlikely stretch of road dominated by strip shopping centers with discount outlets. It's pleasantly appointed with a small bar in the center of the room, stained wainscoting, blue walls on the left side of the room and papered walls on the right both hung with oil paintings. White clothed tables and comfortable chairs complete the charming room.

Groups of six to eight diners are not unusual here, and the room gets noisy. However the mood is more festive than abrasive. Walking into Le Titi can be like walking into a party in progress. On weekends the place bustles and the activity seems to bring out the best in the entire staff.

The kitchen consistently produces excellent food. A long list of interesting specials augments the printed menu. Appetizers include such simple items as fresh oysters and grilled tuna with a beurre rouge and more complicated creations like a cassolette of seafood—grouper, scallops with the coral, shrimp and mussels all cooked in a cream sauce with wild mushrooms and bits of diced eggplant and zucchini—a real winner. Rich lobster bisque from the regular menu with full-bodied lobster flavor makes a good beginning to a meal.

336

Exquisite veal served in a cider sauce with zest of orange is moist, fork-tender and full-flavored. Duck breast cooked rare comes with a currant sauce that balances the earthy gaminess of the meat. Try to resist the temptation to eat all the currants at once; you need to ration them closely to make it through the duck.

The tart, herby vinaigrette dressing on the special salad of mache, chicory, pear, artichoke heart and ripe avocado ties all parts of this excellent dish together. The spinach salad is good, but no match for this special.

Desserts are no less pleasing. An ethereal chestnut mousse sits atop an incredibly light sponge cake "crust" in the chestnut mousse pie. Le Titi's version of Black Forest cake surprises with a dense coat of fine dark chocolate around a whipped cream filling that contains a single brandied cherry—sort of a super high quality Hostess cupcake. This, too comes on a sponge cake foundation. Both desserts sit in creme Anglais.

Attentive efficient servers manage to walk the fine line between friendly and overfriendly. They have a knack for putting people at ease.

French wines dominate the list with a good range of prices.

TONY ROMA'S A PLACE FOR RIBS
American
Rating: Poor

1009 N. Rush St.   642-7427
Hours: Sun–Fri 11–1:30 am, Sat 11–2:30 am
Price range: Moderate
Credit cards: A D M V
Reservations: Accepted for groups of six or more

There are 45 Tony Roma's around the country. All of them, including this new one on Rush Street, pack in customers. People come here while poor little L'Amanguier, a good French restaurant with equally reasonable prices, sits downstairs, virtually empty. Who am I to argue with success? But I must be missing something.

The thing here is supposed to be ribs. Well...these ribs slide right off the bones, indicating that they've been parboiled before barbecuing, a no-no in my book. Moreover, the meat tastes a bit gamey, as if it's old, and the ribs come with no uniform coating of sauce. That's three strikes already. At least the tomato-based sauce tastes tart, but it has precious little spiciness that might add interest to these bland ribs.

Barbecued chicken turns out better, but it's still no great shakes. If you must come here stick with a hamburger probably the best item on the menu—or a steak, and hope it doesn't come out overcooked. (Send it back if it does.) Grilled swordfish carries the same caveat.

As for the side dishes, the onion ring block, billed as unique, is a rip-off of Hackney's classic. The slaw is creamy and flecked with celery seed but was limp the night we had it.

Price is one redeeming factor. The other is Tony Roma's late hours which make it one of the few places to get a bite to eat after a long night of celebrating.

★ TOP NOTCH BEEFBURGER SHOP
American as the dickens

2116 W. 95th St.   445-7218
Hours: Mon–Sat 6:30 am–8 pm, closed Sun
Price range: Inexpensive
Credit cards: No way
Reservations: Forget it
Handicap

The 50's are in fashion these days, so this may be Chicago's most fashionable burger joint despite its diner decor. The menu modestly allows that Top Notch is "the only place to eat beef burgers outside your home—" a claim that the place just might be able to substantiate.

This burger is the genuine 1950s soda fountain item, not one of those puffed-up, too-thick jobs you get in most gourmet burger havens. Don't hold your breath waiting to be asked whether you want your order rare or medium. It's flat and grilled one way; medium well. The bun is plain but toasted. Grilled onions on top are optional.

The fries are good and not too greasy. The shakes are as thick as you remember them and the Coke is the real fountain thing. Burgers come in three sizes: a quarter-pounder, a half-pounder and a three-quarter-pounder. This is a great burger!

Servers are young and fresh, just the way they should be. Enjoy.

★★ TOULOUSE
French

49 W. Division St.   944-2606
Hours: Mon–Thurs 5:30–11 pm, Fri & Sat 5:30–midnight,
*   closed Sun*
Price range: Expensive
Credit cards: A M V
Reservations: Recommended

The one thing I'm asked most often is "Where should I go for a romantic evening?" That all depends on what one considers romantic, of course, something that varies dramatically from person to person. Nevertheless, Toulouse almost always makes my list of restaurants recommended for romance.

There are several reasons for this. First and foremost, David Green, one of Chicago's entertainment treasures, performs most evenings at the piano bar here. The former prize fighter not only plays and sings well, but he's also a walking musical library of pop music. He takes requests from the audience and plays into the wee hours of the morning.

Then there's Victor, the maitre 'd who comes from the old school. He takes care of regulars and makes everyone feel welcomed and pampered.

The room is dark, cozy and elegant. Divided into three distinct parts, the restaurant allows those who want privacy to sit in the far room or along the elevated section in front. Those who want to eat and enjoy Green's act sit in the dining area to the right just inside the door. Or one can drink, watch and listen to Green and perhaps enjoy a light snack at the bar.

Like the maitre d', tuxedoed servers make diners feel comfortable and respect their desired level of intimacy-privacy. Meals flow smoothly from beginning to end.

All items are á la carte. The menu now changes nightly, so a few favored items, such as the lamb with artichokes, no longer appear regularly.

Expect a large number of fresh seafood items sauteed or broiled, often with interesting, creative sauces. But this is not a seafood restaurant. Game usually plays a role in the offerings in fall and winter. Veal, beef and lamb dishes round out the nightly specials.

Careful preparation and beautiful presentation mean dishes look as good as they taste, which definitely adds to the experience here. Desserts range from fresh fruits to tarts with the flakiest of crusts to rich, moist cakes. These also change nightly.

The wine list is good, but the long list of cognacs, armagnacs and other after-dinner liqueurs is outstanding and well worth sampling.

★ ★ ★ LA TOUR
French

In the Park Hyatt Hotel, 800 N. Michigan Ave.   *280-2230*

Hours: Daily breakfast 7 am–11 am, lunch 11:30 am–2:30
*   pm, dinner 6–11 pm*
Price range: Expensive
Credit cards: A C D M V
Reservations: Recommended
Handicap

From the dining room diners can relax and enjoy the spectacular view of the Old Water Tower set in its little park. This stately, refined room shuns theatrics to focus attention on the food, putting to rest once and for all the notion that hotel fare is bland and lackluster.

Large, lavish arrangements of flowers and plants are strategically placed thorughout the room to screen diners and give a sense of privacy. Every white-clothed table has a vase of fresh flowers. A good pianist plays unobtrusively in the bar. Management attends to every detail, down to the bottled water poured at each table.

Prices are high, but the food is worth it. At lunch you can sample at about 20% less cost many of the same dishes found on the dinner menu.

Fresh beluga and sevruga caviar is available for those who want to splurge. Or try the Petrossian smoked Scottish salmon, a wafer-thin slice that covers a 12-inch plate, dotted with leaves of mache, radicchio and watercress.

Other good beginnings include a light Roquefort mousse with grape sauce, sterling soups, seafood terrine and ravioli-wrapped bay scallops. Indeed, it's darned difficult to go wrong with any selection.

Entrees live up to the promise of the starters. Preparations, ranging from simple to highly complex, reflect respect for the ingredients.

Grilled turbot with a light mustard cream sauce lies on a bed of steamed spinach—wonderful. Mild-tasting roast leg and rack of lamb come with the leg meat wrapped around a stuffing of shiitake mushrooms, sun-dried tomato, ham and tarragon. A latticework of braised leeks and red peppers gives chicken breast visual appeal and greatly enhanced flavor.

Sweetbreads and New York duck livers will not win any friends among health nuts, but the mousse-textured meats float like a cloud on the truffled Perigord sauce. A few vegetables decorate the plates of most entrees, but the serious vegetables—like snow peas or carrots—come in a separate covered dish.

The cart of killer desserts provides a fitting finale to the meals here. As if the pastries, cakes and fresh fruits aren't enough, a tray of chocolate truffles with all manner of fillings is placed on the table.

The fine wine list equals the food. A friendly, knowledgable sommelier will help diners decide on a wine that matches their meals in any price range. Be forewarned, however, that few bottles list for less than $20 and may run to $100 and more. Wine can greatly and quickly add to the cost of dining here.

La Tour provides one of the best dining experiences in French cuisine in Chicago.

★★ **TURBOT**
Seafood

1212 N. State Pkwy.   944-1313
Hours: Cafe daily 4:30–midnight, dining room Mon–Sat 5:30–
*   10:30 pm, closed Sun*
Price range: Moderately Expensive
Credit cards: A C D M V
Reservations: Not accepted in the cafe, recommended for the
dining room
Jackets required in dining room
Handicap

Turbot is a combination of Yvette and Toulouse, Bob

Djahanguiri's other two restaurants: half singles bar, half formal restaurant. One enters Turbot through a long hallway, at the end of which is the dining room on the left and the bar on the right. There is entertainment in a large, comfortable, rectangular bar—important points, since waits for a table in the cafe can stretch to an hour or more. A different kitchen serves the more formal dining room (tables by reservation only) but the menus are similar.

The cafe is bright, with blue and beige decor that could have been transplanted from Cape Cod. Big windows, fronted by flower boxes, stand open in warm weather, framing the constant ebb and flow on State Street. This is a place to see and be seen. It's also loud and fairly cramped, packed with tables that are too small to accommodate four diners comfortably. Nevertheless, there's something attractive about Turbot, not the least of which is the food. All of the fish here is fresh and most of it is excellent.

There's no way to go wrong with the beginning of the meal. The appetizers are excellent. The oysters, are fresh, plump and dressed in vinaigrette; the smoked salmon has a nice smoky flavor well complemented by a light dill sauce, capers, chopped eggs and parsley; the poached trout is perfect, as is the salmon and scallop seafood sausage.

The shrimp with asparagus appetizer was the only disappointment one night: the restaurant was out of asparagus, and the dish came without the watercress sauce mentioned on the menu. The shrimp was fine but without the accompaniment the dish was dull. The server should have discouraged this selection. For the most part, service is friendly and attentive, if not always well-informed about the food.

Although most of the fish entrees served in both rooms are usually sauced, they can be ordered without saucing. A plain grilled tuna fillet was perfectly prepared, moist and absolutely fresh. Soft shell crabs covered with almonds are surprisingly good. Swordfish, a difficult fish to cook properly, is perfect. A green seafood pasta is delicious with shrimp and mussels.

Only two of the entrees miss the mark. Curried shrimp with papaya is an unsuccessful combination. Grilled prawns were overdone, unsalvageable even by the excellent tomato sauce. For those who can't abide fish, the restaurant offers steak, chicken and veal. But as the name suggests, fish is the main attraction here.

The chef returns to a classic mode of cooking in the formal dining room, using sauces to add interest to expertly cooked fish, usually successfully. You'll find the dining room less noisy than the cafe. The dark wood and fireplace give the room the feeling of a ski lodge, tables are larger, diners have more room and the dressed-up cuisine command a higher price.

There is a wide selection of desserts, many including fresh fruits. Fresh berries, always available here, may be the perfect way to end a light, healthy meal.

★ ★ ★ LA VICHYSSOIS
French

220 W. Rte. 120, Lakemore   815-385-8221
Hours: Wed–Thurs 5:30–9 pm, Fri & Sat 5:30–10 pm, Sun
*   4:30–9 pm, closed Mon & Tues*
Price range: Moderately expensive
Credit cards: C D M V
Reservations: Accepted
Handicap

Owner-chef Bernard Cretier offers a great value in fine French dining here ("I spend more money on what's on the plate than decor..." Cretier says.) Located outside the city, the modest restaurant has a small service bar and two main dining rooms. Arched, curtained windows overlook a patio; the understated decor is pleasant beige wallpaper, brown carpeting, tables with white cloths and flowers. The seating is comfortable, the service attentive and as unobtrusive as the decor.

Cretier's style is traditional. About half the menu consists of specials that change nightly. Lightly steamed fresh asparagus alternating in layers with delicate flaky pastry with a vermouth cream sauce makes feuillete of asparagus a wonderful beginning. Several country-style patés that always are available come nicely seasoned and moist. The vichyssoise, although thinner than some, is well-balanced and flavorful. The crayfish cassoulet features tender, rich crayfish and sauteed fresh mushrooms in a seductively rich, bisque-like sauce.

An endive, mache and French green bean special salad in raspberry vinegar and walnut oil is interesting and works splendidly. A mix of romaine, tomato and avocado in Dijon vinaigrette constitutes the pleasing house salad. An excellent grapefruit champagne sherbet refreshes the palate before the entrees.

The sherry and red wine vinegar sauce with the roast duck packs a wallop that can clear sinuses. The sauce contrasts well with the duck's richness. Tarragon sauce and rack of lamb work beautifully together. Grilled veal loin steak also is well-served by a full-bodied wine sauce flecked with morel mushrooms. Those looking for a light entree shouldn't look to the lake trout in champagne sauce; the fileted trout drowns in the exceedingly rich, buttery sauce. Vegetables come with all entrees.

Winning desserts include the hazelnut cake, the flourless almond cake with chocolate icing, and a chocolate cheesecake made with quality bitter chocolate. Of the tarts, the lemon is the best. While not extensive, the wine list offers a selection broad enough to suit most tastes. Prices are moderate.

Clearly every attempt is made to create a comfortable environment for the good food at Le Vichyssois. And if waiters lack the polish of some who work in the area's best French restaurants, they also lack the pretensions—a real plus.

★ IL VICINATO
Italian

2435 S. Western Ave.   927-5444
Hours: Mon–Thurs 11 am–10 pm, Fri 11 am–11 pm, Sat 5–11
     pm, closed Sun.
Price range: Moderate
Credit cards: A C D M V
Reservations: Accepted
Handicap

Typical of the many Italian restaurants in this area, Il Vicinato has a bar room in front and a dining room in the back. Friendly waitresses and bright, cheery decor make this a pleasant neighborhood restaurant.

Appetizers outshine most of the other courses here. Start with an order of pizza bread topped with chopped fresh tomatoes (in season) rather than the normal canned puree. Also good is the tortellini in brodo soup, perfectly cooked clouds of pasta filled with sausage in a full bodied chicken broth. The Italian egg drop soup, stracciatella, merits sampling as well. The antipasto here is ordinary, but good. Fried ravioli is amazingly light with a well-seasoned filling.

Care taken with the pasta preparation ensures consistent al dente cooking. Generally excellent sauces, such as the creamy carbonara, make pasta dishes a good bet here.

Veal dishes built around less than the best quality meat leave much to be desired. But chicken Vesuvio turns out succulent and flavorful with its herby olive oil sauce.

The desserts here won't set off fireworks, but the large portions may obviate any need of desserts in the first place.

★ ★ LA VILLITA
Mexican

1403 W. Irving Park Rd.   477-3330
Hours: Daily 10–2 am
Price range: Moderate
Credit cards: A C D M V
Reservations: Accepted

Good food and good times abound at an attractively low price at this neighborhood restaurant. You know the kind of place: Formica-topped tables, Mexican travel posters, a box fan valiantly helping the small window air conditioner propel cool air to the far corners of the room.

One of the restaurant's main attractions is the juke box. Divided roughly 50/50 between Latin tunes and hits from the '40s, it's a world-class selection—and if patrons don't keep the music playing, the owner will.

Baskets of good chips and a fiery salsa come to the table immediately. It's easy to pig out on these but avoid the temptation—portions are huge. Owner Jesus Romo makes a fine margarita to accompany the chips. Don't order them by the liter—they're cheaper that way, but the chipped ice dilutes the punch.

A good fresh guacamole and nachos lead off the appetizer offerings. The crisp corn tortilla chips topped with a puree of refried beans and melted cheese are crowned with guacamole, the best of both worlds. For those who enjoy mole, the chocolate sauce with a spicy kick, La Villita offers a pleasing homemade version. The taste is not for everyone, but thick, dark and rich, this sweet-bitter mole adds interest to nicely cooked chicken parts and to chicken enchilada.

La Villita keeps its excellent chiles relleños simple: two poblano chile peppers dipped in batter arrive steaming hot, stuffed with Mexican chihuahua cheese and topped with ranchero sauce. Somewhat spicy, they're among the best in ea. Three versions of enchilada suizas—beef, chicker and cheese—are offered. Dipped in "La Villita" sauce—? light ranchero sauce of tomato, green peppers, fresh coriander and onions—and topped with Mexican cheese, these tasty suizas come with sour cream.

Naturally, tacos and tostadas are offered. The tacos are well-filled, with a flexible shell that doesn't break. The tostadas have crisper shells. Good refried beans, chopped lettuce, tomatoes, and rice flecked with peas come with all entrees. Beans substitute for meat in several of the dishes.

If you still have room for dessert, the incredibly creamy flan with a sweet golden vanilla sauce is the only choice. For less than $10 a person, plus a dollar for the jukebox, La Villita is a great place for home-cooked Mexican food. Romo always makes sure diners leave satisfied, sending them off with a warm "thank you" and "adios."

★ WALNUT ROOM
American

Seventh floor of Marshall Field's, 111 N. State St.
781-3693
Hours: Daily 10:30 am–3 pm, Mon & Thurs 3–6 pm,
*   Tea Tues, Wed, Fri, Sat 3–5 pm*
Price range: Moderate
Credit cards: A   M   V and Marshall Field's
Reservations: Accepted
Handicap

Most people eat at the Walnut Room once a year if they eat there at all: at Christmas time, when the huge Christmas tree dominates the middle of the room. (Do you know why it looks so big? while the decorations may look the same, they actually dwindle in size as they are placed higher on the tree, creating the illusion that the tree is taller than it really is. Ah, the magic of Christmas!)

It is probably a mistake to visit this room only once a year. For one thing, the room really isn't at its best during the holiday crunch when too many customers suddenly overwhelm the staff. For another, some of the best food available in the Loop at reasonable prices is offered here during the rest of the year. Besides with all that walnut and the two-story ceiling, it's a great old room worth viewing without the obstruction of the tree.

No, I haven't lost my mind after all those artery-clogging dinners. I'm not claiming that the Walnut Room is a great spot for innovative cuisine, only that it deserves to be a year-round option for people who work or shop in the Loop.

The menu is heavily skewed to soups and salads. There are always a few entrees including chicken, fresh broiled fish and red meat.

The quality of the Cobb salad here is a match for any other. Chicken and seafood salads also turn out well. The daily specials are the best bets among the entrees.

Overly sweet, heavy desserts can make the rest of the day pass mighty sluggishly for those headed back to the office or even back home. Skip them and buy a box of Frango mints on your way out instead, for your fellow employees or friends.

Many of the waitresses are efficient and quite nice. However, a few of them are determined to have you do what they want you to do. There's a children's menu and complete bar service; both breakfast and lunch are served. Eight other eateries vie for attention on the 7th floor of Field's, but none of the others can hold a candle to the Walnut Room.

★ THE WATERFRONT RESTAURANT
Seafood

16 W. Maple St.   943-7494
Hours: Mon–Thurs 11:30 am–midnight, Fri & Sat 11:30–1
*   am, Sun 11:30 am–11 pm*

Price range: Moderately expensive
Credit cards: A   M   V
Reservations: Accepted

In it's original Rush Street location, the Waterfront was one of the first restaurants to bring fresh seafood to Chicago. Many devotees of the restaurant mourned when it was closed to make way for a new building. Now it has reopened around the corner on Maple Street with the same dedication to serving exquisitely fresh fish in a relaxed, casual environment. Much of the former staff is back as well, so the place almost seems unchanged.

The somewhat worn copper-top tables are here, along with fishing and wharf murals, lots of wood and bright lighting which give this restaurant the look of an old East-coast seafood house. In many ways, the menu too recalls a bygone era. There are dover sole almondine, pan-fried trout, whole Maine lobsters and even a carpet bagger's steak, broiled sirloin stuffed with seasoned oysters—a dish that can be found in few other places in town.

Simple, predictable appetizers are fresh oysters and clams on the half shell, oysters Rockefeller, clams casino, king crab with avocado, escargot, ceviche, steamers and the like.

The shellfish, either fresh or steamed, probably is the best bet, Ceviche, while not bad, tends to be bland. Unfortunately, the sourdough bread that used to be a highlight at this restaurant has lost some of its punch. Plain salads and rice pilaf come with dinners.

Few complaints can be levied at the entrees, except that they are relatively boring. Fish is fresh, preparations competent and the seasonings relatively bland. Avoid the sole en sacque. This poor filet of sole is completely overwhelmed by sliced ham, shrimp, mushrooms, black olives and cherry sauce. It's cooked wrapped in parchment paper. The best one can say for this dish is that it's very moist. Indeed, the simpler the preparation you choose here—the pan-fried trout, for instance, or broiled red snapper—the better your chances of getting a good meal. Portions are quite large and prices generally lower than many other area fish restaurants. Service may be a mite too friendly but, in general, waiters are concerned and helpful. While the Waterfront is not exciting or innovative, it provides a good alternative to the lesser eateries lining Rush Street waiting to snare the convention trade.

★ ★ ★ WINNETKA GRILL
American

64 Green Bay Rd., Winnetka   441-6444
Hours: Mon–Thurs 5:30–9 pm, Fri 5:30–10 pm, Sat 5–10 pm,
*   Sun 5–9 pm*
Price range: Moderately expensive
Credit cards: C D M V
Reservations: Accepted

This restaurant is small and has no bar to hold any overflow; diners wait in a small area just inside the front door. The restaurant became popular before it was ready to handle the crowds so in the early days, long, fairly uncomfortable waits could be expected on weekends. Most of these problems have been corrected. Even if it takes a while for management to honor your reservation, the wait is worth it.

The odd but enchanting decor and superlative cuisine of part-owner John Stoltzmann make this a special place. In the reception area are four white pillars topped with a gold pyramid, a gold ball and an inverted pyramid, on the floor is painted a geometric design in various colors. Cloud-like murals drift across the walls above fabric-lined booths. The tables, although close together, are large and comfortable.

More than half the entrees come off the mesquite grill and most of it is honest, creative and American, if occasionally inconsistent. The menu changes frequently to reflect seasonal ingredients and currently culinary trends, like New

Orleans cookery. The following dishes represent the type of cooking you can expect, but they may no longer be available.

Usually baby and exotic vegetables, deep fried as appetizers, are quite good. Lake Michigan caviar complements other dishes and is served as an appetizer in a generous portion that is not at all fishy and has a pleasant light burst of flavor. It tastes less salty than most saltwater caviars.

Corn blintzes filled with butternut squash have an intense, pleasing flavor. The portion is large enough for four. Grilled oysters are delightful, served in the shell on a bed of fried parsley, topped with chopped ham in a light, anise-spiked sauce. The bread smells and looks great, but for some reason it doesn't have much flavor.

Striped sea bass grilled over mesquite is excellent, served with a leek and rosemary sauce. Half a Long Island duckling, also grilled over mesquite, is served with a red wine, honey and black peppercorn sauce. The duck is crispy on the outside but a little dry on the inside and overpowered by the sauce, which is too heavy on the honey. Thin pieces of calves' liver done medium rare are a good choice for liver lovers.

Lightly cooked, interesting vegetables come with entrees. The salads are good and creative.

Desserts are not up to the rest of the meal. Chocolate velvet cake, actually a pie, tastes like something you'd find in a corner coffee shop—a Jello-O Pudding-like mousse on an Oreo crust. Better are the pumpkin cheesecake and strawberries in sour cream. Four sherbets are too sweet and not very good. The small wine list emphasizes American wines, most of which cost less than $20.

Service is pleasant and competent. John Stoltzmann has done what many other chefs have tried and failed to do: he has created a menu that comes close to honest American cooking and he's done it well.

WOK'S
Chinese
Rating: Fair

158 E. Ontario St.   664-8633
Hours: Daily 11:30 am–10:30 pm
Price range: Moderate
Credit cards: A C D M V
Reservations: Accepted
Handicap

Competing within a few blocks of House of Hunan and the Szechwan House, two of the better Chinese restaurants, is no easy task. Wok's, which took over the space formerly occupied by a Mexican restaurant, looks promising at first.

The decor rather oddly juxtaposes stucco walls, ornamental wrought iron, interior arches, Mexican tiles, and Oriental waiters serving Chinese fare. But the white-clothed tables and pink walls give the interior visual appeal.

Slow and confused service has plagued the restaurant from the start. There are language difficulties too. All this would not matter so much if the food were superb, but it falls short compared to the nearby restaurants. Not that the fare here is bad; it just isn't very exciting.

Among the appetizers, try the pickled Chinese cabbage, good, flavorful fried dumplings or spring rolls. These turn out better than such starters as the bland shrimp toast, tough beef satay or flavorless fried wonton.

Entrees are uneven. Careful ordering might produce good results, but with the inconsistencies in the kitchen, there's no guarantee of success. Sah cha chicken, moist chunks of chicken in a somewhat spicy sweetened sauce, is a good bet. Moo shu pork also works well. Hunan lamb has little of the spiciness the menu warns about, and not much flavor, either.

Wok's probably will improve over time. At present, however, the slow service and uneven food prevent it from being a good alternative to the other Chinese restaurants in the area.

★ ★ ★ YOSHI'S CAFE
French

3257 N. Halsted St.   248-6160
Hours: Tues–Thurs 5:30–10:30 pm, Fri & Sat 5:30–11 pm,
*   Sun 5–9 pm, closed Mon*
Price range: Expensive
Credit cards: A   M   V
Reservations: Recommended
Handicap

Owner-chef Yoshi Katsumura presides over the kitchen while his wife, Nabuko, manages the front of this pleasant 42-seat cafe. Yoshi's popularity and the tendency of diners to linger over the excellent food may cause a wait for a table, even when you hold a reservation.

While it's small, Yoshi's does not crowd diners. Tables provide ample space and diners have elbowroom even sitting in the middle of the bustling room. Those waiting have to stand in an area about four feet square. The lucky ones get one of the stools at the tiny bar.

With the regular menu and the long list of specials, there are at least 10 appetizers from which to choose. It's a tough choice, although the specials often sound more interesting, they also tend to cost a bit.

Virtually everything is good. Seafood dominates the menu. Don't miss the homemade seafood sausage with prawns and rich, creamy shrimp sauce. Seafood in puff pastry also turns out well. The selection of patés usually offered tastes rich and smooth.

Special soups change nightly but often include onion,

cream of fish chowder au curry and lobster bisque. The onion soup one night was rather ordinary but the lobster bisque was great—rich, sweet and full-flavored.

The entrees are divided between fish courses and meat, game and poultry. The usually large variety of fish includes such items as a moist, lightly sauced, grilled swordfish (although the grill adds little flavor), jumbo shrimp sauteed with garlic and tomato and poached Dover sole with lobster mousse.

The fabulous pork tenderloin en courte is cooked rare; those who cannot tolerate rare pork, be forewarned. The sauteed chicken in tarragon or green peppercorn sauce is delicious—moist, tender and served with a good sauce. Two game dishes—rabbit and roast duck—are at once exciting and somewhat disappointing. The chef has mastered the art of sauces—both accompanying mustard and cherry sauces are excellent—but the meats lack much gamey taste. Entrees are served with fresh steamed vegetables and a house salad, a simple arrangement of fresh leaf lettuce. Entrees also come, usually, with a small vegetable terrine.

A meal of the quality served at Yoshi's should be crowned with an unforgettable dessert but, unfortunately, dessert is the only hit-or-miss course here. Green-tea ice cream is the most interesting item and tastes good. Flourless chocolate cake will satisfy chocolate lovers.

Service is smooth and efficient. Occasionally during the evening Nabuko will make the rounds of the room to make sure all is well. The wine list is limited, but prices are reasonable.

Yoshi started out offering bargain prices. Those who haven't been for a while should be forewarned that prices have risen considerably.

★ YUGO INN RESTAURANT & BAR
Yugoslavian

2824 N. Ashland Ave.   348-6444
Hours: Wed–Sun 5 pm–midnight, closed Mon & Tues
Price range: Moderate
Credit cards: Not accepted
Reservations: Accepted

This place may be the definition of warm and friendly. Its unlikely location on Ashland, where few other businesses are open late at night, may seem a bit foreboding. However, once inside the door, diners are immediately transported thousands of miles away to a charming Yugoslavian neighborhood bar and restaurant.

The bar at the front often has few patrons on weeknights, but the dining room, up a short set of stairs at the rear, usually fills with diners often speaking their native tongues. Dark wood, festive tablecloths, servers in Serbian dress, antiques and art work give this room old-world charm.

Three complimentary hors d'oeuvres begin meals along with a basket of good, crusty fresh bread. The chopped liver has a stronger flavor than most. Kajmak, a spread made from three cheeses and ajvar, a wonderful dip of seasoned chopped pepper and eggplant, are better bets.

Given the large portions to follow, additional appetizers may not be necessary. However, both the fresh, deep-fried smelt or the crisply battered fried squid merit sampling.

Entrees include Serbian specialties such as mozak brains, riba, fresh fish and sarma, stuffed cabbage. Both the cabbage and stuffed peppers taste fresh, but bland. Try the musaka or one of the grilled dishes instead.

Cevapcici, ground beef and veal rolled into a sausage shape and grilled, has a bit too much salt, but it comes out moist and flavorful. Pljeskavica, ground round steak in the shape of a hamburger, has a rubbery texture, but great flavor. Raznjici, a shish kabob of pork, beef or chicken with pepper and onion, features large chunks of moist meat on a bed of rice. The dish is hardly unique as the menu claims.

Dinners come with a choice of soup, salad and dessert, as well as the complimentary appetizers. The soup changes daily, but tends to be a hearty broth, like chicken with big pieces of vegetables. Salads are a mix of cucumbers, onion, tomato and feta cheese.

Desserts include a good chocolate rum torte, ice cream and ordinary jam-filled crepes. The wine list is composed of three or four fruity Yugoslav wines priced at less than $15.

For comfort and value, the Yugo Inn has few rivals in Chicago. The food is generally a notch or two above the norm.

★ YVETTE
French bistro

1206 N. State Pkwy.   280-1700
Hours: Cafe daily 11:30-1 am, dining room Mon–Thurs 5:30–
*   11 pm, Fri & Sat 5:30 pm–midnight, Sun 5:30-10 pm*
Price range: Moderate
Credit cards: A D M V
Reservations: Accepted
Handicap

More popular watering hole than serious restaurant, Yvette serves credible, if simple, French fare at extremely reasonable prices for the Rush St. area.

The little cafe to the right of the entrance has sliding glass doors that open onto State Street in warm weather. This cafe abuts the bustling pick-up bar, where two pianists entertain most evenings. Tile floors, dark wood, glass globe lamps, mirrors and paintings with Art Deco feeling give the atmosphere of a bustling French bistro.

A long hallway leads to a tiered dining room in the rear. Again, the feeling is bistro, but a bistro that is quieter, with white-clothed tables and less of a crowd.

The food ranges from dressed-up burgers to classic French

specialties like as steak and fries, with a good deal of fresh seafood filling in the gaps.

Starters like snails, oysters, cream of mussel soup and simple patés are good . Main courses might include a pasta special with seafood, roast duck, lamb with artichoke heart or broiled or poached fresh fish with a simple sauce. None of the food is outstanding, but then neither are the prices.

Desserts tend to be excellent. There are good pastries, tarts and tortes, as well as fresh fruits. The wine list is limited, but priced in accordance with the rest of the menu. Servers are attentive and pleasant.

Yvette is definitely a place to see and be seen, more than a great restaurant. But neither the food nor the prices will kill you.

★ ZODIAC
Continental

Neiman-Marcus, 737 N. Michigan Ave.
642-5900, ext 2365
Hours: Lunch Mon–Sat 11 am–4 pm, afternoon tea 3–5 pm
Price range: Moderate
Credit card: Neiman-Marcus only
Reservations: Accepted
Handicap

Despite Neiman-Marcus's outrageously sophisticated reputation, its dining room has a disappointingly conservative decor and a fairly conservative approach to food.

One enters the restaurant through the food department. Set off to the left is a smashing jet-black bar, most often deserted. This is a great place to relax from the rigors of shopping or disappear with a business associate for a private discussion. Straight ahead is the dining room, with lots of banquettes done in boring greys and beiges.

Of course, the overall effect is the one desired: class and

comfort. Service is attentive, polished and professional.

The food has had its ups and downs since the Zodiac opened. The menu changes, but generally includes appetizers like chicken liver mousse, steamed shrimp or a snack of fresh beluga caviar (more than $30 an ounce at press time).

A large number of salads, from the typical offerings to a good seafood pasta salad and an excellent smoked turkey and shrimp mixture, lead the menu. A few sandwiches offer the lowest priced options.

There are a number of specials and nearly a dozen entrees. Entrees include fresh broiled fish with simple saucing, beef and poultry. In general, these offerings are far more ambitious than those found at any other department store restaurant. While they work well enough, these dishes should excel since the average price for lunch is more than $10 a person.

Desserts, from the light fresh fruits to the rich, flourless chocolate cake and pastries, will send most diners away smiling.

On most days there is live piano music, another lunchtime extra. Also models may stroll by wearing the latest fashions, to remind you what you're really there to do.

EAU CLAIRE DISTRICT LIBRARY